MICHELLE WOOD & PAUL WOOD

SILENT MEDITATION *and the* GOSPELS

A Weekly Practice with the Sunday Readings

First published in Australia in 2024
by Quiet Communion
Website www.quietcommunion.org

© Michelle Wood and Paul Wood 2024

The right of Michelle Wood and Paul Wood to be identified as the authors of this work has been asserted by them under the Copyright Amendment (Moral Rights) Act 2000.

This work is copyright. Apart from any use as permitted under the Copyright Act 1968, no part may be reproduced, copied, scanned, stored in a retrieval system, recorded, or transmitted, in any form or by any means, without the prior written permission of the copy right owner and publisher.

A catalogue record for this book is available from the National Library of Australia.

ISBN 978-0-646-70330-5 (paperback)
ISBN 978-0-646-70331-2 (ebook)

Cover design by Nada Backovic
Cover images: Olga Thelavart/Unsplash and Shutterstock

Typeset by Nada Backovic

Foreword

by Laurence Freeman OSB,
Director of the World Community for Christian Meditation

Christianity is awaiting a new reformation. Better to say, perhaps, it is awakening to a radical liberation from the past and empowerment for the future that has been underway for some time. It is significant that of the many prophets of this evolution, two of the most influential—I am thinking of Dietrich Bonhoeffer and Simone Weil—died before the age of forty, in a time of catastrophe for Western civilisation. They delivered their message from a profound mystical vision interwoven with the signs of their time and from the margins of the institutional church.

They preceded and influenced major internal eruptions of the Holy Spirit in Christianity during the twentieth century. Not least was the Second Ecumenical Council of the Vatican, which was the twenty-first of its kind. Among its many fruits was a recovery of much that had been repressed or forbidden in the Christian tradition. Included in these essential components of the Christian calling were the universal call to holiness, the spiritual equality of clerical and marital-life vocations, the bridge of faith between contemplation and action as exemplified in the Martha and Mary episode in Luke and the life-giving experience of the Scriptures. For long, holiness seemed restricted to an elite, celibacy was regarded as higher than conjugality and contemplatives were cloistered. Regarding access to the word of God, two thirteenth-century councils forbade lay people from reading the Bible in their own language.

Go figure, as a young person of our time might say.

I refer to this aspect of Christian history, sadly often covered by the shadow of institutional egotism and an abuse of power, to show what a wonderful affirmation of the radical change of direction in Christian life and spirituality is witnessed by this book you are reading. It is a sign of the renewal of Christian wisdom in our time.

Significantly, too, Michelle and Paul are both contemplative priests. They suggest that theology, which has largely been written over the past two millennia by celibate males, is putting out new and necessary branches. Their calling to ministry has given them the opportunity to study the tradition more than might be possible for others. They have put this opportunity to great use in the accessible, yet informed, short commentaries they have written together for the annual liturgical cycle.

Very importantly, they write from their own experience of the powerful connection between *lectio* (spiritual reading) and what the early Christian teachers often called *oratio pura*. Pure prayer, or the prayer of the heart or meditation understood in its original sense, is nourished by all dimensions and expressions of prayer. These are not hierarchically or even sequentially organised. By this, I mean that one form is not in itself better than another and you don't have to master one level before moving to another. The long-dominant theory was that you were not ready for contemplative prayer until you had endured the arid complexities (as many found them) of over-cerebral 'discursive meditation'. As this was the formula for most seminary training, it had a disastrous effect on the level of spirituality of the clergy, who were seen as requiring a higher level of knowledge and practice and, by contagion, on the congregations they served. Some churches are still stuck in this spiritual Catch-22, and others are still extricating themselves from its long-lasting effects.

Christian theology, as it took shape in the first centuries, was the product of the fission and fusion of contemplative prayer, taught by Jesus and practised in the 'inner room', and the reading of the Scriptures, the 'living and active word of God'. There is a distinction between these two aspects of prayer but also a union in the silence, stillness and simplicity of contemplation in which thoughts, words and images are surrendered and transcended. In his reflection on the vision of St Francis, *The Journey of the Mind to God*, St Bonaventure speaks of prayer as leading to the suspension of all the operations of the mind, both rational and imaginative. Cassian—Benedict's teacher—similarly speaks of the mantra that leads into the 'grand poverty' of the spirit, a long-lost practice of Western Christianity that John Main powerfully helped to recover.

Michelle and Paul have learned what this practice means on the journey of meditation through their experience and by sharing the teaching with others. This book guides us through the readings of the Sunday liturgy in the light of this inner journey. It is a fruit and a sharing of the journey of the mind and heart to God.

Laurence Freeman OSB
Bonnevaux
October 2023

How to Use This Book

This book is to help you learn and practise silent meditation in the Christian contemplative tradition, ideally within a supportive group context. Although meditation is a rhythmic withdrawal into solitude and silence, it is also beneficial that we belong to a community because:

- meditating with a group of others holds one to the task; like the banks of a river, it contains the discipline
- it enables us to narrate our experience and understandings
- it keeps us in relationship with the Church Universal.

The format we suggest is to begin with the short talk, then practise twenty minutes of silent meditation, followed by the sacred story from the forthcoming Sunday gospel. Silent meditation before the gospel, rather than after, enables a deeper receptivity to the gospel.

The following words or similar may be used to prepare for meditation.

Let us prepare for our practice of twenty minutes of silent meditation. A bell will be rung at the beginning of the meditation period and at the end to close the meditation.

If you already have a meditation practice, please continue to use it and join with us. If you are new to meditation, read some simple instructions on how to meditate from the World Community for Christian Meditation.[1]

Sit still with your back straight. Close your eyes lightly. Then, interiorly, silently begin to recite a single word—a prayer word. We recommend the ancient Christian prayer word *maranatha*. Say it as four equal syllables:
ma-ra-na-tha.
Breathe normally and give your full attention to the word as you say it, silently, gently, faithfully and—above all—simply.
Ma-ra-na-tha.
Stay with the same word during the whole meditation. The essence of meditation is simplicity.

---

[1] https://wccm.org/meditate/how-to-meditate/.

About the Authors

Michelle is an Anglican priest and narrative therapist with thirty years of experience counselling individuals and families. She is a registered professional supervisor with the Australian Counselling Association and provides supervision and consultation to professionals in the counselling, health, legal, religious, government, business, community and education sectors.

Michelle completed postgraduate studies in Zen Buddhism and creative writing. In 2017, she was awarded a PhD from the University of Kent, Canterbury. Her doctorate explored how to narrate the transformative effects of silent meditation, walking in nature and reading literature. She obtained her theological qualifications in biblical studies from Trinity College, Melbourne. In 2018, she was awarded The Catherine Laufer Award for Excellence in Systematic Theology. She has served in parishes as priest-in-charge and honorary associate.

Paul was ordained an Anglican priest in 1988 and has served as priest-in-charge in several parishes in Australia and the United Kingdom. He worked as a counsellor for eight years in a community health setting. He is a keen student of C. G. Jung. He walks, writes and paints.

Acknowledgements

We wish to acknowledge the members of Quiet Communion, who have meditated and reflected in open discussion with these talks over the last four years: Anamaya Milner, Beth Page, Philip Huggins, Bryn Jones, Denise Thamrin, Eden Libby Nicholls, Emily Payne, Ethne Green, Gabrielle Seaton, Helen Bensley, Jan White, Jean Henderson, Jennifer Jones, Judith Moore, Justine Shelton, Kaaren Smethurst, Kate Neal, Ian Thompson, Kristy Thompson, Kylie Webster-Percival, Sandra Halford, Marion Bennett, Marita Pille, Meredith Ure, Michelle Walker, Patricia Hendricks, Rhonda Holden, Richard Merton, Rod Bensley, Rosalind Brown, Sheila Brennan and Suzie Don Leonard.

Contents

Foreword by Laurence Freeman OSB, Director of the World Community for Christian Meditation	iii
How to Use This Book	v
About the Authors	vi
Acknowledgements	ix
Introduction: Silent Meditation and the Lectionary	1
YEAR A. THE YEAR OF ST MATTHEW	3
Advent (Year A)	4

FIRST SUNDAY OF ADVENT (YEAR A) — 4
Nepsis (Watchfulness)
by Michelle Wood

SECOND SUNDAY OF ADVENT (YEAR A) — 5
In the Wilderness of the Self
by Paul Wood

THIRD SUNDAY OF ADVENT (YEAR A) — 7
Are You the One?
by Michelle Wood

FOURTH SUNDAY OF ADVENT (YEAR A) — 9
Dreams and Visions
by Paul Wood

THE BIRTH OF OUR LORD (YEAR A) — 11
Silently, How Silently, the Wondrous Gift is Given
by Michelle Wood

THE EPIPHANY OF OUR LORD (YEAR A) — 13
Journey to the Heart
by Paul Wood

SECOND SUNDAY AFTER EPIPHANY (YEAR A) — 15
Gentleness
by Michelle Wood

THIRD SUNDAY AFTER EPIPHANY (YEAR A) — 16
Letting Go of Entanglements
by Paul Wood

FOURTH SUNDAY AFTER EPIPHANY (YEAR A)   18
A Way of Being the Beatitudes
by Michelle Wood

FIFTH SUNDAY AFTER EPIPHANY (YEAR A)   21
The Saltiness of Silence
by Paul Wood

SIXTH SUNDAY AFTER EPIPHANY (YEAR A)   23
Reconciling Inner and Outer,
*   from the Sermon on the Mount*
by Paul Wood

SEVENTH SUNDAY AFTER EPIPHANY (YEAR A)   24
A Consciousness Not Based on Retribution
by Michelle Wood

EIGHTH SUNDAY AFTER EPIPHANY (YEAR A)   27
The Highest of All Values
by Paul Wood

LAST SUNDAY AFTER EPIPHANY (YEAR A)   29
A Young Woman's Zen Pilgrimage up a Mountain and the Transfiguration
by Michelle Wood

Lent (Year A)   32

FIRST SUNDAY IN LENT (YEAR A)   32
Loving Attention as a Way of Prayer
by Michelle Wood

SECOND SUNDAY IN LENT (YEAR A)   33
Going up the Mountain
by Paul Wood

THIRD SUNDAY IN LENT (YEAR A)   34
The Well Within
by Michelle Wood

FOURTH SUNDAY IN LENT (YEAR A)   35
From Darkness to Light
by Paul Wood

FIFTH SUNDAY IN LENT (YEAR A)   37
Miracles and Home Meditation
by Michelle Wood

SIXTH SUNDAY IN LENT (YEAR A)   38
Entering In
by Paul Wood

Easter (Year A)   40

EASTER SUNDAY (YEAR A)   40
An Essential Easter
by Michelle Wood

SECOND SUNDAY OF EASTER (YEAR A) — 41
Resurrection from Inside
by Paul Wood

THIRD SUNDAY OF EASTER (YEAR A) — 42
Seeing and Recognising: The Road to Emmaus
by Michelle Wood

FOURTH SUNDAY OF EASTER (YEAR A) — 44
Ego, Robbers and the Good Shepherd
by Paul Wood

FIFTH SUNDAY OF EASTER (YEAR A) — 45
Why Meditate? Opening to Christlikeness
by Michelle Wood

SIXTH SUNDAY OF EASTER (YEAR A) — 46
Indwelling
by Paul Wood

SEVENTH SUNDAY OF EASTER (YEAR A) — 48
What's Missing with Zoom? Experimenting with a Guided Entrance
by Michelle Wood

Pentecost (Year A) — 50

DAY OF PENTECOST (YEAR A) — 50
Breath
by Paul Wood

TRINITY SUNDAY: FIRST SUNDAY AFTER PENTECOST (YEAR A) — 52
The Trinity: Our Maker, Keeper and Everlasting Lover
by Michelle Wood

SUNDAY BETWEEN 5 AND 11 JUNE (YEAR A) — 53
Silence within the Drama
by Paul Wood

SUNDAY BETWEEN 12 AND 18 JUNE (YEAR A) — 55
Authority over Unclean Spirits
by Paul Wood

SUNDAY BETWEEN 19 AND 25 JUNE (YEAR A) — 55
The Sword and the Mantra
by Michelle Wood

SUNDAY BETWEEN 26 JUNE AND 2 JULY (YEAR A) — 56
Three Methods of Silent Meditation
by Paul Wood

SUNDAY BETWEEN 3 AND 9 JULY (YEAR A) — 59
Becoming Gentle and Humble of Heart
by Michelle Wood

SUNDAY BETWEEN 10 AND 16 JULY (YEAR A) — 60
The Sower
by Paul Wood

SUNDAY BETWEEN 17 AND 23 JULY (YEAR A)   61
Let the Weeds Be
by Michelle Wood

SUNDAY BETWEEN 24 AND 30 JULY (YEAR A)   62
What is the Kingdom of Heaven Like?
by Paul Wood

SUNDAY BETWEEN 31 JULY AND 6 AUGUST (YEAR A)   64
To Nourish with Nothing
by Michelle Wood

SUNDAY BETWEEN 7 AND 13 AUGUST (YEAR A)   65
A Cry from the Heart
by Paul Wood

SUNDAY BETWEEN 14 AND 20 AUGUST (YEAR A)   67
Heart as the Centre of Practice
by Michelle Wood

SUNDAY BETWEEN 21 AND 27 AUGUST (YEAR A)   68
The Confession of St Peter and Coming to the Heart of the Matter
by Paul Wood

SUNDAY BETWEEN 28 AUGUST AND 3 SEPTEMBER (YEAR A)   69
Meditation and the Divine Life
by Michelle Wood

SUNDAY BETWEEN 4 AND 10 SEPTEMBER (YEAR A)   70
The Value of the Individual
by Paul Wood

SUNDAY BETWEEN 11 AND 17 SEPTEMBER (YEAR A)   72
Forgive from Your Heart Again and Again and Again
by Michelle Wood

SUNDAY BETWEEN 18 AND 24 SEPTEMBER (YEAR A)   73
The Guardians of Silence
by Paul Wood

SUNDAY BETWEEN 25 SEPTEMBER AND 1 OCTOBER (YEAR A)   75
Silence, Inner Authority and Uncritical Love
by Michelle Wood

SUNDAY BETWEEN 2 AND 8 OCTOBER (YEAR A)   77
The Stone
by Paul Wood

SUNDAY BETWEEN 9 AND 15 OCTOBER (YEAR A)   78
The Inner Wedding Banquet
by Michelle Wood

SUNDAY BETWEEN 16 AND 22 OCTOBER (YEAR A)   80
Be in the World but Not of the World
by Paul Wood

SUNDAY BETWEEN 23 AND 29 OCTOBER (YEAR A) — 82
The Way of Love and Small Breaths
by Michelle Wood

SUNDAY BETWEEN 30 OCTOBER AND 5 NOVEMBER (YEAR A) — 83
Immortal, Invisible, God Only Wise
by Paul Wood

SUNDAY BETWEEN 6 AND 12 NOVEMBER (YEAR A) — 84
Our Busy Minds – Half In, Half Out
by Michelle Wood

SUNDAY BETWEEN 13 AND 19 NOVEMBER (YEAR A) — 86
Life as an Egg
by Paul Wood

SUNDAY BETWEEN 20 AND 26 NOVEMBER: CHRIST THE KING (YEAR A) — 87
Sorting through Ourselves
by Michelle Wood

YEAR B. THE YEAR OF ST MARK — 89

Advent (Year B) — 90

FIRST SUNDAY OF ADVENT (YEAR B) — 90
Maranatha – Awake, Alert, Expectant and Full of Hope
by Paul Wood

SECOND SUNDAY OF ADVENT (YEAR B) — 91
Beginnings
by Michelle Wood

THIRD SUNDAY OF ADVENT (YEAR B) — 93
Restoring the Image of God
by Paul Wood

FOURTH SUNDAY OF ADVENT (YEAR B) — 94
Creating a Meditative Womb
by Michelle Wood

THE EPIPHANY OF OUR LORD (YEAR B) — 95
Journey to the Heart
by Paul Wood

FIRST SUNDAY AFTER EPIPHANY (YEAR B) — 96
The River and the Practice of Silent Meditation
by Michelle Wood

SECOND SUNDAY AFTER EPIPHANY (YEAR B) — 97
Between Earth and Heaven
by Paul Wood

THIRD SUNDAY AFTER EPIPHANY (YEAR B) — 99
'Follow Me' and 'I Will Make You'
by Michelle Wood

FOURTH SUNDAY AFTER EPIPHANY (YEAR B)   100
   Exousia
   by Paul Wood

FIFTH SUNDAY AFTER EPIPHANY (YEAR B)   102
   Meditation: A Deserted Place
   by Michelle Wood

SIXTH SUNDAY AFTER EPIPHANY (YEAR B)   103
   Touching the Leper
   by Paul Wood

SEVENTH SUNDAY AFTER EPIPHANY (YEAR B)   105
   Released from Paralysis
   by Paul Wood

EIGHTH SUNDAY AFTER EPIPHANY (YEAR B)   106
   New Wine in New Wineskins
   by Paul Wood

LAST SUNDAY AFTER EPIPHANY: THE TRANSFIGURATION (YEAR B)   109
   Gaining Altitude
   by Paul Wood

Lent (Year B)   111

FIRST SUNDAY IN LENT OR ASH WEDNESDAY (YEAR B)   111
   The Inner Wilderness Pilgrimage
   by Michelle Wood

SECOND SUNDAY IN LENT (YEAR B)   112
   The Cross and Transcendence
   by Paul Wood

THIRD SUNDAY IN LENT (YEAR B)   114
   Our Body a Temple
   by Michelle Wood

FOURTH SUNDAY IN LENT (YEAR B)   115
   The Spectre of the Cross (Snake on a Pole)
   by Paul Wood

FIFTH SUNDAY IN LENT (YEAR B)   117
   A Seed Knows How to Wait
   by Michelle Wood

PALM SUNDAY (YEAR B)   119
   Entrance into Holy Week
   by Paul Wood

MAUNDY THURSDAY (YEAR B)   127
   Love, the Only Thing That Gets Us Through
   by Michelle Wood

Easter (Year B) — 129

SECOND SUNDAY OF EASTER (YEAR B) — 129
The Locked Room
by Paul Wood

THIRD SUNDAY OF EASTER (YEAR B) — 130
The Hidden Harmony
Michelle Wood

FOURTH SUNDAY OF EASTER (YEAR B) — 131
The Good Shepherd Leading Us up: The Great Resurrection Harvest
by Paul Wood

FIFTH SUNDAY OF EASTER (YEAR B) — 133
Abiding
by Michelle Wood

SIXTH SUNDAY OF EASTER (YEAR B) — 135
Inner Guidance
by Paul Wood

ASCENSION DAY (YEAR B) — 136
The Great Silence of God
by Paul Wood

Pentecost (Year B) — 139

DAY OF PENTECOST (YEAR B) — 139
Blow Our Minds
by Michelle Wood

TRINITY SUNDAY (YEAR B) — 141
The Holy Trinity
by Paul Wood

SUNDAY BETWEEN 5 AND 11 JUNE (YEAR B) — 142
Binding the Strong Man
by Paul Wood

SUNDAY BETWEEN 12 AND 18 JUNE (YEAR B) — 144
Love Keeps Breaking Through
by Michelle Wood

SUNDAY BETWEEN 19 AND 25 JUNE (YEAR B) — 145
Crossing over the Sea
by Paul Wood

SUNDAY BETWEEN 26 JUNE AND 2 JULY (YEAR B) — 147
Touching the Holy
by Michelle Wood

SUNDAY BETWEEN 3 AND 9 JULY (YEAR B) — 149
Authority over Unclean Spirits
by Paul Wood

SUNDAY BETWEEN 10 AND 16 JULY (YEAR B) — 150
Silent Meditation and Sweetness of Heart
by Michelle Wood

SUNDAY BETWEEN 17 AND 23 JULY (YEAR B) — 152
A Little Cove of One's Own
by Michelle Wood

SUNDAY BETWEEN 24 AND 30 JULY (YEAR B) — 154
Withdrawal into the Mountains
by Paul Wood

SUNDAY BETWEEN 31 JULY AND 6 AUGUST (YEAR B) — 156
Being Living Bread
by Michelle Wood

SUNDAY BETWEEN 7 AND 13 AUGUST (YEAR B) — 158
The Basics of Meditation
by Paul Wood

SUNDAY BETWEEN 14 AND 20 AUGUST (YEAR B) — 160
Union with Christ
by Paul Wood

SUNDAY BETWEEN 21 AND 27 AUGUST (YEAR B) — 162
Meditation and Eternal Life
by Michelle Wood

SUNDAY BETWEEN 28 AUGUST AND 3 SEPTEMBER (YEAR B) — 163
The Light of the Gospel
by Paul Wood

SUNDAY BETWEEN 4 AND 10 SEPTEMBER (YEAR B) — 165
Take Off Your Rhinoceros Head, Smell the Spring Blossoms and Offer Healing Wherever You Can!
by Michelle Wood

SUNDAY BETWEEN 11 AND 17 SEPTEMBER (YEAR B) — 167
The Cross: In This Place and At This Time
by Paul Wood

SUNDAY BETWEEN 18 AND 24 SEPTEMBER (YEAR B) — 168
The Poetry of Smallness
by Michelle Wood

SUNDAY BETWEEN 25 SEPTEMBER AND 1 OCTOBER (YEAR B) — 171
The Winds of Change
by Paul Wood

SUNDAY BETWEEN 2 AND 8 OCTOBER (YEAR B) — 172
Receive as a Child
by Michelle Wood

SUNDAY BETWEEN 9 AND 15 OCTOBER (YEAR B) — 174
The Narrow Way
by Paul Wood

SUNDAY BETWEEN 16 AND 22 OCTOBER (YEAR B)   176
   Making a Throne of Humility and Peace
   by Michelle Wood

SUNDAY BETWEEN 23 AND 29 OCTOBER (YEAR B)   177
   The Practice of Emptiness
   by Paul Wood

ALL SAINTS' DAY (YEAR B)   179
   The Saints: Mystics, Monastics, Artists and Poets
   by Michelle Wood

SUNDAY BETWEEN 6 AND 12 NOVEMBER (YEAR B)   181
   The Widow's Mite
   by Paul Wood

SUNDAY BETWEEN 13 AND 19 NOVEMBER (YEAR B)   183
   Birth Pangs
   by Michelle Wood

SUNDAY BETWEEN 20 AND 26 NOVEMBER (YEAR B)   184
   The Feast of Christ the King
   by Paul Wood

YEAR C. THE YEAR OF ST LUKE   187

Advent (Year C)   188

FIRST SUNDAY OF ADVENT (YEAR C)   188
   A Way to a Light Heart
   by Michelle Wood

SECOND SUNDAY OF ADVENT (YEAR C)   189
   The Spirituality of the Wilderness
   by Paul Wood

THIRD SUNDAY OF ADVENT (YEAR C)   191
   The Amour of Light
   by Paul Wood

FOURTH SUNDAY OF ADVENT (YEAR C)   193
   The Visitation
   by Paul Wood

CHRISTMAS DAY (YEAR C)   194
   Drawing Near to the Centre of Existence
   by Michelle Wood

THE EPIPHANY OF OUR LORD (YEAR C)   195
   Journey to the Heart
   by Paul Wood

FIRST SUNDAY AFTER EPIPHANY (YEAR C)   195
   Prayer
   by Michelle Wood

SECOND SUNDAY AFTER EPIPHANY (YEAR C) — 198
Water into Wine and the Transformation of Consciousness
by Paul Wood

THIRD SUNDAY AFTER EPIPHANY (YEAR C) — 200
Christ's Manifesto and Meditation
by Michelle Wood

FOURTH SUNDAY AFTER EPIPHANY (YEAR C) — 202
Seeing in the Dark
by Paul Wood

FIFTH SUNDAY AFTER EPIPHANY (YEAR C) — 204
Put Out into Deep Water
by Michelle Wood

SIXTH SUNDAY AFTER EPIPHANY (YEAR C) — 205
The Silence of the Beginning
by Paul Wood

SEVENTH SUNDAY AFTER EPIPHANY (YEAR C) — 207
Mercy and the Moulin Rouge
by Michelle Wood

EIGHT SUNDAY AFTER EPIPHANY (YEAR C) — 209
Love Your Enemies, How…?
by Michelle Wood

LAST SUNDAY AFTER EPIPHANY (YEAR C) — 212
A Cloud of Grace
by Paul Wood

Lent (Year C) — 215

FIRST SUNDAY IN LENT (YEAR C) — 215
The Beloved in the Wilderness
by Michelle Wood

SECOND SUNDAY IN LENT (YEAR C) — 217
Jerusalem, Jerusalem
by Paul Wood

THIRD SUNDAY IN LENT (YEAR C) — 219
The Secret Life Within
by Paul Wood

FOURTH SUNDAY IN LENT (YEAR C) — 221
All That Is Mine Is Yours
by Michelle Wood

FIFTH SUNDAY IN LENT (YEAR C) — 223
The Devotional Life
by Paul Wood

PASSION SUNDAY (YEAR C) — 225
The Gardens of Eden, Gethsemane and Paradise
by Michelle Wood

Easter (Year C) — 227

EASTER SUNDAY (YEAR C) — 227
The Resurrection Life: What Is It?
by Paul Wood

SECOND SUNDAY OF EASTER (YEAR C) — 228
Resurrection from the Inside
by Paul Wood

THIRD SUNDAY OF EASTER (YEAR C) — 229
Boundless Love
by Michelle Wood

FOURTH SUNDAY OF EASTER (YEAR C) — 230
Finding Your Way
by Paul Wood

FIFTH SUNDAY OF EASTER (YEAR C) — 232
A New Commandment
by Paul Wood

SIXTH SUNDAY OF EASTER (YEAR C) — 233
On the Edge
by Paul Wood

SEVENTH SUNDAY OF EASTER (YEAR C) — 235
Making Known Love
by Michelle Wood

ASCENSION DAY (YEAR C) — 237
The Great Silence of God
by Paul Wood

Pentecost (Year C) — 238

DAY OF PENTECOST (YEAR C) — 238
Breath
by Paul Wood

TRINITY SUNDAY (YEAR C) — 238
The Glint of God within Us
by Michelle Wood

SUNDAY BETWEEN 5 AND 11 JUNE (YEAR C) — 240
Compassion in the Temple of the Holy Spirit
by Paul Wood

SUNDAY BETWEEN 12 AND 18 JUNE (YEAR C) — 243
Praying as a Woman Who Shows Great Love
by Michelle Wood

SUNDAY BETWEEN 19 AND 25 JUNE (YEAR C) — 244
The Demoniac of the Gerasenes
by Paul Wood

SUNDAY BETWEEN 26 JUNE AND 2 JULY (YEAR C)   **246**
   To Follow without Distraction
   by Michelle Wood

SUNDAY BETWEEN 3 AND 9 JULY (YEAR C)   **248**
   Pairs of Love and Peace
   by Michelle Wood

SUNDAY BETWEEN 10 AND 16 JULY (YEAR C)   **249**
   The Wounded Self
   by Paul Wood

SUNDAY BETWEEN 17 AND 23 JULY (YEAR C)   **250**
   There Is Need of Only One Thing
   by Michelle Wood

SUNDAY BETWEEN 24 AND 30 JULY (YEAR C)   **252**
   The Lord's Prayer as a Ladder
   by Paul Wood

SUNDAY BETWEEN 31 JULY AND 6 AUGUST (YEAR C)   **255**
   Being Rich towards God
   by Michelle Wood

SUNDAY BETWEEN 7 AND 13 AUGUST (YEAR C)   **258**
   Making Purses for the Kingdom
   by Paul Wood

SUNDAY BETWEEN 14 AND 20 AUGUST (YEAR C)   **260**
   Silent Meditation and Eternal Time
   by Michelle Wood

SUNDAY BETWEEN 21 AND 27 AUGUST (YEAR C)   **262**
   A Sabbath Rest
   by Paul Wood

SUNDAY BETWEEN 28 AUGUST AND 3 SEPTEMBER (YEAR C)   **264**
   Vying for a Place at the Head of the Table
   by Michelle Wood

SUNDAY BETWEEN 4 AND 10 SEPTEMBER (YEAR C)   **265**
   Meditation and Dying
   by Paul Wood

SUNDAY BETWEEN 11 AND 17 SEPTEMBER (YEAR C)   **266**
   The Marriage of Creation and Christ as Centre and Climax of our Salvation
   by Michelle Wood

SUNDAY BETWEEN 18 AND 24 SEPTEMBER (YEAR C)   **269**
   Meditation – A Single Point of Focus
   by Paul Wood

SUNDAY BETWEEN 25 SEPTEMBER AND 1 OCTOBER (YEAR C)   **271**
   The Little Girl at My Gate
   by Michelle Wood

SUNDAY BETWEEN 2 AND 8 OCTOBER (YEAR C)   273
    Faith the Size of a Mustard Seed
        by Paul Wood

SUNDAY BETWEEN 9 AND 15 OCTOBER (YEAR C)   274
    Returning to Give Thanks – My Prayer Practice This Week
        by Michelle Wood

SUNDAY BETWEEN 16 AND 22 OCTOBER (YEAR C)   276
    The Widow and the Corrupt Judge
        by Paul Wood

SUNDAY BETWEEN 16 AND 22 OCTOBER (YEAR C)   278
    Humility
        by Michelle Wood

SUNDAY BETWEEN 23 AND 29 OCTOBER (YEAR C)   280
    Jesus Blesses Little Children
        by Michelle Wood

SUNDAY BETWEEN 30 OCTOBER AND 5 NOVEMBER (YEAR C)   282
    Zacchaeus and Dehiscence
        by Paul Wood

SUNDAY BETWEEN 6 AND 12 NOVEMBER (YEAR C)   283
    Stripping Away Intellectual Peacocking and Returning to a Living Centre of Love
        by Michelle Wood

SUNDAY BETWEEN 20 AND 26 NOVEMBER (YEAR C)   285
    The Feast of Christ the King
        by Paul Wood

Bibliography   287

List of Figures

Figure 1: Entry into Jerusalem	120
Figure 2: The Bridegroom	121
Figure 3: Maundy Thursday. The Washing of Feet	122
Figure 4. The Mystical Supper	123
Figure 5: The Crucifixion	124
Figure 6: Holy Saturday	125
Figure 7: The Resurrection	126

Introduction: Silent Meditation and the Lectionary

Silent meditation in the Christian contemplative tradition is a prayer practice of learning the art of listening. To listen, one must do three things: be still, put self aside and be attentive. If one can do these three things, one will discover a depth of listening. Stillness and silence allow space for receiving. This book will focus on how these enable one to receive the gospels.

This book was conceived by a twofold practice of silent meditation and listening to the gospels. We initially asked ourselves three questions: What, if anything, do the gospels teach about the prayer of silence? How could the prayer of silence help us hear the gospel of love? Does the prayer practice of silent meditation expand the mind and heart to receive the word of the gospel as Benedictine monk John Main expounded? According to him, 'What we do in meditation and in the lifelong process of meditation is to refine our perception down to the single focal point, which is Christ. Christ is our way, our goal, our guide. But he is our goal only in the sense that once we are wholly with him, wholly at one with him, we pass with him to the Father ... It is through Jesus that we pass over from everything that is dead, from everything that is restricted, mortal, finite, into the infinite expansion of God which is the infinite expansion of love.'[2]

We explored these questions by following the lectionary cycle and writing a thematic homily each week for three years.[3] We shared these reflections at our silent meditation practice group Quiet Communion. We crafted each homiletic reflection with exegetical awareness but remained faithful to the questions: How can stillness and silence influence our reception of the gospels, and what can the gospels teach about the prayer of silence? We have also interwoven the reflections with writings from the canon of contemplative Christian literature.

While there is a long tradition of contemplative prayer within the Christian tradition, there is no modern systematic theology that links the lectionary cycle—that is, the Great Prayer of Christian Churches (Anglican, Orthodox and Roman)—to the practice of silent meditation. It is paramount that this link is made so that the prayer of silence is anchored to, participates in and is a unique expression of the Church Universal.

Former archbishop of Canterbury Rowan Williams and Pope Francis gave some cautionary and wise advice in relation to spiritual practices that

---

2   John Main, *The Inner Christ* (London: Darton, Longman and Todd, 1987), 117–18.
3   Anglican Church of Australia, *A Prayer Book for Australia* (Mulgrave, Victoria: Broughton Publishing, 1995).

reflect a type of contemporary personalised mysticism. Pope Francis wrote that Gnosticism and neo-Pelagianism, both of which feed into 'spiritual worldliness', have the following effects: 'The first shrinks Christian faith into a subjectivism that "ultimately keeps one imprisoned in his or her own thoughts and feelings" .... The second cancels out the role of grace and "leads instead to a narcissistic and authoritarian elitism, whereby instead of evangelizing, one analyses and classifies others, and instead of opening the door to grace, one exhausts his or her energies in inspecting and verifying".'[4]

While Pope Francis highlighted what we should avoid, Williams offered a way forward in his writing *Participating in Divinity, Entering Emptiness: The Shape of Transformation*. He suggested, 'we need to reconceive encounter with God as something beyond a confrontation of "selves" (that) relativizes what I say, sense or believe about myself and its supposed needs and wellbeing'.[5]

It is in the cautionary and wise spirit of these two contemporary leaders of the Christian faith that we encourage the Christian meditator, beginner to experienced, to receive our reflections. The Christian practitioner of silent meditation is invited to both let go of their worldly constructed personal subjectivity and conjoin with the Spirit of Christ. From this solidarity in Christ, one is led deeper and deeper into union with God, people and the whole of Creation. Just as the Indigenous people of this land have songlines that tell great sacred stories, Christian sacred stories are found in the texts of the Hebrew Old Testament and the New Testament, particularly in the gospels.

Whether you are an Indigenous person, a Buddhist, Jewish, Islamic or Christian, your spiritual wisdom is embedded in history, landscape and people. It is communicated through dance, text, song, story and ritual. There is no reality to individualised Christianity, just like there is no reality to a tree cut off from its roots. There is only an authentic expression of a received living tradition, revealed in communion across time present, time past and time eternal. The revelation is always the same: love. God loves God's people and all of Creation. Love is God's transformative language.

It is imperative that Christianity be a living tradition that engages with the wide breadth and depth of humanity. Our homiletic reflections thereby seek to learn from and create dialogue with other religious and artistic traditions. A Christian theology in dialogue and transformed by other wisdoms is not one that is watered down. Far from it, it is rather illuminative of the power and inclusiveness of the heart of Christ.

---

4   Francis, *Apostolic Letter Desiderio Desideravi of the Holy Father Francis: To the Bishops, Priests and Deacons, to Consecrated Men and Women, and to the Lay Faithful: On the Liturgical Formation of the People of God* (Rome: Dicastero per la Comunicazione, Libreria Editrice Vaticana, 2022).
5   Rowan Williams, *Looking East in Winter: Contemporary Thought and the Eastern Christian Tradition* (London: Bloomsbury Continuum, 2021), 96.

YEAR A. THE YEAR OF ST MATTHEW

Advent (Year A)

FIRST SUNDAY OF ADVENT (YEAR A)
Matthew 24:36–44

Nepsis (Watchfulness)
BY MICHELLE WOOD

I had a new insight into the gospel reading this week. It is a reading that I have not really liked in the past. At a surface level of reading, it seemingly creates a dichotomy of the chosen and the left-behinds. However, I believe there is a deeper depiction of internal psychological and cosmic transformation in the symbolic arc of this gospel.

The text calls us to be awake and watchful of the divine presence that is on the edges, coming. It asks us to be attentive, ready to receive the love and mystery that is breaking into our ordinary life. It could happen at any time, like bumping into the one with whom you fall in love. You cannot orchestrate or predict it, but you can be alert to when it appears. To respond to a big love story, even at the human level, there is a leaving behind of the mechanistic, purely material and superficial ways of participating in life to enter a more sacred reality.

I notice that the more time I spend in my meditation cell, so to speak, the more I am changed. I am more watchful. I notice the tiniest things in nature, from the beginning blooming of billy buttons to the scent of a ripe apricot in late summer. I can touch the edges of small joys and experience bliss in ways that I was not able to before. Being alert, watchful and awake changes us.

Silent meditation is a practice of developing the muscles of watchfulness (*nepsis*). By being attentive to our breath or prayer word for twenty minutes, we observe what our mind does when directed to focus. We watch its cunning ways of disrupting and distracting our focus. Like a shepherd guarding her sheep from a fox, we watchfully guard our attention. Through this process of watchfulness, we learn to pay attention.

In his book, *Looking East in Winter: Contemporary Thought and the Eastern Christian Tradition*, Rowan Williams wrote a theology of why the practice of contemplative prayer and silent meditation are crucial to our development as humans. He bases much of his thought on the *Philokalia*, a collection of the early writings of the desert fathers and mothers from the third and fourth centuries.

A touchstone in all the *Philokalia* writings is the practice of *nepsis*, which means watchfulness. Inner watchfulness and self-awareness are the two eyes of the contemplative, and they are underscored in our reading this week.

Drawing on the work of Evagrius, Williams describes *nepsis* as a state of angelic awareness. He wrote that the practice of *nepsis* teaches us to ask of each impression or sensation how far we are turning it into something other than itself by applying its significance to our needs and projections.[6]

Being watchful of our thoughts and looking towards the edge of our consciousness, we wait, ready to receive new realities with angelic awareness.

SECOND SUNDAY OF ADVENT (YEAR A)
Matthew 3:1–12

In the Wilderness of the Self
BY PAUL WOOD

John the Baptist was a wild man. He wore camelhair with a leather belt about his waist and ate locusts and wild honey. As a wilderness man, he was not bound by the conventions and expectations of culture and polite society. He was a man close to nature and close to God.

So, what has John the Baptist to do with meditation? Well, two things. First, many meditators seeking solitude are close to nature. They often feel they are like John the Baptist: 'the voice of one crying out in the wilderness'.[7]

Second, John the Baptist is not the main event, for the main event is the coming of Christ. John is simply the forerunner, and he occupies that primal and empty space before the event. He stands in the tradition of prophets of the Old Testament and points beyond himself 'to One who is coming'.

There is a sense in which by meditation we also stand in that place within ourselves that is before the event, before we display our behaviour, before we speak our words and before we act—a place that is a little like the wilderness in that it is unbound by the whims of others, a place within ourselves where the wind blows free and that has not yet been brought to heel by the conventions of society and the external world. This is a place where our minds might roam freely in the great wilderness of the inner self. This is the wilderness place all meditators come to know.

---

6   Williams, *Looking East in Winter*, 31.
7   John 1:23.

When we are in the wilderness of the self, we are in the place of raw experience. We are a little closer to our primal and primitive being, for it is a place that reveals our secret thoughts to ourselves. It is a place where our intentions are displayed before our very eyes. It is a place that confronts us with the truth of ourselves, as we really are, before the truth of God, as God really is. So, we need a shepherd, a guide and a protector if we are to roam in the wilderness of the self.

In the Old Testament, Moses and the 'pillar of cloud and fire' led the children of Israel through the wilderness to the Promised Land. In the New Testament, Jesus and the Holy Spirit lead us through the wilderness of our soul and into resurrection. That is the journey!

When we meditate, we close our eyes and so we close the door of our cell. Rather than fumbling about in our inner selves going everywhere—and going nowhere—we instead bring our minds to focus with single intent on our prayer word or phrase. This keeps one's mind attentive in one place, and this is like the pillar of fire, leading the children of Israel out of slavery into freedom.

For example, one prayer phrase we might use is *maranatha*, which in Aramaic, the language that Jesus spoke, means 'Come Lord'. John Main, the Benedictine monk behind the World Community for Christian Meditation, said it is the earliest Christian prayer and has the right phonic qualities to keep our minds attentive in one place.

Alternatively, we may use the greatly loved Jesus Prayer, 'Lord Jesus Christ, Son of God, have mercy on me, a sinner.' The prayer phrase keeps us from wandering about in the wilderness in no particular direction, going everywhere/nowhere. It keeps us facing east, as it were, towards the Promised Land. It also keeps us in right relation to 'the Shepherd and guardian of our souls'.[8]

Just as John the Baptist was a wilderness man, close to nature and close to God, we as meditators also belong to that wilderness spiritual tradition. So, let us leave for a moment the busy streets of the world, and for twenty minutes withdraw into the windswept expanse of the wilderness within ourselves. Remember, as Kenneth Leech so clearly demonstrated in his study of 'The God of the Desert', the wilderness is the primary source for knowing God.[9]

---

8   1 Pet. 2:25.
9   Kenneth Leech, *True God: An Exploration in Spiritual Theology* (London: Sheldon Press, 1985), 127–61.

THIRD SUNDAY OF ADVENT (YEAR A)
Matthew 11:2–11

Are You the One?
BY MICHELLE WOOD

In this week's sacred story, a question is put to Jesus by John the Baptist. Are you the One? The One for whom we have been waiting? The One of whom Isaiah wrote to the people:

> *He will come and save you.*
> *Then the eyes of the blind shall be opened,*
> *and the ears of the deaf unstopped;*
> *then the lame shall leap like a deer,*
> *and the tongue of the speechless sing for joy.*
> *For waters shall break forth in the wilderness,*
> *and streams in the desert.*[10]

John had been locked in a cell in the fortress palace of Machaerus, overlooking the Dead Sea for twelve months when he uttered the question: 'Are you the One?' I wonder with what tone of voice he asked this question.

Perhaps in that dark stone cell he felt alone, vulnerable, with doubts creeping in. Perhaps he had had enough of everything and had come to the end of himself. Perhaps he was questioning his life's meaning. A meaning that hangs on an answer to that question, 'Are you the One?'

Folk singer Leonard Cohen also grappled with this question in his last album, *You Want it Darker*. In a song called 'It Seemed a Better Way', he wrote:

> *I wonder what it was*
> *I wonder what it meant*
> *First he touched on love*
> *Then he touched on death*
> *Sounded like the truth*
> *Seemed the better way*
> *Sounded like the truth*
> *But it's not that truth today*
> *I wonder what it was*
> *I wonder what it meant.*[11]

---

10   Isa. 35:4–6.
11   Leonard Cohen, 'It Seemed the Better Way', recorded between April 2015 and July 2016, track 7 on *You Want It Darker*, Columbia Records, 2016, compact disc.

At the time of writing, Cohen was facing death, darkness and doubt. Cohen, brought up Jewish, asks with curiosity, 'Was Jesus the Messiah?' He does not have the answers but, like John the Baptist, is willing to ask the question: 'Are you the One?'

To grapple with questions is to open oneself. To receive the answer to this question has huge consequences. Former archbishop of Canterbury Rowan Williams wrote, 'To the extent that any praying Christian becomes truly open to the act of God in Christ, they become a sign and foretaste of the end things: they signify what happens when the materiality of this world is given over to Christ.'[12]

Another way of explaining this is that by opening to the act of God in Christ, one meets the end of things as they appear in a consumerist, scientific, rationalistic world. Things are not material objects for our narcissistic exploits. Instead, all is divine, exuding a sacredness.

This opening to the act of God in Christ is utterly transformative and psychologically apocalyptic. Apocalyptic, in the literal sense of the Greek word, means 'uncovering'. It not only transforms how we view the world, but also who we are. As St Paul wrote in his letter to the Galatians, 'It is no longer I who live, but it is Christ who lives in me. And the life I live in the flesh I live by the faith of the Son of God who loved me and gave himself for me.'[13]

When John the Baptist opened himself to the act of God in Christ, he became the fullest expression of whom he was created to be: the messenger to prepare the way. In silent meditation, we practise opening to God. At times, it is an act of doubt, questioning and vulnerability.

This giving over to God involves, in part, ending entertaining our thoughts and mental constructions and returning to a simple prayer word or breath practice. Evagrius, a desert father, explained it this way: 'If … you wish to behold and commune with God who is beyond sense-perception and beyond conception, you must free yourself from every impassioned thought.'[14]

By quietening our thoughts, we can come to feel the living stream in the wilderness of ourselves. It is not always easy to sit and pray in this way. Perhaps, like John the Baptist, we sometimes come to the end of self, where doubts lay bare and anxieties heighten, where we ask questions such as, 'Has all my churchgoing, studies, meditation practice and prayers amounted to naught?'

---

12 Williams, *Looking East in Winter*, 250.
13 Gal. 2:20.
14 Nikodimos and Makarios, *The Philokalia: The Complete Text, Vol. 1*, trans. G. E. H. Palmer, Philip Sherrard and Kallistos Ware (New York: Farrar, Straus and Giroux, 1979), 57.

When our silence has us facing uncomfortable uncertainties and the hypocrisies both inside us and in the world, we can take some solace in the words of St Benedict: 'Prayer is not just quiet time; it is an invitation to grow. It breaks us open to the designs of God for life.'[15]

So, let us in this time of silent meditation give ourselves over to the mystery of the One, who says, 'Listen, and see the good news.'

FOURTH SUNDAY OF ADVENT (YEAR A)
Matthew 1:18–25

Dreams and Visions
BY PAUL WOOD

An angel of the Lord appeared to Joseph in a dream and said, 'Joseph, do not be afraid to take Mary as your wife, for the child conceived in her is from the Holy Spirit.'

This is a rich reading with many themes, such as the cultural ethics around marriage, the vulnerability of women and the judgements of society. We could also talk about St Joseph, an example to all men to 'do the honourable thing' and protect their woman. However, what shines out for me is Joseph's dream in solving his complex dilemma.

Our biblical tradition has an exceptionally long history of dreams being a way through which God reveals things to us, insights about the nature of things or warnings and directions about the future. A basic search of the Bible will reveal over three hundred references to dreams, some that refer to normal night dreams but others that refer to waking dreams called visions. For example, we all know the story of Jacob's ladder, his dream of a 'ladder set up between earth and heaven with angels ascending and descending upon it.'[16] We have all heard the story of Joseph the dreamer and his coat of many colours and how Joseph became the prime minister of Egypt because he could interpret dreams.[17]

Prophets throughout the Old Testament had dreams and interpreted dreams, like the great dreams throughout the Book of Daniel, which tell of the rise and fall of kingdoms. Other prophets had visions of the glory of the

---

15 Joan Chittister, The Rule of Benedict: A Spirituality for the 21st Century (New York: Crossroad, 2010), 19.
16 Gen. 28:10–17.
17 Gen. 41.

Lord, such as Isaiah's vision in the temple[18] or Ezekiel's on the banks of River Chebar[19] and his amazing vision of the Valley of Dry Bones.[20] We all know that the Book of Revelation is a vision, a vision that John had on the island of Patmos that tells of the close of the age and the coming of the Kingdom of Christ.

So, it is little wonder that among all these narratives is the Christmas Nativity story, full of dreams, angels, stars and prophecies. Our Christian tradition takes both dreams and visions very seriously, and so, one might ask oneself, 'How is my dream life? Is it rich? Is it fruitful? Is it healing?'

Psychoanalysts such as Freud and Jung believed that dreams reveal to us what is happening in our unconscious minds. Both spent many hours interpreting dreams as a healing cure and recommended listening to dreams for psychological growth.

What really attracts me about dreams is that they come from the inside; they are very private and personal. They come from that same mysterious place from which thoughts originate, that mysterious place from which creativity arises, that mysterious place hidden somewhere within each person from which life begins.

Dreams are like the intertidal zone between our consciousness and the immense ocean of God. When we pray, we consciously and intentionally enter this intertidal zone. However, when we dream, the intertidal zone comes to us. In the ebb and flow of waking and dreaming, many bits and pieces and strange things can be found in and recovered from this intertidal zone. An extremely significant part of prayer life is paddling about in that intertidal zone, just on the edge of everyday consciousness and just on the edge of the great mystery of God.

There are many ways one can do this: Bible reading, verbal prayer, liturgy and creative activities such as journalling, painting, playing music or writing poetry or fiction. Something that I have practised for over thirty years now is writing and developing a dream story, a process Jung called 'active imagination', which has become a rich source of personal revelation to me.

To be a contemplative is to sit on the edge of one's conscious mind, in the intertidal zone as it were. Perhaps 'beachcombing' is a good metaphor to describe what we are doing. Perhaps 'fishing' is another, waiting for a dream, an idea or a new insight.

When we practise meditation, we are doing two things. First, we are becoming absolutely still and silent within ourselves. This involves getting

---

18   Isa. 6.
19   Ezek. 1.
20   Ezek. 37.

rid of the clutter and fluster of the world, bringing us to the water's edge as it were. Second, we are learning to become attentive and receptive before the great mysterious ocean. By reciting our prayer word, we become focused, attentive and receptive.

THE BIRTH OF OUR LORD (YEAR A)
Titus 3:4–8a

Silently, How Silently, the Wondrous Gift is Given
BY MICHELLE WOOD

Who do you really love? Picture them. If you could give them anything, what would you give them?

I really love my husband, and if I could give him anything I would give him the health of his twenty-year-old former self, buckets of energy and a long life with me (I am a fair bit younger and fear life without him). I really love my children. What would I give them if I could give anything?

Well, I have five adult children. To one, I would give freedom from anxiety. To another, I would give a workplace that allowed her to grow and work with others rather than struggle on her own. To the third, I would give the gift of courage, and to the fourth, relationship discernment. To the last, who is about to have a baby, I would give the gift of excellent health, safety in delivery and fulfilment in being a mother, plus solid love with her partner as they begin to build a family. Apart from my family, who else in my life do I really love?

Well, I really love the people that I work with in counselling. What would I give some of them? For one young woman, who had terrible abuse as a child, I would give her internal and external safety, a future in which she is never harmed again, an abundance of real love, opportunities to study, learn and use all her gifts. Abuse robbed her of so much! I would also give her one friend, a genuine friend who was her age. I think that would make her really happy.

To the beautiful young couple with two small children who are questioning their early marriage because of infidelities, I would give the gift of forgiveness, healing and faithfulness. To the older man who has been recently dumped in love and who is quite lonely, I would give a new companion who would love and adore him back to good health.

It is interesting to think about what we would give and what difference that would make. It strikes me that these gifts of love also give life. For what blocks life are loneliness, anxiety, isolation, fear, confusion, violence, dishonesty and lack of care when vulnerable. However, love unblocks a person, enabling life to flourish.

In our reading from Titus today, we are told that 'when the goodness and loving kindness of God our Saviour appeared, he saved us … according to his mercy'.[21] God's mercy is a constant and generous flow of love and goodness, like sunlight. In the birth of Jesus, God came to feed the whole of humanity with goodness and loving kindness, to feed us with these treasures like a mother feeds her baby.

Jesus was born in Bethlehem. Bethlehem is a Hebrew word that means 'house of bread'. It is no coincidence that the one who would go on to proclaim, 'I am the bread of life, they who come to me will not hunger',[22] was born in the place called the house of bread. 'I came so that you may have life and have it abundantly'[23] is how Jesus describes his coming to us.

God's intimate gift to us is his Son, who has come to us, to love us, touch us, heal us, feed us and dwell in us and among us. It is a gift of never-ending nourishment, surprising us with small joys each day that give life. The more we can receive the gifts of God's goodness and loving kindness, the more we will be transformed into bearers of love for others.

How do we receive this wonderous gift? St Jerome, an early Church father, gave us an idea. He recommended that we make a Bethlehem heart, a little humble manger within. He wrote, 'Blessed are those who possess Bethlehem in their hearts and in whose hearts Christ is born daily.'[24]

It is a beautiful idea, this Bethlehem heart; how might we come to develop it? What shape could our lives take if in our hearts Christ is born daily? Perhaps we would be a little more able to give some of those gifts to the ones whom we love. Perhaps we could extend our giving to those who we have no personal connection with but who really need it. May our practice of silent meditation strengthen our Bethlehem heart, our little manger within.

---

21   Titus 3:4.
22   John 6:35.
23   John 10:10.
24   Robert Atwell, *Celebrating the Saints* (London: Canterbury Press, 2016), 457.

THE EPIPHANY OF OUR LORD (YEAR A)
Matthew 2:1–12

Journey to the Heart
BY PAUL WOOD

This week, we celebrate the Epiphany, the revelation of Christ to the gentiles. It is the story of the Magi. There are two reasons that this story of the Magi, the visitors from the East, can teach us something about Christian meditation.

First, the Magi did not follow the Hebrew scriptures. Instead, they followed a star! The significance is that they were gentiles; they came from outside the Jews, outside the covenant that God has with Abraham and his descendants. They were not circumcised. They did not have the Scriptures to guide them. They did not have the stories of the patriarchs, the Law of Moses, the Ten Commandments or the writings of the prophets, and they did not know of the coming Messiah. They were not Abraham's descendants. Rather, they were outsiders who found their way through life, not through the special revelation of the Scriptures but through the general revelation of God in nature. They were pagans and were schooled in the arts of observing the stars and seasons. These skills brought them to the Holy Land, seeking the newborn king. Here they inquired further and learned, from those who did know the Scriptures, that the Christ was to be born in Bethlehem. With that confirmation, they continued to follow the star until it came to a stop—over the house where the Christ Child was.

In many ways, this is what meditation is. It is like following a star. We journey by faithfully following a prayer word, a prayer phrase or the breath, like footsteps following the star of Bethlehem—right foot, left foot, a rhythm—and this is how we stay focused, how we are led to the Christ Child.

So, for example, in meditation one might use the Jesus Prayer as one's prayer phrase. 'Lord Jesus … have mercy'. As we focus on our prayer, we follow it as if it is the star of Bethlehem. This practice, so the desert tradition tells us, will bring us into the heart, into the centre. At the centre is the Logos that holds the whole of the created order together, without which there is disintegration into chaos. St John stated that Christ is the Logos, the Eternal Word of God.[25]

At the centre, there is no Jew and gentile divide. There is no 'us and them', for the centre, like the Logos, holds all things together in one place.

This universal vision of Christ is the mystery that St Paul explained 'was hidden for ages past but is now revealed' and that the 'gentiles are fellow heirs

---

25   John 1:1–3.

and members of the same body'.[26] Thus, when we meditate, we are coming to the centre, to the heart, where we also find Christ 'who is before all things and in him all things hold together'.[27]

The second reason that this story fits with meditation is that at the end of the journey, the Magi entered the house and saw the child with Mary, his mother, and they kneeled and worshipped the Christ Child, the One they had been searching for their whole journey. Opening their treasure chests, they offered him gold, frankincense and myrrh.[28]

The end of their journey was surrender and adoration: falling in worship and offering the gifts they had been carrying since their journey began. This 'adoration and surrender' is what the meditator seeks to cultivate. This is particularly so if one practises the surrender methods of meditation, in which the discipline is to become empty of self through self-surrender. Thus, thoughts that arise are not held onto or entertained but simply let go of and surrendered. Each thought, each feeling, each distraction is surrendered. Finally, your whole self is surrendered to God.

Often people discover that their minds are like a puppy that wants to follow every smell that comes its way. The prayer word is an intervention to break this habit and stay attentive to one thing. The task is to remain in that posture of surrendering to God. When you drift away from it, caught up in a thought, then your prayer word, like the star of Bethlehem, will remind you to come back on track.

This practice of focusing and pouring out all of your treasures and surrendering them into the eternal, that's the journey! Let us now move into a short season of meditation.

Let us gently close our eyes. Let us become absolutely still in body and still in the mind. Because the mind will always wander, we use a prayer phrase to keep it tethered in one place: *Lord Jesus, have mercy. Lord Jesus, have mercy.* Like left foot, like right foot. *Lord Jesus, have mercy.*

As we surrender our thoughts and feelings, we allow release as all tensions slip away. Our intention is to be open-hearted before the great mystery of Christ at the centre of existence. Let us stay with this intention for twenty minutes.

---

26 Eph. 3:1–13.
27 Col. 1:17.
28 Matt. 2:11.

SECOND SUNDAY AFTER EPIPHANY (YEAR A)
John 1:29–42

Gentleness

BY MICHELLE WOOD

Contemporary theologian Miroslav Volf narrated a story about a golden nib pen. The pen was exceptionally beautiful and crafted with the utmost of care. It was an object of immense pleasure, so slick and smooth to use. However, the depth of its pleasure came from more than its functionality and beauty; it came from the story he carried in relation to it. For the golden nib pen was a gift from his father. Each time he used this pen, he connected to the depth of love with which it was given and the depth of love that he had for his father.

In this simple story, we can deduce how objects become symbols of something more. So, let us think about this in relation to the practice of silent meditation. What are the symbols that inform and envelop this practice?

In this week's sacred story, we are offered a symbol to consider that runs deeply through the Old Testament, the Gospel of John and the Book of Revelation.

Jesus walked towards John the Baptist, who declared, 'Here is the Lamb of God who takes away the sin of the world!'[29]

The lamb in the Christian sacred stories is a symbol of innocence, purity and gentleness. Its roots reach as far back as the Book of Exodus, when the lamb was sacrificed to protect and save the people of Israel, and as far forward as the poetic Lamb that sits on the throne at the end of all time in the Book of Revelation. The gentle Lamb, the Christ, who by sacrificing himself overcame all violence and evil.

Gentleness of heart, mind and action is central to a Christian path. Evagrius the Solitary, a desert monk from the fourth century, underscored this in his *153 Texts on Prayer*. He made the key statement that 'prayer is the flower of gentleness and freedom from anger'.[30]

In the practice of silent meditation, we are attentive to this flowering gentleness, the indwelling Spirit of Christ. We authentically contend with all that is within us that distracts from this union.

Letting go of those distracting thoughts and feelings is a psychological sacrifice. In obedience to reciting a prayer phrase or following our breath,

---

29 John 1:29.
30 Nikodimos and Makarios, *Philokalia*, 57.

we practise the art of dying to solipsism, egocentricity and judgementalism, dying to our feelings of anger, pride, greed, rivalry and hatred.

Silent meditation in a Christian sense is not a personal improvement plan but rather a practice of surrendering into the love of God, just like the Lamb of God. Through this prayer act of sacrificial love, we are transformed.

Gentleness is the flower of silent prayer. Freedom from anger and violence is the way of the Lamb. When we sit in silent meditation, beyond the obvious physical discipline, we stretch towards a symbolic and sacred connection to the Lamb of God, the peace of Christ.

By praying in this way, our hope is to deepen and strengthen this awareness so that we can live not only at a functional golden nib pen level but also through attentively offering small or large acts of sacrificial love in our day-to-day lives to bring more gentleness to what is so often a harsh world.

THIRD SUNDAY AFTER EPIPHANY (YEAR A)
Matthew 4:12–25

Letting Go of Entanglements
BY PAUL WOOD

The Epiphany continues. The people who walked in darkness have observed a great light, and John the Baptist has preached his message: 'One is coming.' And so, the light of the gospel is spreading. As he went about preaching in synagogues and healing the sick, Jesus' first message was, 'Repent, for the kingdom of God is near.'[31] So, all the towns in Galilee were abuzz with the good news. In this context, 'Jesus walked by the Sea of Galilee. He saw two fishermen. And he said to them, follow me. And immediately they left their nets and followed him.'[32]

The word 'immediately' has always bothered me. It seems all too easy. Letting go of your nets, your livelihood, your family. Letting go to follow Jesus. My experience is that letting go is difficult. In fact, my following Jesus has been more like dragging my nets along, tangled up with a whole lot of baggage that I cannot let go. So, I'd like to discuss letting go. Of course, letting go is only the first of many 'letting goes' that comprise the Christian spiritual journey, but this is the first and the primal one.

We see this, for example, in the story of Abraham in the Old Testament. Abraham is called the 'father of the faith' because biblical faith began with

---

31   Matt. 3:2.
32   Matt. 4:18–22.

him. This is how his story began. 'Now the Lord said to Abram, "Go from your country and your kindred and your father's house to the land that I will show you"'.[33] Faith begins with leaving, by letting go of present contingencies to journey to that place that the Lord will show.

Letting go can also be found in the story of Moses and the ancient Hebrews as they journeyed to the Promised Land. It began by leaving Egypt. It was difficult to extract them from Egypt. In fact, it involved a whole drama, including plagues, but in the end, they were let go. Leaving, letting go, detaching, breaking away, being set free are all part of the Christian journey to claim the freedom of one's own agency so that one can journey to the Promised Land.

The desert mothers and fathers of the early Church taught that one should not just leave the entanglements of this world but should flee from them. Flee into the desert and learn the ways of solitude, freedom and intimacy with God to become purified of heart and more Christlike.

Let go. Detach. Flee! Remember, we are attached not just to possessions, like the rich young man who wanted to follow Jesus but could not do so because he could not let go of his wealth. We also have psychological attachments, be they hurts, resentments, ideas, habits, identities or assumptions. Sometimes the self becomes so entangled with the culture of this world that we need to be reminded of our baptisms: that we have died to the world and have been raised anew with Christ. Letting go is like a death and resurrection.

As I reflected on this apparent ease with which the disciples were able to let go of their nets and follow Christ, I came to understand that they were able to let go because they were inspired by love, because it is only love that will take you beyond yourself. Everyone who has fallen in love knows that love makes you do crazy things. Love will inspire you to cross mountains, rivers and seas. Love is a long journey, which, if you remain faithful to it, will bring you to the Cross, where you must break with the selfish self to stay in relationship with the one you love. Love will cause you to journey beyond yourself, beyond the things of this world and ultimately return into the divine. Thus, it was the inspiration of love that enabled the disciples to simply let go and follow Jesus.

As we come to meditate, let us for a while let go of our mental constructions and other distractions and instead allow our hearts, like a compass, to point the way, for the flow of love is always returning to the source, the Creator.

---

33   Gen. 12:1.

FOURTH SUNDAY AFTER EPIPHANY (YEAR A)
Matthew 5:1–12

A Way of Being the Beatitudes
BY MICHELLE WOOD

Mother Maria Skobtsova of Paris was born in Russia in 1891. She was an intellectual and a poet. Divorced twice, she had three children and entered monastic orders at the age of forty-one on the condition that she would not be cloistered but be able to live alongside the people.

Mother Maria worked with refugees and destitute people in France in the 1930s and was a courageous defender of Jewish people during the German occupation of Paris.[34] Her life was one of a contemplative in action, sustained by the Beatitudes. She wrote, 'Not only do we know the Beatitudes, but at this hour, this very minute, surrounded though we are by a dismal and despairing world, we already savour the blessedness they promise.'[35]

I have three thoughts on why Mother Maria is a model and an inspiration for us as practitioners of silent meditation, but first let us explore her living the Beatitudes.

Blessed are the poor in spirit, for theirs is the kingdom of heaven.[36]

Mother Maria's day typically began with a journey to Les Halles to beg for food or buy cheaply whatever was not donated. The cigarette-smoking, beggar nun became well known among the stalls. She would return home with a sack of bones, fish and overripe fruit and vegetables to provide up to 120 meals each day at her house of hospitality in Paris for people in need.[37]

Blessed are those who mourn, for they will be comforted.[38]

When she was thirty-six years of age, Maria lost her second child, Anastasia, who was three years old, to influenza. This wound of love and grief enabled her to closely identify with the grief of Mary, the mother of Jesus.

From this she developed a theology about caring for others, not on the basis of moral duty, ethics or purity of spiritual advancement, but rather one rooted in the flesh of our shared humanity and relationships. Mary grieved for Jesus not because it was the right thing to do but because she loved him. Mother Maria's catchcry was that love must be at the centre of all our actions.

---

34   Williams, *Looking East in Winter*, 216.
35   Jim Forrest, 'The Challenge of a 20th Century Saint, Maria Skobtsova', Pravmir.com, last modified 31 March 2015, https://www.pravmir.com/the-challenge-of-a-20th-century-saint-maria-skobtsova/.
36   Matt. 5:3.
37   Forrest, 'Challenge of a 20th Century Saint'.
38   Matt. 5:4.

Blessed are the meek, for they will inherit the earth.[39]

I am not sure if Mother Maria was that meek or gentle! Perhaps if we gaze into her face, we can sense a gentleness in its softness. Metropolitan Anthony of Sourozh provided an impression of what Mother Maria was like in those days: 'She was a very unusual nun in her behaviour and her manners. I was simply staggered when I saw her for the first time. I was walking along the Boulevard Montparnasse. In front of a café, there was a table, on the table was a glass of beer, and behind the glass was sitting a Russian nun in full monastic robes. I looked at her and decided that I would never go near that woman. I was young then and held extreme views.'[40]

Blessed are those who hunger and thirst for righteousness, for they will be filled.[41]

During Germany's occupation of Paris, many Jews came to Mother Maria's house of hospitality to seek refuge, shelter and a baptism certificate to be spared arrest and persecution. She worked tirelessly with her assistant priest Friar Dimitri to forge certificates and the church baptismal register. They were convinced that Christ would do the same in such circumstances.

Blessed are the merciful, for they will receive mercy.[42]

When the nuns in her community complained about others not complying with prayer or their liturgical duties, Mother Maria responded, 'Piety, piety … but where is the love that moves mountains?'[43]

Blessed are the pure in heart, for they will see God.[44]

Mother Maria wrote, 'The vocation of hospitality is much more than the provision of food, clothing, and a place to sleep. In its depths, it is a contemplative vocation. It is the constant search for the face of Christ in the stranger.'[45]

Blessed are the peacemakers, for they will be called children of God.[46]

Mother Maria wrote, 'Love is purposive, aiming at transfiguration. But this can only happen when we enter the "inner atmosphere" of the other … "Attention, sobriety, and love" should characterize our engagement—neither beginning from a fixed model of how change should come about, nor being "sentimentally" affirming the given state of the other.'[47]

---

39 Matt. 5:5.
40 Forrest, '20th Century Saint'.
41 Matt. 5:6.
42 Matt. 5:7.
43 Forrest, '20th Century Saint'.
44 Matt. 5:8.
45 Forrest, '20th Century Saint'.
46 Matt. 5:9.
47 Williams, *Looking East in Winter*, 229.

Blessed are those who are persecuted for righteousness' sake, for theirs is the kingdom of heaven.[48]

In Paris, 12,884 Jews were arrested en masse in 1942. Of these, 6,900 (two-thirds of whom were children) were brought to a sports stadium just a kilometre from Mother Maria's house on Rue de Lourmel. Held there for five days, the captives received only water from a single hydrant. From there, the captives were to be sent to Auschwitz.

Mother Maria had often thought her monastic robe a godsend in aiding her work. Now it opened the way for her to enter the stadium. Here, she worked for three days comforting the children and their parents, distributing what food she could bring in, even managing to rescue a number of children by enlisting the aid of garbage collectors and smuggling them out in trash bins.[49] Her house was closed by the Gestapo, and Mother Maria, her son Yuri and her assistant priest Friar Dimitri were all arrested.

Blessed are you when people revile you and persecute you and utter all kinds of evil against you falsely on my account.[50]

Mother Maria was killed at Ravensbrück concentration camp in Germany on Holy Saturday in 1945. A fellow prisoner wrote of Mother Maria, 'She radiated the peace of God and communicated it to us.'[51] She was canonised St Maria of Paris in 2004.

So, three thoughts on how the spirit and writings of St Maria of Paris can inform our practice of silent meditation.[52] First, St Maria, while a great intellectual and person of deep contemplation, was able to just freely connect with and love people.

Our meditation practice hopefully helps us to connect better with other people. As we practise letting go of worldly constructions that distance and divide us from others, hopefully we are clearing the way for, as St Maria put it, the 'showing through of love' in our everyday lives.

Second, we practise attentiveness, a giving over of self, a letting go, making space for God. Perhaps this is the very training that may help us enter the 'inner atmosphere of the other' as Mother Maria put it. I certainly have experienced becoming a better listener and counsellor through the practice of silent meditation.

Third, the prayer of silent meditation opens us to our rootedness in Christ and, therefore, our solidarity with all people. Through this very opening to

---

48   Matt. 5:10.
49   Forrest, 'Challenge of a 20th Century Saint'.
50   Matt. 5:11.
51   Forrest, '20th Century Saint'.
52   Skobtsova, Maria, *Mother Maria Skobtsova: Essential Writings*, trans. Larissa Volokhonsky and Richard Pevear (Maryknoll, NY: Orbis Books, 2003).

transformation and communion, we grow the potential to see as St Maria saw: 'Each person is the very icon of God incarnate in the world.'[53]

FIFTH SUNDAY AFTER EPIPHANY (YEAR A)
Matthew 5:13–20

The Saltiness of Silence
BY PAUL WOOD

You are the salt of the earth, but if salt has lost its taste, how can its saltiness be restored?[54]

As I ponder this saying from the Sermon on the Mount, I find myself wondering how it might apply to silent meditation and ask: What is our 'saltiness'? How does promoting silence enhance the world, our community and each other? Are we in danger of losing our saltiness?

First, I would like to suggest that our saltiness has something to do with a sense of the sacred, a sense that there is something special, something different from what is ordinary and common, something transcendent, something holy. Having a sacred sense gives an edge to that which is ordinary and everyday, in the same way that salt flavours food.

In the Hebrew scriptures, the word for sacred has its root in 'to cut' or 'to separate', because when something is made holy, it is cut off from the ordinary and set aside for the purposes of God. It is made distinct and different from what is normal and everyday. Of course, as meditators, we have consecrated silence. Silence is special. We have made it like a sacrament and a vehicle of God's grace. Thus, we would hope that our saltiness is that we carry this sacred silence within us amid the great drama of life.

Second, our saltiness has a distinct narrative. The story that the ordinary secular world offers our children is that we come from nothing, and we return to nothing. In contrast, our story is that we come from the great mystery of God who is love, and we return to this great mystery of God who is love. If we have a good narrative that joins all the dots of experience for us, a narrative that embodies our values and creates our meanings, it will offer something of real value that enriches all the flavours of the world.

It is important that such a narrative include the ancient stories that connect us all the way back to the dawn of consciousness, stories about God's

---

53   Forrest, '20th Century Saint'.
54   Luke 14:34–35.

love and stories about human folly. Stories about how love works through confession and forgiveness and the importance of recreation and salvation. A grand narrative that embraces the mysteries of how we came to be, what we are doing here, where it is all going and what the point is. Our challenge is to have a narrative that is true and legitimate, consistent and orthodox. So, our question must be: 'What is the place of silence in the Christian narrative?'

Here is a sketch. Silence is the canvas upon which the whole drama of life happens. The opening sentence of the Bible is a silent place of darkness and emptiness before the first word, 'Let there be light.' Silence is the backdrop to the biblical drama of the Word. In this place of emptiness, the Spirit of God brushes over the face of the waters. In silent meditation, we enter the narrative in that place before the great drama of life begins, just before the first word.

So, also, in the Elijah narrative. Elijah was a prophet of great drama, but it was only once Elijah had come to the end of himself and learned that God is not in the drama that he 'hears the sound of sheer silence'.[55] Only then does he receive clear direction from the Lord about what to do next. When we meditate, we come to the end of our own drama as we sit within the 'sound of sheer silence'. By this, we de-dramatise ourselves so we are more able to receive true directions from God.

So, also, we find silence of God in the gospel narrative. Silence is that space in between the drama of Good Friday and the new life of resurrection. The silence of the tomb is like the womb from which comes the new birth of resurrection. Silence precedes that which is new and pristine.

So, also, we find a silence between the Ascension and Pentecost, when the physical presence of Jesus has come to an end and before the coming of the Holy Spirit, when the disciples are told to wait in the city. This waiting for God to act is about entering into the great silence of God.

Silence comes after the end and before the new beginning. Thus, silence gives us a glimpse of the great canvas upon which the spectacle of life happens. As we learn how to rest ourselves in the great silence of God, we also deepen our understanding of ourselves and the gospel narrative. In this way, silence enriches the world, just as salt flavours our food.

---

55   1 Kings 19:12. The 'sound of sheer silence' is the translation of the New Revised Standard Version. Other translations, such as the King James Bible, translate this as 'a still small voice'. The Hebrew is unclear. I like to use the New Revised Standard Version translation because I think it makes the best sense of the narrative.

SIXTH SUNDAY AFTER EPIPHANY (YEAR A)
Matthew 5:21–37

Reconciling Inner and Outer, from the Sermon on the Mount

BY PAUL WOOD

Our reading on Sunday continues with the Sermon on the Mount. The sense I make of it in this section has something to do with the integrity of who I am on the inside compared with who I am on the outside. It seems to me that hypocrisy is the thing that Jesus is exposing: 'You have heard that the law says you must not murder, but I say to you that if you are angry with your brother, you have murdered him in your heart and are liable in the final judgement.'[56]

Outside appearances are not enough (because people can pretend). It is the heart that matters. It is the same with sexual sins. On the outside, you appear like this, a good faithful man, caring of others, but inside you are more like a gigolo. Watch out; it can cause a lot of destruction. Inside and outside. Private and public. Life is complex, and we need to learn to navigate it with care. Much of the spiritual journey is about healing the difference between the inside and outside.

Jungian psychology speaks of how we all have our persona, which is one's public face, the mask that one wears to face the world, and how that is different from how you are in yourself, when you are alone and looking in the mirror. There is the mask, and then there is the self. If these two are contradictory, then life is a bumpy ride that one needs to navigate with care, principally through confession and forgiveness, bringing gradual healing to the whole.

How does this work? When we pray, we leave our mask behind and do as Jesus teaches us: 'Whenever you pray, go into your room and shut the door and pray to your Father who is in secret; and your Father who sees in secret will reward you.'[57] So we bring ourselves as we really are before the truth of God as God really is. No masks! So begins the path of healing. The healing proceeds through confession and forgiveness, like right foot, left foot, confess and forgive.

When we meditate, we are coming back into the centre of the union between ourselves and God. In a busy persona-driven world, we repeatedly

---

56   Matt. 5:21–22.
57   Matt. 6:6.

return, centring ourselves in God, so that we belong more and more here, in the place of being at one.

In the next part of the Sermon on the Mount, Jesus spoke of the importance of love, of walking the extra mile and the generosity of spirit that delves beyond what is expected. It ended with Jesus saying you must be perfect, even as your Heavenly Father is perfect. The word for 'perfect' here is *telos*, which does not mean perfect in terms of squeaky clean. Rather, it means perfect in terms of completeness. Both inside and outside complete and one with God.

SEVENTH SUNDAY AFTER EPIPHANY (YEAR A)
Matthew 5:38–48

A Consciousness Not Based on Retribution
BY MICHELLE WOOD

Surfing is the metaphor that I would like to use to explore this week's sacred story.

To set the mood, a quote from Australian novelist and surfer Tim Winton:

> *I will always remember my first wave that morning. The smells of paraffin wax and brine and peppy scrub. The way the swell rose beneath me like a body drawing to air. How the wave drew me forward and I sprang to my feet, skating with the wind of momentum in my ears. I leant across the wall of upstanding water and the board came with me as though it was part of my body and mind. The blur of spray. The billion shards of light. I remember the solitary watching figure on the beach ... as I flew by; I was intoxicated. And though I've lived to be an old man with my own share of happiness for all the mess I made, I still judge every joyous moment, every victory and revelation against those few seconds of living.*[58]

To contemplate deeply Jesus' teachings from the Sermon on the Mount is to contemplate the revelation of the highest level of love that we can live. To ride these great teachings, even for one instant or one relationship, will be, for the practitioner of silent meditation, our measure of joy and victory, our partaking in the revelation. To ride the swell of this wave of wisdom, we need mercy, purity of heart, peace-making and inner strength. This wave rises and pitches by proposing subtle understandings about the origins of anger,

---

[58] Tim Winton, *Breath* (London: Penguin Group, 2008), 29–30.

inappropriate objectification of women, divorce, holding of grudges and making of false oaths. Honesty and simplicity are our legs to stand on, and silent meditation is our surfboard. As the demands of the teachings rise, an agile surfer soon begins to sense the steepening wave; riding it to the highest level of human consciousness will require a daring and unique courage that sets its heart to the sky, heavenward. As this wave peaks, how can the practice of silent meditation be a source of steadiness, centredness and love?

Let's paddle out into the depths and see.

Jesus teaches:

> *Do not resist an evildoer. If anyone strikes you on the right cheek, turn the other also.*[59]

Just as a surfer must plant their feet firmly on their board, so must the meditator still their body, still their mind, still their spirit and focus on the rising and falling of the breath. Being one with your practice will allow you to ride this God-like wave. What will it take for a human being to ride this wave? Nothing less than a God-like perfection.

> *Be perfect ... as your Heavenly Father is perfect.*[60]

'Perfect', in this context, does not equate to a great exam score, but rather, its meaning is more accurately found in concepts such as the wholeness and completeness of an evolved human being: in other words, Christlikeness.[61]

Silent meditation is training, therefore, in creating a space so that we don't react out of animalistic, automatic fight responses or populist mob mentalities. Rather, we stay unified with the Spirit of Christ and ride this teaching wisdom wave to follow the flow of the love of God.

If we practice regularly, every morning and evening, for twenty minutes, we develop enough inner space and inner constraint to not impulsively react in heedless ways. We stay on our board, riding the wisdom wave of love—in all times, steady, in every encounter, especially the most inhumane, proclaiming the gospel of love. This is our highest, fullest, most complete self because we are one with the wave, the impulse of God, in whom rests the harmony of all, something much greater than our own reactions.

---

59 Matt. 5:39
60 Matt. 5:48
61 The Hebrew word translated as 'perfect' is *tamim* and means, among other things, 'whole, sound, healthful' and 'having integrity'. The Septuagint—the Greek translation of the Old Testament—uses the word *teleios* (the same word used in Matthew 5:48) to mean perfect in the sense of 'complete' and 'entire'. See Frank F. Judd Jr., '"Be Ye Therefore Perfect": The Elusive Quest for Perfection', in *The Sermon on the Mount in Latter-day Scripture*, eds. Gaye Strathearn, Thomas A. Wayment and Daniel L. Belnap (Salt Lake City: Deseret Book, 2010), 123–39.

Back to surfing: in surfer parlance, they say, 'hang loose', which means, 'stay relaxed'. If we are to stay relaxed and at ease, we will find it helpful to let go of possessiveness towards our belongings. Your brand of surfboard or wetsuit is not important if you ride this wave; the lighter you are, the better and freer you will be. So:

> *If anyone wants to sue you and take your shirt, give your coat as well.*[62]

Length and duration are important. Think about how far you can go with your meditation practice. Skilful application of this practice will allow the wind of sweet mercy to carry you far. You will find an energy beyond what you have known:

> *If anyone forces you to go one mile, go also the second mile.*
> *Give to the one who asks of you, and do not refuse*
> *anyone who wants to borrow from you.*[63]

Surfers say that one must respect the power of the ocean. The power of God's generosity is great. To ride the wave of it will bring great joy and healing to other human beings. Openness to this generosity is the key to a good ride. In surfing, when at a point break, the whole wave breaks at once, in all its fullness, it carries the rider home; it is exhilarating.

Jesus' teaching peaks with the saying:

> *You have heard that it was said, 'You shall love your*
> *neighbor and hate your enemy.' But I say to you: Love your*
> *enemies and pray for those who persecute you.*[64]

To ride this wave is to stay close to the most powerful source of love. There is no way back when riding it. It is pure surrender; it is near impossible, beyond comprehension; it will take a 'single mindedness and a drying up of every dollop of commonsense', a spirit Tim Winton describes well.[65] This is what it is to surf the ultimate wave. People caught up in the powers and principalities of this world won't understand it; they will think you nuts! When you travel along this wave of eighty thousand feet at a speed of eighty kilometres per hour, there is no thinking or judging—just pure love, just pure surfing, on the heartbeat of God.

> *That was the simple objective, being airborne, up longer, up higher, more*
> *casually and with more … elegance than anyone else in the world. I never*

---

62 Matt. 5:40.
63 Matt. 5:41–42.
64 Matt. 5:43–44.
65 Winton, *Breath*, 148.

understood the rules or the science of it but I recognized the singlemindedness it took to match risk with nerve come what may. Some endeavours require a kind of egotism, a near-autistic narrowness. Everything conspires against you—the habits of physics, the impulse to flee—and you're weighed down by every dollop of commonsense dished up. Everyone will tell you your goal is impossible, pointless, stupid, wasteful. So you hang tough. You back yourself and only yourself. This idiot resolve is all you have.[66]

So, as we enter the rising waters of our silent meditation practice, as the surfer reminds us, we hang tough. Even though the world thinks it is pointless, we back ourselves and rely on our idiot resolve, for we seek to love perfectly in this vast ocean.

EIGHTH SUNDAY AFTER EPIPHANY (YEAR A)
Matthew 6:22–34

The Highest of All Values
BY PAUL WOOD

> *The eye is the lamp of the body, so if your eye is healthy, your whole body will be full of light.*

This teaching is about seeing correctly, about seeing what is true, what is real and what is just. It is not that the world is simply there to be seen or that all we need to do is look at it. Seeing is more than just the eye being a biological camera that mirrors what is there. What is out there, in terms of raw data, is infinite and needs to be selected, interpreted, processed and understood by the viewer before anything like 'seeing' can happen. This is literally true, as discovered by robotic engineers. An array of light waves entering a camera lens is chaos until it is processed; shapes need to be identified, and edges must be made distinct from the foreground, background and empty space. Colours and hard and soft shadows must first be identified if the robot is to begin to see the world not as a jumble of light and colours but as something akin to what a human experiences. This is a massively complex undertaking. But when we come to the world of human beings, things become exponentially more complex.

For example, how do we see injustice? Or how do we see truth, goodness or beauty? How do we see what is right and what is wrong? Seeing in this

---

66   Winton, *Breath*, 148–49.

way requires, among other things, a set of values gleaned from experience, education, culture, history and traditions. These are the stories that operate within us as interpretive lenses and enable us to see. These values must be ordered into a hierarchy because some values are more consequential than others, some more significant than others and some more fundamental than others. Here, Jesus places the kingdom of God as the highest of all values: 'Seek first the kingdom of God.'

And so, we can only see truly if our 'eye' is healthy, that is, if our interpretive lens is healthy. Then, our whole lives are full of light. But if we see falsely and are unable to see the truth, our whole lives are full of darkness.

Jesus goes on to explain how we become clear-sighted, teaching us that we cannot serve two masters—God and wealth (mammon). He paints a picture of what living by faith in God looks like when we are not serving wealth. He describes how we are then like the birds of the air, without anxiety or concern for tomorrow.

Jesus concludes with the clear-sighted call to orient our life to the highest value possible: 'Seek first the kingdom of God, and all these things will be added to you.'

How does this fit with the meditator? All of us are, no doubt, entangled in this world where we must serve wealth: we cannot do without it. We may be inspired by stories of people who have left all and lived by faith, like St Francis, who gave away all his possessions and became literally naked for the sake of the kingdom. We may be inspired by a myriad of Christian saints or just simple examples of monks or nuns who live without any personal possessions in a community. Or maybe we are inspired by those explorers who live off the grid in the bush and practice self-sufficiency—which, in truth, is never as self-sufficient as they might claim and certainly not as easy as for the birds of the air, but rather very, very hard. I cannot help but feel that the Sermon of the Mount is an ethic that we must all strive for and place at the highest point of all our values while at the same time recognising that it is an aspirational ethic and we will all, without exception, fall short of this ideal.

However, as meditators, we live as the birds of the air for twenty minutes at each sitting when we orient our hearts towards the highest of all values. Here, for twenty minutes, we seek to simply be—at one with nature and at one with ourselves—and rest among the blessings of Creation as our Heavenly Father has ordered it for today. We sit in single-minded faith, free from the anxieties of wealth, free from the pressure of life, at one with ourselves, our history and our breath. We are simply as we are: in this place, at this time. Let us simply sit.

LAST SUNDAY AFTER EPIPHANY (YEAR A)
Matthew 17:1–9

A Young Woman's Zen Pilgrimage up a Mountain and the Transfiguration
BY MICHELLE WOOD

The Polish nun entered. Her face glowed translucent like a thin skin about to split. Her spirit was spilling out, splashing the forest walls with light. I looked at her and with courage asked, 'After a lifetime of meditating, what have you learned?' The nun replied, 'That every moment is different.'

This excerpt is from a story I wrote about an epic pilgrimage I undertook when I was thirty years old, some twenty years ago now, to a tiny island off the coast of Northern China. I climbed up a mountain, following a track called The Wisdom Path. Up and up the winding mud-stained track I climbed. There the monsoon rains fell like diamonds. I was travelling to stay in a remote Zen monastery.

There is something magical about mountains, their height and grandeur. Richard White, a famous Australian black-and-white photographer, spent many years photographing the mountains of the High Country. He wrote, 'To be in one of these places, listening to the silence as dawn breaks, is almost heaven itself.'[67]

Throughout the Bible, mountains are places where mystical experiences occur, where one encounters God—from Moses on Mt Sinai to Elijah on the Holy Mountain and Jesus on Mt Tabour in this week's reading with Peter, John and James. It is on the mountain that the disciples entered that heavenly sphere where the veil between our physical perceptions is split open to see that which is numinous.

It is important to note that this is not a type of spiritual experience whereby the physical body disappears. Our physical bodies matter and are part of our journey to divine nearness. One of the great things about practising silent meditation is that it involves our bodies. It is not a mental task nor another clever idea; it is an embodied practice of prayer.

In silent meditation, we leave behind the busyness of the world on the plains and metaphorically climb an inner mountain, breath by breath, opening to the divine nearness. This week, I read a wonderful piece of theology written

---

67 Richard White, *The High Country: Australia* (Mansfield, Victoria: Zone I Productions, 2014).

by Karl Rahner and entitled 'Revelation by Way of the Body', which illuminated for me the importance of our bodies as sites for transfiguration:

> *Through bodiliness the whole world belongs to me from the start, in everything that happens ... we must not get the impression in this connection that our body stops where our skin stops, as if we were a sack containing several different things, which clearly ceases to be what it is where its 'skin', the sacking, stops. No. Let us think in quite simple terms ... about modern physics. In some sense we are an open system. Of course, I can say, 'This chair is not part of my body.' But when we ask in terms of physics what that actually means, then the matter becomes very obscure ... what I want to say (is)—we are all living in one and the same body—the world.*[68]

I love this sense that the divine 'stuff' by which we are made renders us one with all of Creation—all of us radiating beyond the skin we live in, all living in the same body—the world: 'Through bodiliness the whole world belongs to me from the start.'

Meditation is a bodiliness awareness practice. The spiritual journey of a Christian is twofold: first, going up and expanding our consciousness; and second, staying grounded in our bodies because our bodies matter, and the body of this precious world matters.

What would a body transfigured by the radical love of Christ be? Something beyond our comprehension at one level, but at the material level, it would be a body of action, a messenger of love, of peace and healing. I imagine it to be as actively attentive as the Polish nun perceiving the uniqueness of every moment, sensing the unity with all that is, glowing this love through the body. With that in mind, I would like to begin our meditation practice with a body scan.

Begin by closing your eyes and bring your awareness to your face. Release all the tension you have in your face, relax your forehead, eyebrows, eyes, cheeks, lips, throat, shoulders and arms and rest your palms facing up as you release all the tension in your hands. Let it drain away.

Now bring your attention gradually down your body. If there is tightness or pain or discomfort in your pelvis, back or buttocks, try to release it. Relax your muscles. Gently bring your attention to your legs, relaxing the muscles to the feet, and let the tensions slip away. Now feel your weight pulling down to the earth, as the earth upholds you in equal amount.

Pause for a moment of silence.

---

[68] Karl Rahner, *Theological Investigations*, vol. 17, trans. Margaret Kohl (Limerick, Ireland: Mary Immaculate College, University of Limerick Centre for Culture, Technology and Values, 2004), 11.

Now bring the light of your consciousness into a global awareness of the whole of your body and sense the outline of it—all of it, all at once.

Observe the sensation of your living body as a sense of 'glee'. My body is alive! Sense where your living body ends and the outside world begins. Observe the sense of glow that you feel extending just beyond the boundary of your skin.

If you do not sense this, then imagine a glow extending beyond your body like a halo.

This is your living presence.

I have this life.

I indwell this life.

I can observe this life with my consciousness.

I can give thanks to God for this life.

Loving God, you bless this body in which I dwell with the light of your presence. I open my self to you in this time of meditation.

Lent (Year A)

FIRST SUNDAY IN LENT (YEAR A)
Matthew 4:1–11

Loving Attention as a Way of Prayer
BY MICHELLE WOOD

To build a relationship with anything, we begin by giving it our attention. The deeper we can give our attention to another, the deeper the relationship grows. In fact, if we are distracted or preoccupied with self, we cannot be in genuine relationship with another. To choose to give our full attention is an act of love. The Christian mystic Simone Weil said that 'the whole of prayer could be summed up as loving attention directed to God'.[69]

So, if we wonder what we are attempting to do in the practice of silent meditation, one way to understand it is as a way of growing the muscles to give this quality of undivided loving attention. If we can practise the art of being still, focused, alert, aware and at peace, we will be more available to receive the presence of God and give loving attention to other people in our everyday lives.

Some guidance for preparing to meditate. If you are new to meditation, a simple instruction from the Christian tradition according to the teaching of John Main OSB is as follows: 'Sit down. Sit still and upright. Close your eyes lightly. Sit relaxed but alert. Silently, interiorly begin to say a single word. We recommend the prayer phrase '*maranatha*'. Recite it as four syllables of equal length. Listen to it as you say it, gently but continuously. Do not think or imagine anything—spiritual or otherwise. If thoughts and images come, these are distractions at the time of meditation, so keep retuning to simply saying the word.'[70]

Ma-ra-na-tha.

Be faithful to your mantra amid the temptations and distractions of your mind, just as Jesus was faithful to God in the wilderness.

---

[69] Simone Weil, *Waiting for God*, trans. Emma Craufurd (New York: Perennial Classics, 2001), 57–58.
[70] Main, *Inner Christ*, v.

SECOND SUNDAY IN LENT (YEAR A)
Matthew 17:1–9

Going up the Mountain
BY PAUL WOOD

For our meditation teaching this week, I wish to use the metaphor of going up a mountain. I chose this because our Sunday gospel reading is about Jesus going up the mountain to commune with his Heavenly Father, just as Moses and Elijah went up the mountain and communed with God. This is a useful symbol because prayer is not just talking to God. It is also about raising our consciousness to a higher level. This is because the kind of mindset that we need to navigate the world below is vastly different from the mindset we need to navigate our approach to God.

The world of the everyday is full of concerns, attachments and responsibilities, some of which hurt the ego, some of which inflate the ego. The world of the everyday is a world of subject and object. The world of the everyday requires us to judge, measure and proceed with caution, wisdom and cunning.

However, our approach to God is through faith, openness and receptivity. It requires vulnerability, devotion and love. As we rise above the things of the world, we become more aware of spaciousness, freedom, limitlessness, universals, peace, bliss and joy. The view from the mountain top is full of sky.

But we need both. Sometimes we must be immersed below to work in the world, but we also need to know how to detach from that stuff and rise higher to commune with the divine. So, how do we gain altitude? Well, Benedictine monk John Main, the teacher behind the World Community for Christian Meditation, is quite pragmatic about how we meditate. It is not complicated. In fact, simplicity is of the essence.

He teaches us to recite a single word or phrase. The word he recommends is the Aramaic word *Maranatha*. Recite your word in four equal syllables.

Ma-ra–na-tha.

That is it. That is how you reach the top of the mountain. If you asked a mountaineer how to climb to the top of the mountain, he might reply, 'Well, you place one boot in front of the other, one at a time, and keep on at it.' Stay faithful to that process. That's how you get to the top. You do not have to know how it works or why it works; that will come in time. The important thing is that you do it, and that's how you get to the top.

Of course, you may find that you begin with good intentions by saying your word, but at some point, you suddenly wake up to find you are off somewhere else daydreaming. This is quite common, but the important thing is that when you become aware that you have wandered off daydreaming, you simply let go of that daydream, no matter how juicy it is at the time, and return to your path. That is, return to your word.

Ma-ra-na-tha.

Be faithful in saying your word and that's how you reach the top.

THIRD SUNDAY IN LENT (YEAR A)
John 4:5–42

The Well Within

BY MICHELLE WOOD

The Christian path teaches three important things:

1. Each person is made in the image of God.
2. The Holy Spirit dwells within each person.
3. Nothing can separate one from the love of God.

The practice of silent meditation can help us experience these deeper realities. Most of the understandings we have about ourselves are created from living on the surface through culture and our dealings in the world. While important, they do not necessarily reflect the depths of who we really are. They are partial snippets—I am a counsellor, a mother, a gardener, retired, an artist—but they are never the whole.

In his conversation with the Samaritan woman at the well, Jesus went beyond the partial snippets of identity—Samaritan, Jew, woman, man, married, unmarried, moral, immoral—to speak with her. He saw beyond the categories constructed by the world. He saw her as she was truly meant to be seen: a person reflecting the image of God and someone who no matter what she had done was never separated from God. They conversed deeply and explored together.

He spoke to her of living water, a wellspring within, that never dries up, which gushes up to eternal life. In the practice of silent meditation, we are opening to that divine gift of living water to feel that wellspring within.

To do this, we need to strip away the superficialities, surface distractions, worldly divisions and noise so that we can reach the depths.

How to meditate

Sit still with your back straight. Close your eyes lightly. Then interiorly, silently begin to recite a single word—a prayer word. We recommend the ancient Christian prayer word *maranatha*. Say it as four equal syllables. Breathe normally and give your full attention to the word as you say it, silently, gently, faithfully and, above all, simply.

Ma-ra-na-tha

The essence of meditation is simplicity. Stay with the same word during the whole meditation.

FOURTH SUNDAY IN LENT (YEAR A)
John 9:1–4

From Darkness to Light
BY PAUL WOOD

The gospel reading this Sunday is about Jesus healing a blind man and Jesus being the 'Light of the World'. So, the metaphor I use for our meditation teaching today is about the journey from darkness into light.

The spiritual journey is often understood as a journey from the darkness of this world and into the light of God. It is a journey of waking up and opening our eyes, for this world is often described as being in darkness. It is in darkness because it is so difficult to see what is true, what is good and what is beautiful. The reason it is so difficult to see what is true, good and beautiful is because there is so much clutter in our minds that stops us seeing what is truly there.

We all have things that blind us. We all have:

- prejudices, likes and dislikes
- false assumptions
- things we fear, avoid and bury
- attachments and pet theories to justify our position
- tendencies to project and blame, often in ways of which we are not even aware.

All these things get in the way of seeing things truly as they are. To add to the confusion out there in the public marketplace of ideas, our blindness is further magnified and distorted by various interest groups, ideologies, financial greed, group think, fake news and so on.

Thus, it is exceedingly difficult to see things as they truly are, to see what is true, real, good, just and beautiful. As St Paul said, 'We see in the mirror dimly—but then (when we finally get to God) we will see God face to face.'[71] However, at the moment, we see as in a mirror dimly.

When we come to meditation, it is not about filling our heads with more information, more content and more clutter. Rather, it's about gently leaving thoughts aside and coming into the heart. It is about:

- simplicity
- having single intent
- coming to the centre
- stillness
- peace.

We do this by bringing our attention to our Lord Jesus in prayer through using the ancient prayer word *ma-ra-na-tha* ('Come Lord') as a way to focus our attention in one place, leave behind all the complexity of our distorted thinking and simply allow the light of God to gently infuse our being. So, we journey from darkness into light. It is like a gentle waking up to the universal light of God, seeing better what is true, what is good and what is beautiful.

Here is an ancient Celtic prayer from the *Carmina Gadelica* that illustrates something of this:

> *O God, who brought me from the rest of last night*
> *Unto the joyous light of this day,*
> *Be Thou bringing me from the new light of this day.*
> *Unto the guiding light of eternity.*
> *Oh! from the new light of this day.*
> *Unto the guiding light of eternity.*[72]

---

71 1 Cor. 13:12.
72 Alexander Carmichael, *Carmina Gadelica: Hymns and Incantations* (Edinburgh: Floris Press, 1992), 44.

FIFTH SUNDAY IN LENT (YEAR A)
John 11:32–45

Miracles and Home Meditation
BY MICHELLE WOOD

Someone once asked how I established a regular daily practice of silent meditation. I can remember saying that the first step was to create a spot at home. It was unbeknown to me when I uttered those words in one of our first Quiet Communion meditation sessions how relevant they would become.

In 2020, all churches were suddenly closed because of the COVID-19 pandemic; all Quiet Communion meditators were in lockdown. Prior to the pandemic, we had been meeting weekly at a local church. Paul and I had to quickly think how we could offer this practice. Suddenly, all of us had to think more about spiritual practices in the home.

At that time, during what seemed like the death of Quiet Communion, we discovered a home-based miracle. We found that we could practise silent meditation together online, and it was beautifully connecting, prayerful, comforting and deep. Within this context, I remember encouraging people to create their own home meditation spot (even if it was in front of a computer).

I suggested, where possible, to place some things that helped mark this as a sacred spot—a candle, an icon, a flower, a special knee rug, a shawl or a Bible, whatever made it comfortable and connected one to the spirit of peace and prayer. It was with joy that I saw, in that first session, each meditator's face in its Zoom cell pop onto my screen like a lemonade bubble. It felt like a miracle.

Miracle is a beautiful word. Its roots are in the idea of wonder; something wonderful happens beyond what we could have hoped. Although scoffed at in the modern scientific era of rationalism, miracles are as necessary for us today as love. We need miracles when faced with darkness, loneliness, fear and death.

This week's gospel is the raising of Lazarus, which is the story of Jesus' greatest miracle. The death of Lazarus and the pain of grief for his family and friends were very real. We can all relate to such times. It is human. Lazarus was dead; all seemed lost. It was too late, and there was great weeping.

Then Christ came, the human face of God, the Light of the World, and there was a miracle. From death comes life, from pain comes joy, and relationships are restored.

It is a miracle, a wonderful story. One doesn't need to nitpick for proof and validity in the same way as one does not have to nitpick whether love exists or not. What matters is not proof but the miracle that delivers the wonderful ending, a transcendent ending, the type of ending for which we all long.

Life without miracles would be pretty bleak. Can you imagine witnessing the constant destruction and violence in the world without a miracle—such as the newborn baby pulled alive from under rubble after the earthquake that struck Syria on 6 February 2023? Born in an earthquake, still alive, so precious, hope for all those people on the frontline searching for their loved ones. To cries of joy, this little miracle was dug out, her mother dead and she still attached by the umbilical cord, her faint cries heard by those looking for the miracle. In the darkest of dark, this little baby, a miracle of all, became fuel for the devastated heart.

A story of this calibre is food for our soul. It connects us to the love and goodness that is beyond the pain and suffering of this human world. May our practice of meditation strengthen us to see the tiny, invisible, often overlooked miracles.

SIXTH SUNDAY IN LENT (YEAR A)
Matthew 21:1-11

Entering In

BY PAUL WOOD

On Sunday, we celebrate Palm Sunday, when the Church throughout the world commemorates Jesus' entry into the Holy City of Jerusalem, the crowds welcoming him with palm branches and crying 'Hosanna'. Our Palm Sunday celebrations are our way of entering 'Holy Week', our most sacred week of the year.

The operative word is 'entry'—Jesus enters the Holy City of Jerusalem; the Church enters Holy Week—so this evening I wish to use the metaphor of 'entering' as a description of what we are aiming for in meditation.

When we meditate, we are entering not into the external world in which we normally dwell but rather into the world within, with the aim of finding our way to the very heart of our life, the dwelling place of God within, the place of peace, rest and salvation.

We must remember that when Jesus entered Jerusalem, it was incredibly significant, because while there were Jewish synagogues all over the ancient world where the Scriptures were read and expounded, there was only one temple, and that temple was in Jerusalem. There was only one place where sacrifices were made; that was within the temple of Jerusalem. Deep inside the temple, behind a veil, was a place called the Holy of Holies. It was so sacred that nobody was allowed to enter except for the high priest, who could only enter once a year on the Day of Atonement. So, the Holy of Holies is the most sacred place in the land and represents the dwelling place of God, which is why in apocalyptic literature when an invading army desecrates the Holy of Holies it is then the end of the world.

Now, as we meditate, as we enter into ourselves, I wish to parallel that with Jesus' entry into the Holy City. Here, there are a number of rather interesting parallels. First, Jesus entered on a donkey, not on a warhorse as the worldly kings would. This is a reminder that the practice of meditation requires humility and simplicity. It is not a grand thing. It is only a donkey!

Second, the crowds are like all the distractions the meditator inevitably has. Many people, particularly beginners, are beguiled by distractions. These may be outside noises, but more likely they come from one's own mind—here's another great idea, here's another fascinating thought. These are distractions, and one must not become caught up in them. Our destination is not the voices of the crowds. We can have those any other time. Our destination is the dwelling place of God within. We must go deeper. Jesus came to the temple and cleansed it by driving out all the moneychangers: 'Do not make my father's house into a den of thieves!'[73] As we come into our heart, we also need to cleanse it from attachments and idols because these, too, are distractions, before we can finally enter the most holy place.

Finally, Jesus went into the Holy of Holies, not into the symbolic earthly temple but into the real objective dwelling place of God through his death on Mt Calvary. Thus, he entered the real Holy of Holies. Now, this is the place we hope to enter into as meditators, a place of rest and quietude.

As the letter to the Hebrews says, 'Therefore, my brothers and sisters, since we have confidence to enter the sanctuary by the blood of Jesus, by the new and living way that he opened for us through the curtain (that is, through his flesh)'.[74]

Meditation is simply a technique, a donkey and one of many. However, the World Community for Christian Meditation teaches us this way to bring our consciousness into that most holy place, the place of peace and wholeness that Jesus has already won for us.

---

73 Luke 19:46.
74 Heb. 10:19–20.

Easter (Year A)

EASTER SUNDAY (YEAR A)
Matthew 28:1–10

An Essential Easter
BY MICHELLE WOOD

During the COVID-19 pandemic, when churches closed and symbolic actions shut down, it seemed more important than ever to get to what is essential about Easter. We heard a lot in the COVID-19 news about the differences between essential and non-essential activities. I wondered during that time: What would an essential Easter look like? I wondered what we would discover without all the hype of holidays and layers of dogmatic religiosity.

I think the practice of meditation helps one to sit in the stripped backedness and bareness to discover the essential. Silent meditation requires, for a brief period, a type of death—the death of our worldly self, a self that is constantly tossed in emotional currents and snagged in thoughts.

During silent meditation, we sit still and in darkness, like Christ in the tomb, waiting. Once we have quietened, we notice the smallest things—the sound of our word, the feel of our breath, the life that was always there but drowned out by the babble of the world inside our head. In silent meditation, our breathing itself is a prayer, an essential Easter proclamation:

Each breath out is a death; each breath in is new life.
Christ has died, Christ is risen, Christ will come again.
Each breath out is death; each breath in is new life.
Christ has died, Christ is risen, Christ will come again.

We pray the prayer word *maranatha*, an ancient Aramaic word meaning 'Come Lord'.

Christ has died, Christ is risen, Christ will come again.

Let us prepare for our practice of twenty minutes of silent meditation. Sit still with your back straight. Close your eyes lightly. Then, interiorly, silently begin to recite a single word—a prayer word. We recommend the ancient Christian prayer word *maranatha*. Say it as four equal syllables. Breathe normally and give your full attention to the word as you say it, silently, gently, faithfully and, above all, simply.

Ma-ra-na-tha.

The essence of meditation is simplicity. Stay with the same word during the whole meditation.

SECOND SUNDAY OF EASTER (YEAR A)
John 20:19–23

Resurrection from Inside
BY PAUL WOOD

Inside and outside. In this reflection, I would like to think of prayer as something within and not limited by the physical laws of space and time. Within the inner world of prayer, you can travel in time, to the past, to the future and anywhere in the world that your imagination takes you. Internally, we are free from the physical laws of space or time that rule the outside world. It is this internal/external distinction that awakens my interest when I read the Sunday gospel.

The disciples are in lockdown. Out of fear, they have barricaded themselves into a room, fearful that those who killed Jesus would be after them next. Hiding from the outside world, bolting the windows and doors so nobody can come in. They were afraid and in lockdown. It is into this locked room that the Risen Christ appeared and stood among them. He said, 'Peace be with you.'[75] He did not come in through the door, window or down the chimney. No. He just appeared as if he were already there, for the Risen Christ is not bound by the laws of space and time, as was the physical Jesus of Nazareth. Rather, the Risen Christ is free from those limitations. As the Risen Christ appeared among them, their experience was real and tangible because they all experienced it together simultaneously.

The point that I wish to make is this: the Risen Christ comes from the inside, not from the outside. In fact, many things come from the inside. Life itself comes from the inside. Organic growth grows of itself from the inside out. You cannot make life from the outside. You can make a machine or robot, but not life. Life emerges from within itself.

Also, love emerges from the inside, and you cannot impose it from the outside.

So, also, consciousness emerges from within.

So, also, creativity comes from the inside, not the outside.

So, also, free will comes from the inside, as does moral choice.

So, also, faith comes from the inside, and so on.

---

[75] John 20:21.

It is strange that we need years of schooling and socialisation to navigate the outside world, but little time is given to learning to navigate the internal world, which is, I suspect, just as complex and perhaps more so. This is what prayer and meditation are about: learning to navigate the internal world.

So, when we pray, we close our eyes, and so we close the door on the outside world and pray in secret.[76] We become still in the body, and through focused attention using our prayer word, we also become still in the mind. Free from distractions of movement in body and mind, our consciousness moves to the heart or the centre of ourselves. Here we sit, with openness and attentive receptivity, to receive the presence of the Risen Christ, who is already here, within and among us, and who greets us with 'Peace be with you'. All this emerges from the inside and is already present.

How to meditate according to the World Community for Christian Meditation

Sit still with your back straight. Close your eyes lightly. Then interiorly, silently begin to recite a single word—a prayer word. We recommend the ancient Christian prayer word *maranatha*. Say it as four equal syllables. Breathe normally and give your full attention to the word as you say it, silently, gently, faithfully and, above all, simply.

Ma-ra-na-tha.

The essence of meditation is simplicity. Stay with the same word during the whole meditation.

THIRD SUNDAY OF EASTER (YEAR A)
Luke 24:13–35

Seeing and Recognising: The Road to Emmaus
BY MICHELLE WOOD

Every moment we see things. We are bombarded by the visuality of life, so much so that our brain, in an effort to cope with all that we see, conflates and takes shortcuts. When we look at a flock of sheep, we just see generic sheep, but each sheep has a unique face and is different from all the others. If we were to really look and see, we would recognise that reality.

However, so much of our lives are lived in the realms of shortcuts and generalisations, thought obsessions and habitual frames. We see in limited, partial, disjointed patches, often caught up in our own insular bubbles. What meditation can offer to help us see more fully is two things.

---

76   Matt. 6:6.

First, it enables a clean reboot of our minds so that we stop seeing out of our habitual well-worn tracks to see afresh. Our minds are like a blackboard that is full, and meditation is like cleaning with a duster. Second, it opens the floodgates of seeing—the frame widens, and yet our capacity to hold the minute details of difference between things is possible.

I can remember meditating by the banks of the Murray River, arriving hassled at the close of day. Busily organising a spot to meditate before the sun went down, I was oblivious to the river. Fiddling around with my books and bells, the river was there, but I barely noticed it. Blindly and blusteringly, I organised my timer, seat, notebook and scarf. My seeing was probably the size of a postage stamp. Then I meditated. I went into the silence (or the process of silencing my mind), into the darkness, slowly letting go of all my preoccupations. When I opened my eyes, I really saw the river. I saw a thousand eyes twinkling at me, each little wave made by light, wind and water. I saw so many shades of green in the swaying eucalyptus branches. The beauty of the scene kept on pouring into my eyes until I felt I would almost burst. The seeing kept growing larger, and yet the capacity to hold the beauty of detail was also possible. This is a gift of meditation. This capacity for slow seeing, drinking in beauty, is one reason for practising silent meditation. However, as a spiritual practice, it is not about one's own boutique experiences but rather training one's attention so that one can attend to every moment of life, including the horrific, hard and ugly moments, in this way.

I call it to live out of a resurrection consciousness, to see and recognise the pulsating life of God through all and in all, to see as if you are seeing for the first time, just like the song *Morning Has Broken*: 'Morning has broken like the first morning blackbird has spoken like the first bird.'[77]

To live out of resurrection consciousness is to really see and recognise our partners, friends, children, neighbours, animals and the natural world, to see them as if we are seeing for the first time, full of curiosity, aliveness, preciousness. Noticing the fullness of their being. Not being blinded by past baggage nor dulled down to only see the generic sheep, but rather seeing that is full of new noticing—the first wrinkle, grey hair, latest growth—noticing that every moment is new, every moment is life, every moment is a resurrection moment to celebrate, delight in and join with.

---

77 Eleanor Farjeon, 'Morning Has Broken', in *Songs of Praise*, ed. Percy Dearmer, Ralph Vaughn Williams and Martin Shaw (London: Oxford University Press, 1931), 30.

FOURTH SUNDAY OF EASTER (YEAR A)
John 10:1–5

Ego, Robbers and the Good Shepherd

BY PAUL WOOD

Here's a question: I wonder what you do with your ego when you meditate? By ego, I mean your everyday conscious self. The 'me' of your life. The 'I' that leads and decides and that becomes upset when it is not acknowledged. The 'me' that takes centre stage. Of course, the New Testament does not use the word 'ego'. Rather, it uses the word 'self'. Jesus said that if anyone wants to be a follower, let them deny themselves, take up their cross and follow him. The path of Christ is the way of selfless love; in other words, 'egoless love'. This quality of love requires us to love 'the other', even when no rewards are being paid to the 'ego self'. This is the way of the Good Shepherd who lays down his life for the sheep.

The practice of meditation is like a gymnasium for the soul, where we attempt to decentre the self from its usual position of centre stage and allow Christ to take centre stage instead. It is the practice of selflessness. When we first begin to meditate, we become aware of the behaviour of the ego, which does not like being sidelined or de-platformed. It just wants to be centre stage, and it will play all sorts of dirty tricks to recentre itself into that position.

Initially, the ego argues that meditation is a waste of 'valuable time' (even when you have plenty of time on your hands) or that although it may be suitable for others, it is not for you. Even once you have managed to negotiate with the ego just twenty minutes of being decentred, to be still, to remain silent, just twenty minutes, and after that it can do whatever it likes; even then, it will still sneak in when you are not paying attention, steal your meditation away and turn it into a wonderful daydream: 'Oh, how lovely are the beaches in Honolulu, the sea, the sun, the coconuts.' When this happens to me, as it does often, I am reminded of the disciples who, when Jesus asked them to pray with him in his hour of need, all fell asleep. The self sneaks in and takes away our prayer.

Keep awake! Keep alert! Be watchful! This is a sentiment often expressed by the early Christian contemplatives. St John of Sinai was one such person who, in the Egyptian desert, described the importance of vigilance during meditation and solitude: 'Take up your seat on a high place and watch, if only you know how, and then you will see in what manner, when, whence, how many and what kind of thieves come to enter and steal your clusters of grapes. Watch, solitary monk, be vigilant at the times when wild beasts prowl; otherwise, you will not be able to adapt your snares to them.'[78]

This watchfulness of the sneaky nature of the self is part of the work in the early stages of prayer—learning not being distracted, to not lose your grapes to the thieves.

In our reading today, Jesus the Good Shepherd teaches that he is the gate into the sheepfold. Once the sheep are safely through the gate, they are in the fold. They are protected from thieves and robbers.

Meditation is a prayer practice that is like a narrow gate through which we are brought into the fold. Once in, we are safe and protected from distractions, we are free to open ourselves to the great and mysterious love of God.

FIFTH SUNDAY OF EASTER (YEAR A)
John 14:1–14

Why Meditate? Opening to Christlikeness
BY MICHELLE WOOD

Why would Christians meditate? When we think about meditation, we might immediately conjure in our minds Buddhist monks sitting cross-legged, lotuses or Indian gurus in flowing saffron robes chanting *om*, images seemingly far from the Christian practices of kneeling in cold old churches and listening to Bible stories. It is often easy when we glance only at the surface of things to observe differences. If we penetrate a little more deeply, a little more respectfully, we might be surprised to discover something more.

The path of Christian prayer is one of opening in humble surrender to the love and goodness of God so that we may become agents of selfless love. That is the way of Christ. If that is the path, I find I ask myself two questions: Who keeps me opening to love and goodness? And what spiritual practices keep me opening to selfless love?

I delight in meeting people who reveal a Christlikeness: a heart of selfless love and joy. They seem to be able to really listen to another, not just to their words but to their needs, and to respond rather than impose. There is a directness in their actions that meets the mark. I am curious as to what

---

[78] John Climacus, 'The Ladder of Divine Ascent: Step 27: On Holy Solitude of Body and Soul', SermonIndex.net, n.d., https://www.sermonindex.net/modules/articles/index.php?view=article&aid=41415.

holds them steady and aware and sustains them. I am curious about their spiritual practices.

Christian spiritual practices vary from praying, churchgoing, engaging in public rituals and rites of passage, singing hymns, walking in nature, reading the Scriptures, making art, spiritual writing and engaging in acts of charity or social justice, to name but a few.

Tonight, we practise one—silent meditation. Silent meditation offers a way that is not so much about concepts of the head but about opening the heart. It is not so much about action, but one would hope that it prepares one for action by uniting one to Christ, who embodies the human face of universal love. We still our bodies and still our minds. We let go momentarily of thinking about 'me and mine' to open a little more towards Christ.

Through meditation we let go of our small-minded thoughts, petty prejudices and stifling repressions to open our hearts to that which is unseen, marginalised, rejected, going into the depths, widening our gaze more inclusively, generously, receiving more to take on our own Christlikeness.

'I am the way, the truth and the life', said Christ.[79]

Meditation is simply a practice of just sitting and opening to the way of love, the truth of love and the life of love … soaking in it, brewing, like tea in a pot.

SIXTH SUNDAY OF EASTER (YEAR A)
John 14:15–19

Indwelling

BY PAUL WOOD

We spend so much of our time plugged into the demands of the external world, which can be so loud and authoritative, so much so that we forget our own internal world. We must not ignore the internal world, for the creative powers of love, faith and hope all come from the inside.

This Sunday, our gospel begins to tell the story of Jesus' departure from this world. He said, 'I am going away, you will no longer see me, but you will not be left orphaned, for the Father will send you an advocate who will indwell you'.[80] This Spirit of Truth 'is with you' (now in the person of Jesus) 'and will be in you' when he goes away.

---

79   John 14:6.
80   John 14:18.

This is highly significant in the sense that up to this point, their faith had been about following an external authority, that is, following the physical external Jesus. However, now the locus of authority was about to change from external to internal. You will be on your own, but not entirely so, for the Father will send the indwelling Spirit who will be your guide. Now when we meditate, the locus authority changes from external to the internal, and our guide is the Spirit of Truth.

To navigate the complexities of the internal world, the World Community for Christian Meditation offers us a method as a guide, but in the end, we must all find our own way. Isn't it interesting that when Jesus left his disciples, he did not give them any external authority to follow? He did not write his teachings down and say, 'now follow that'. They had done that for centuries with the Ten Commandments and it never really worked. No. He did not give them another external authority to follow. Rather, he entrusted his teachings to their living soul, and so he breathed into them and said, 'Receive the Holy Spirit.' He entrusted the gospel into their living hearts.[81]

The Church was born in the context of the Roman Empire, which was a terrifyingly powerful external authority. It modelled itself on that, and so Rome became the central external authority for all Christians. When the Protestants came along, they did the same thing and preached another powerful external authority pointing to the written word of the Bible.

However, this is the thing. Only having a powerful external authority might mean that we never develop awareness of our own internal guide of the Spirit of Truth. We may become lazy and dependent upon external authority to navigate the complexities of the world for us. If this happens, we have fallen asleep and have become robotic.

So, let us awake and let us turn inward. Let us close the door on the external world for a time and close our eyes. Let us pray to our Father in secret, in communion with the advocate, the Spirit of Truth.

---

81 John 20:22.

SEVENTH SUNDAY OF EASTER (YEAR A)
John 17:1–11

What's Missing with Zoom? Experimenting with a Guided Entrance

BY MICHELLE WOOD

We log on, fumble with microphones, unstable internet connections, frozen pictures and neighbours' barking dogs for the flat-screened Zoom Quiet Communion meditation group. It is a delight to see faces each week. In some mysterious way, the experience of connecting and practising together this way works, yet I also find myself questioning what is missing from the Zoom online meditation experience.

In the Zoom meditation space, unlike being in a church or a sacred place together, we are not surrounded by the symbols that direct the mind and heart towards the transcendent. There is something odd about being met with a flat screen.

Whenever one enters a sacred place, steeped in centuries of prayer, one enters with reverence—perhaps with a bow, perhaps making the sign of the Cross or taking off one's shoes, entering quietly—to acknowledge that one is entering a holy place. Entering the holy is not like entering the railway station or museum.

When entering a holy space, the architecture does a good deal of the work for us—the art, the stained-glass windows, the altar and the symbols. Since their inception, humans have created physical structures to gather in worshippers, from the fires of corroborees to cathedrals and temples. These are outer signposts of the spiritual that lies within.

To begin our meditation this evening, for those of you who are unable to gather in a place of worship or who are far from what you may call your spiritual home, I invite you to join in the following visualisation to reconnect with the postures of the heart and mind towards which your sacred places take you.

Close your eyes. Picture a church or sacred place known to you. Imagine you are about to enter this church or sacred place.

Take a moment to see the doorway. As you enter, notice what is inside. Take a moment to perhaps bow, make the sign of the Cross, take off your shoes and light a candle. Find a seat, adjust yourself, settle and quieten. Prepare your body for meditation. Sit still, with your spine upright, hands gently on your lap.

Then interiorly, silently begin to recite a single word—a prayer word. If you have your own prayer word or breath practice, please continue to use that.

If you are new to meditation, we recommend the ancient Christian prayer word *maranatha*. Say it as four equal syllables.

Ma-ra-na-tha.

Breathe normally and give your full attention to the word as you say it, silently, gently, faithfully and, above all, simply.

Ma-ra-na-tha.

Stay with the same word during the whole meditation. The essence of meditation is simplicity.

Pentecost (Year A)

DAY OF PENTECOST (YEAR A)
Acts of the Apostles 2:1–4

Breath

BY PAUL WOOD

The breath, the wind, the spirit—all the same word in Hebrew and Greek. On the day of Pentecost, the disciples gathered. 'Suddenly there was from heaven the sound of a rushing mighty wind which filled the house where they were sitting.'[82] And so the Church was born.

Something like 580 years before that, Ezekiel was in a valley of dry bones: 'Mortal man prophesy to the wind and say to the breath—Thus says the Lord God come from the four winds and breathe upon these slain that they may live.'[83] A prophecy of the restoration of Israel.

Going further back to the beginning of the Bible: 'Then the Lord God formed man out of the dust of the ground and breathed into his nostrils the breath of life and man became a living soul.'[84] Going even before that, in the opening verses of the Bible, 'darkness was on the face of the deep while the breath of God moved over the face of the waters.'[85] Breath, wind or spirit; these three English words are all the same word in Hebrew and in Greek, and they are often identified with the invisible presence of God.

The Ten Commandments tell us not to take the name of God in vain. We often assume that this means that we should not misuse the name, but there is a tradition in Judaism that says it means that we should not even utter the name! One must not sound the name at all. Why? Because the moment that you have done that, you have made something that is the equivalent of an idol, for you have entered the world of forms, images and names. However, God, by definition, is beyond all worldly forms, images and names. One way we can talk about God is to say that God's invisible presence is like the wind, which has no form and yet is ever present.

---

82   Acts 2:2.
83   Ezek. 37:9.
84   Gen. 2.
85   Gen. 1:1–4.

The name of God when written looks like this: YHWH. Some scholars have noted that the letters YHWH represent breathing sounds or aspirated consonants. When pronounced, it sounds like breathing. *Yah* (inbreath) and *weh* (outbreath). Thus, some claim that the sound of the name of God has within it the sound of breath before the tongue has shaped it and the lips have clipped it into segments, creating distinct words, names, ideas or idols.

God is like breath, and everything is breathing: every man, every woman and every child. All animals are breathing, all the way down to the tiniest insect and even the most invisible microbe. Every living thing is breathing, in and out, including everything in the plant world. Plants breathe in what we breathe out, and we breathe in what they breathe out. All of life is breathing. It is the rhythm of living things.

In and out.

When we were born, the first thing we did was to breathe in, and when we die, the last thing we do is to breathe out. It is as if the whole of life is breath. We are in it, just as it is in us.

The breath, the spirit, the wind

Perhaps this Pentecost weekend, we might meditate with the breath. We can only do this if we leave the world of form—ideas, words, thoughts and images—and return to that which is the most primal of all, the formlessness of spirit, wind and breath.

Anthony De Mello, the Indian Jesuit meditation teacher, taught that when one meditates on the breath, one should not focus on the lungs but rather focus on the sensation of the breath going in and out of the nostrils.[86] Pay attention to the sensation of breath passing in and then out. Being aware of the sensation, you may notice there is a temperature difference between the inbreath and the outbreath or the quantity of air difference in each nostril. This meditation asks one to focus on a sensation rather than a word.

Stay with the sensation, in and out. Breathe normally and allow the breath to be your prayer word for this Pentecost session.

---

86   Anthony de Mello, *Sadhana: A Way To God*, 19th ed. (Anand, India: Gujarat Sahitya Prakash, 1988).

TRINITY SUNDAY: FIRST SUNDAY AFTER PENTECOST (YEAR A)
Matthew 28:16–20

The Trinity: Our Maker, Keeper and Everlasting Lover

BY MICHELLE WOOD

The mystic St Julian of Norwich described the Blessed Trinity as our Maker, our Keeper and our Everlasting Lover.[87] Whatever metaphors are used, the Christian Triune God is always depicted as three entities. For example:

- Father, Son and Holy Spirit
- Creator, Living Word and Life-giving Spirit
- Eternal Source, Redeemer and Sanctifier.

So, as practitioners of silent meditation, what is our relationship to the Triune God?

Jesus says, 'I am in God, you are in me, and I in you.'[88] How can we notice a little more that we live within these three relationships that are one?

- Christ in God
- we in Christ
- Christ in us

Within the hiddenness of the Blessed Trinity, we move and exist. Although it is a mystery we can never fully apprehend, Jesus paves a way for us towards it, saying, 'Those who love me will keep my word, and my Father will love them, and we will come to them and make our home with them.'[89]

This *keeping of his word* means to love as Jesus loves—unconditionally. As St Paul writes, this is made possible because 'God's love has been poured into our hearts, through the Holy Spirit that has been given to us.'[90]

---

[87] Karen Anita Manton and Lynne Muir, *The Gift of Julian of Norwich* (Mulgrave, Victoria: John Garratt Publishing, 2005), 46.

[88] John 14:20.

[89] John 14:23. Note that *The Jerome Biblical Commentary for the Twenty-First Century* states that the 'word' in the Johannine sense is very much the living word or the example of love for all that Jesus embodies. See John J. Collins, Gina Hens-Piazza, Barbera Reid and Donald Senior, eds., *The Jerome Biblical Commentary for the Twenty-First Century* (London: T&T Clark, 2020), 1834.

[90] Rom. 5:5.

I don't know about you, but my head becomes cluttered with many thoughts and worries, and silent meditation helps me settle and pay attention to that which is in my heart.

So, a story from my practice.

This week I felt fairly hassled mentally about a whole range of things. So, I went to the garden, sat still, closed my eyes and breathed. I paid attention to only this. Soon enough, I felt the sun warm my eyelids and my spidery lashes flicker, shading my eyes.

Evagrius the Solitary wrote, 'If a jar of wine is left in the same place for a long time the wine becomes clear and settled and fragrant.'[91]

I descended into deeper stillness; my mind settled, becoming clearer. I then heard dozens and dozens of little birds singing in the hedges. Had this concert been going on all morning, but I had simply not heard it? So insular is the mind when hijacked by constant thoughts.

When I finally opened my eyes, there was not a bird to be seen in the dense hedges, but the songs continued.

Somehow, it is in these moments that I am taken towards the mystery of the Triune God.

I experience a welling of love in my heart, a gift of grace, and, in some way, I get a glimpse that:

- my life is within Christ
- Christ is within me
- Christ is within God, permeating the whole of Creation.

I sense that I am, in some small way, a part of these relationships, this grand mystery that ungirds all of life, where God is Maker, Keeper and Everlasting Lover of all.

SUNDAY BETWEEN 5 AND 11 JUNE (YEAR A)
Matthew 9:9–13, 18–26

Silence within the Drama
BY PAUL WOOD

When reading a gospel story, one can take many different perspectives to unpack its meaning.

---

[91] Nikodimos and Makarios, *Philokalia*, 35.

One may stand in the shoes of Jesus and be the teacher and bringer of healing, restoration and salvation.

Alternatively, one may stand in the shoes of the person being healed or receiving the gospel, be it the blind man, the leper, the outcast or the would-be follower, and see the world from their point of view.

One may also stand with the crowd of onlookers, who may be wondering in amazement, 'Who is this man?' and may be approving, disapproving or criticising.

Then again, one could take a global perspective and observe the scene from a distance. I believe that this is what we often do, which is perhaps a shortcoming of the academic approach: looking on from a dispassionate and rational distance, treating it forensically and judging this and that about it.

Our gospel today covers a range of stories, and there are a number of different perspectives and places we can stand in the story. It might be interesting to note where you stand. Maybe you will want to stand in a number of different places at once and 'hog the board', so to speak, identify with everyone, thereby glossing over many perspectives. It may be good instead to identify just one place to stand, then intuitively feel how the story unfolds for you and the dilemmas it creates for you.

Perhaps this is one way through which we can bring the gospel into ourselves and a new living way, because within each one of us there is a drama going on. We especially know this if we spend time alone, for what we discover is not the silence and peace we might have hoped for but rather the drama, the stories within the stories, the explanations within the explanations, the justifications, memories, perceptions, understandings, the voices of the past, the voices of the future and the voices that one never dares to speak. There is a great drama within! Perhaps one way of sorting through our 'stuff' within is to bring the gospel story into ourselves. As an ordering principle, it will bring with it a transcendent presence and will gradually lead the drama towards a peaceful resolve.

As we practise the discipline of silent meditation, we do not focus on the drama within; rather, it is time spent untangling ourselves from the drama within to discover the silence of the centre, the still point, the silence before the drama began, the silence that is after the drama is over, the silence that is behind the drama, the backdrop to the drama. It is this silence that is the landscape upon which the drama happens. When we identify that silence within ourselves, we become less obsessive, less fanatical, less trapped in the drama and more able to operate with greater wisdom and freedom.

This is why in Quiet Communion we meditate first, to cleanse our minds before we hear the gospel, so that when we hear the gospel, we do so with pristine freshness, like the first day of Creation, unclouded by our own stuff.

And then, in our discussion afterwards, we can begin to identify where we are in our story and intuitively and imaginatively allow the gospel to work its healing powers within us.

And so, let us meditate.

SUNDAY BETWEEN 12 AND 18 JUNE (YEAR A)
Matthew 9:35–10:8

Authority over Unclean Spirits
BY PAUL WOOD

See Mark 6:6b–13 and page 149.

SUNDAY BETWEEN 19 AND 25 JUNE (YEAR A)
Matthew 10:24–39

The Sword and the Mantra
BY MICHELLE WOOD

Jesus said, 'Do not think that I have come to bring peace to the earth; I have not come to bring peace, but a sword.'[92]

Here, Jesus uses the word *sword* as a metaphor. It is a sword not of violence but of clarity. The symbolic sword that Christ brings is that which cuts through divisive psychological and cultural harms so that we can journey to the depths of our heart, cutting away unjust power conventions to find the truth of love. Hebrews states that 'the word of God is living and active, sharper than any two-edged sword, piercing until it divides soul from spirit, joints from marrow; it is able to judge the thoughts and intentions of the heart.'[93]

Our minds are riddled with fears and rigid habits that are skilled at keeping us living in anxious conflict with ourselves and one another.

Every time we use the mantra or breath to focus our meditation, we are in fact taking up a symbolic sword and returning our attention to the indwelling Spirit of Christ. We are attempting to let go of distracting thoughts and dramas to enter the realm of the heart: 'Do not think that I have come to bring peace to the earth; I have not come to bring peace, but a sword.'[94]

---

92 Matt. 10:34.
93 Heb. 4:12.
94 Matt. 10:34.

In our internal psychological worlds, we need a symbolic sword of clarity whenever we:

- feel angry
- wish to belittle others
- feel self-important or self-satisfied
- seek self-indulgent praise
- wish to describe the faults of others
- feel a need to blame others
- wish to speak harshly and cause disputes.

In meditation, whenever such thoughts arise, we use the mantra or the breath like a sword to cut them off. Rather than sitting in smug, self-absorbed inner peace, we actively and attentively sit in the light of Jesus' words: 'Do not think that I have come to bring peace to the earth; I have not come to bring peace, but a sword.'[95]

Perhaps the cross that we, as modern people, take up to follow Christ is to responsibly carry what goes on in our own minds, for our thoughts are forerunners to our actions. We are called to be people of love, to keep a commandment of love, and this I believe is only possible when we have cut away from our hearts all thoughts that cause harm to self and others.

Therefore, in your practice, hold firm your sword and cut off all thoughts, moment by moment, focusing on your mantra or your breath.

Sit still and attentively, guided by 'the word of God ... living and active, sharper than any two-edged sword, piercing until it divides soul from spirit, joints from marrow; ... able to judge the thoughts and intentions of the heart'.[96]

SUNDAY BETWEEN 26 JUNE AND 2 JULY (YEAR A)
Matthew 10:40–42

Three Methods of Silent Meditation
BY PAUL WOOD

Jesus is speaking to his disciples: 'Whoever welcomes you, welcomes me and whoever welcomes me, welcomes the one who sent me.'[97]

---

95 Matt. 10:34.
96 Heb. 4:12.
97 Matt. 10:40.

There is a lineage. We are connected through time, through our teachers, back to Christ and back even further to God the Father.

And so, as I was thinking through these meanings in relation to our prayer practice of silent meditation, I thought it would be beneficial to look at the lineage in which we stand.

There are essentially three schools of contemporary Christian meditation practices, which I have borrowed from Cynthia Bourgeault's book *Centering Prayer and Inner Awakening*. These three contemporary methods of silent meditation can be categorised as:

- concentration methods
- awareness methods
- surrender methods.[98]

Let me draw out the distinctive characteristics of each one.

Concentration methods
When using a concentration method, the mind is given a simple task on which to focus. This may be the repetition of a simple word such as *maranatha*, or it may be to concentrate on one's breath. Concentration methods are mantra methods.

The World Community for Christian Meditation, founded by Fr John Main and now led by his disciple Fr Lawrence Freeman, builds on the foundation of the mantra to provide a focus for one's attention. Rather than allowing the mind to wander where it wills, it is anchored steadily and constantly in the simple repetition of the task. In the words of Cynthia Bourgeault, 'The mind stays alert and present while the deeper waters of one's being are refreshed in the numinous presence which the mantra invokes.'[99]

In most concentration methods, the meaning of the word is not important; rather, it is the faithful practice of repeating it and paying attention to it.

Repeating a sound such as *maranatha* or focusing on the breath are examples of the concentration method.

Awareness methods
Awareness methods involve aligning yourself with your inner observer, where you simply observe your thoughts and feelings coming and going, like clouds drifting across the sky. These methods teach you to not become attached to your thoughts or immersed in them, rather to simply witness them passing by. Using

---

[98] Cynthia Bourgeault, *Centering Prayer and Inner Awakening* (Lanham, MD: Cowley Publications, 2004), 19–30.
[99] Bourgeault, *Centering Prayer*, 20.

these methods, you learn that you can either be *in* a thought, meaning you are possessed by it and cannot see it clearly, or you can stand back, as it were, and observe the thought from the outside, watching it come and watching it go.

In our everyday conscious state, we are immersed in our thoughts and action, where we are not mindful of what we are doing or thinking. It is only when we stop and become aware of our inner observer, the silent witness within, that we can simply observe and become mindful. It is this silent observer with whom we stand. Many Buddhist schools teach awareness methods. In secular contemporary culture, they are known as 'mindfulness'.

The first time I came across a Christian meditation teacher was in the 1980s. Anthony de Mello was an Indian Jesuit priest who taught much of this tradition. His book *Saddhana: A Way to God*[100] contains numerous awareness exercises designed for people to awaken, observe and become aware of themselves, their thoughts, their breath and their feelings. He taught me to stop and observe.

Surrender methods
Surrender methods are taught by Fr Thomas Keating and the Episcopalian priest Cynthia Bourgeault and are often referred to as 'centring prayer'. Here, one aims for surrender, letting go of all thoughts as they arise. The emphasis is not so much on focused attention or witnessing; rather, it is about orienting the heart in surrender to God. The heart is likened to a valve, where it can be either closed or open in surrender towards the beloved.

I believe that a body posture that reflects this orientation of the heart is the 'orans' posture, where the arms are stretched out sideways and the palms are open and facing up, exposing the chest. This is what a priest does at the altar. Many other meditation methods teach the joining of hands or touching the thumb and forefinger together, perhaps to keep the energy within. The orans posture, in contrast, suggests an openness to the cosmos and the great mystery of God. Rather than keeping the energy within, one is surrendering to the great mystery of God from whom we give and receive, similar to breathing. So, the emphasis here is not so much upon attention of the mind but on an openness of the heart. And as each thought arises, it is surrendered to God.

In the centring prayer method, suggests Cynthia Bourgeault, you can use any word, not as a rhythmic mantra but as a reminder, like a piece of string attached to your finger. When you become aware that you are caught up in wandering thoughts, the word reminds you to turn back and reopen yourself to God. Many different words can be used—it could be 'Jesus' or more generic words such as 'let go' or 'trust' or 'love'—to remind the practitioner to surrender the heart and be open to giving and receiving.

---

100   de Mello, *Sadhana*.

So, the three contemporary methods are concentration methods (as taught by the World Community for Christian Meditation), awareness methods (also known as mindfulness) and surrender methods (as taught in *Centering Prayer and Inner Awakening*). And I suspect, in practice, there may be an overlapping of these different traditions.

Let us now practice twenty minutes of silent meditation in whatever tradition you feel comfortable with.

SUNDAY BETWEEN 3 AND 9 JULY (YEAR A)
Matthew 11:25–30

Becoming Gentle and Humble of Heart
BY MICHELLE WOOD

Only once, in all of his years of teaching, did Jesus explicitly use the expression 'learn from me.'[101] In Sunday's gospel he says, 'Learn from me, for I am gentle and humble in heart.'[102] The word 'gentle' has its roots in 'gene' or 'to give birth'. Gentleness gives birth to peace, calm and consistency of character. It is not volatile or abrupt in its response to the world. A gentle temperament is not something everyone is born with, but it is something we can learn. The practice of silent meditation is a way of gentleness. Through the doors of quietness and stillness we learn to pause rather than to react. Gentleness makes room for others and cools anger and hot-headedness. Gentleness has time; it does not rush people; it is generous. It is a quality extolled by James, who writes, 'Who is wise and understanding among you? Show by your good life that your works are done with gentleness born of wisdom.'[103] 'Learn from me', says Jesus, 'for I am gentle and humble in heart.'[104]

The word 'humble' has its origins in the Latin word *humus*, meaning the earth or the ground. To be humble is to be 'down-to-earth'. The heart of Christ is down-to-earth; it is in the marketplace, the fields and the inns; it is at weddings and festivals; it is where people are sick, where people are suffering and dying.

The humbleness of heart of which Jesus speaks is not a humility of the head but rather a quietness in the core of our being, a quiet knowingness of who we are, so that we can give of ourselves freely. Humbleness of heart is being

---

101 Matt. 11:29.
102 Matt. 11:29.
103 James 3:13.
104 Matt. 11:29.

honest with ourselves and others, meeting situations in a down-to-earth way, as they truly are, without adding false projections or subtracting from them.

Just as the breath gives us vitality and life, gentleness and humbleness of heart give us inner wisdom and loving action. They are a perfect coupling for the Jesus lesson.

SUNDAY BETWEEN 10 AND 16 JULY (YEAR A)
Matthew 13:1–9, 18–23

The Sower

BY PAUL WOOD

In the book of Genesis, in the story of Creation, the first act of God is the creation of light. It is interesting that light was created before the sun, moon or stars were, even though light does not exist apart from that radiated by the sun, moon and stars. So, what is this light that was created before everything else?

We can understand this light as the primordial undifferentiated consciousness, the canvas upon which the Lord God begins the work of creating. Creating through making distinctions, differentiating one thing from another: light from dark, the waters above from the waters below, the sea from dry land, plants from animals, animals from humans, the distinction of time by the sun and moon. Through these differentiations, the world as we know it is created by God.

Thus, Creation emerges from the primordial canvas of undifferentiated light, the consciousness that exists before distinctions are made. Now, as meditators, it is this 'undifferentiated consciousness' that we seek.

Our normal everyday awareness is about making judgements, differentiating this from that. It is how we navigate a complex world: this concern over here, that responsibility over there. But it is exhausting, and it drives some people crazy because there is no break from it!

However, in the meditative consciousness, one does not make distinctions or judgements but attempts simply to stay alert and awake in an undifferentiated state of awareness.

The everyday mind constantly moves from one thing to another. It never stops; it is like a torch in a dark room, shining onto one item, then the next. Onto this concern, then that concern, this memory, then that fear or anxiety, this love or those hopes, always moving about. But meditative consciousness is not like a torch moving about from one thing to another; rather, it is like switching on a light, which falls on everything equally, all at the same time. Everything is simply there, and it is simply as it is.

I first encountered this consciousness in a monk whom I had visited when I was stressed because of conflicts in my parish. He listened to my pain but appeared unmoved by it. I felt indignant. He seemed to be saying to me, 'There is light and there is dark, there is night and there is day; things are as they are. Why should you expect it to be any different?' Now this may not be the advice of a doctor, but it is a deep spiritual truth about accepting things as they are, a truth that also needs to be heard. Jesus said, 'Let anyone with ears listen!'[105]

God is like this: God makes the sun shine on the good and bad alike, God sends rain on the righteous and the unrighteous alike. He makes no distinctions. Jesus teaches that our love must be the same: 'Be perfect (in love), therefore as your Heavenly Father is perfect.'[106] Our role is simply to give good news to all and sundry without distinction and without judgement. 'Judge not', says Jesus, 'that you be not judged.'[107] In the Parable of the Sower, Jesus throws out the seed of the gospel to all and sundry. The Sower does not judge each bit of ground as being worthy or unworthy of his precious seed, he broadcasts the seed to all without judgement. Just like God's love.

If the practice of meditation is the gymnasium for the soul, then for twenty minutes we are training ourselves in pure undifferentiated consciousness without the anxiety of making judgements.

SUNDAY BETWEEN 17 AND 23 JULY (YEAR A)
Matthew 13:24–30

Let the Weeds Be
BY MICHELLE WOOD

Each of us carries within ourselves a tiny seed of meditation, like a tiny seed of wheat. I wonder if you can remember when you first felt the seed within you. I wonder what you were seeking at that time. What were you opening towards? What were you responding to?

John Main, founder of the World Community for Christian Meditation, describes this seed as a search for depth and rootedness in Christ. People who

---
105 Matt. 13:9
106 Matt. 5:48
107 Matt. 7:1

take up the path of meditation, says Main, have heard the gospel of love but seek to respond to it at their deepest level of being.[108]

Main says that the overarching aim of Christian meditation is 'to allow God's mysterious and silent presence within us to become more and more … *the reality* in our lives; giving us meaning, shape and purpose in everything we do, to everything that we are'.[109]

Developing a meditation practice is a process, much like growing a tiny seed. In each meditation sitting, through the silence and stillness, we try to listen more deeply to God's mysterious and silent presence within us. Our minds are often noisy and clogged up with distractions or 'weeds'.

We are encouraged in this week's reading to let the weeds be, to live in the imperfection of things, to grow in the paradoxes that life presents.

The weeds are just there—while we don't need to feed them, we also don't need to violently rip them out because, as Jesus cautions, we may uproot the wheat with them. Sometimes it is difficult to discern the weeds from the wheat because they grow entwined.

As we come to our own meditation garden this week, may we come with tolerance and patience, trying to stay awake, with our prayer word or mantra—our little seed, if you like. Let us try to not be distracted by the weeds, just letting them be, trusting in God's ultimate goodness, giving ourselves time to grow, leaning a little more into the earth of God as the very ground we are planted in.

SUNDAY BETWEEN 24 AND 30 JULY (YEAR A)
Matthew 13:31–33, 44–52

What is the Kingdom of Heaven Like?
BY PAUL WOOD

Parables of the kingdom of heaven are the stories that Jesus tells a disenfranchised people by the shores of Lake Galilee. Interestingly, they also speak profoundly to the meditator.

So, what is the kingdom of heaven like?

Well, it is like a mustard seed, the tiniest of all seeds, and yet it grows into a mighty tree, which becomes a home for many birds. As meditators, we like to notice tiny seeds. Once all of the loudness and demands of the world, the restlessness of the mind and the cries of the flesh are put aside, we begin

---

108 Main, *Inner Christ*, 10.
109 Main, *Inner Christ*, 15.

to notice the tiny things. The gentle breeze on our cheeks, the warmth of the sun's rays, the deep colour of the sky, the numerous shades of green, the sound of leaves, the gentleness of breathing, the miracle of life. These small 'noticings' are seeds that may grow into a great consciousness, giving shelter to all of those around us.

Again, what is the kingdom of heaven like? Well, it is like the yeast in bread dough, a hidden presence. Although you cannot see it, it is there, quietly working away and gently leavening the bread. Our meditative consciousness is like this. You may not be able to distinguish between those who meditate and those who do not, but meditation influences us all—how we notice things, how we listen to things, how we are less reactive or caught up in the drama, how we are more centred within ourselves. Thus, we become better listeners, noticing things that others do not; better seers, seeing things that we never saw before; more at peace, more spacious, less hassled. Others may not know you meditate, but your practice will quietly and secretly leaven those around you.

And again, what is the kingdom of heaven like? It is like a treasure hidden in a field. Jesus often speaks about hiddenness. For example, he speaks of storing treasure in heaven rather than on earth, where you already have your reward. He also talks about praying in secret rather than in public because our Heavenly Father sees in secret. The external world deals only with the visible, the known, the obvious and can become dominated by the loud and the strong. But the roots of spiritual life run deep beneath the surface, deep into that which precedes the world of thought, that which precedes the world of feelings, deep into the hidden source of life within, like a treasure buried in a field.

Again, the kingdom of heaven is like a merchant in search of fine pearls. When he finds 'the one', he sells all that he has to buy it. The pearl of great price! Meditation is not the pearl; meditation is simply a technique to help us identify the pearl. It is, as it were, a pair of spectacles to help us see more clearly so that we can find that which our hearts truly desire. The kingdom is what our hearts desire—a place of perfect order within an economy of love. This is the pearl of great price, and meditation may help us find it.

And again, the kingdom of heaven is like a net cast into the sea, embracing all kinds of fish, the good and bad alike. In meditation it is important that we do not judge our thoughts but leave all judgement to the angels and God at the end of time. Rather, it is ours to embrace the diversity within us and among us and simply practise love.

For those who are concerned about understanding these little parables correctly, Jesus concludes his teachings by saying they are adaptable and should be used creatively: 'Every scribe who has been trained for the kingdom of heaven is like the master of a household who brings out of his treasure what is new and what is old.'[110]

SUNDAY BETWEEN 31 JULY AND 6 AUGUST (YEAR A)
Matthew 14:13–21

To Nourish with Nothing
BY MICHELLE WOOD

A few years ago, in my work as a school counsellor, I counselled a six-year-old boy. His head barely reached the door handle of my office when we first met. His father had suddenly died, and I was to walk a journey of grief with him, his eight-year-old brother and his mother. A journey full of tears, great sadness, pain and confusion.

One day, the little boy came to see me after a difficult week at home and said, 'I would like to give a present to my mum and my brother.' I looked silently around my counselling room, thinking that I did not have much to offer. I asked the boy what sort of present he would like to give. He looked around the room, then set his eyes on the table in front of him. He said he could write them letters thanking them for taking care of him, and that we could wrap them up like 'real' presents.

And so, he set about the task of making these letters and asking for help to spell the words of 'love', 'thanks', 'care' and 'letting me play with you'. I managed to find some string, and he folded his picture letters carefully, wrapped them into two little parcels and decorated each with bright, cheery colours. He placed them on the table and smiled, and then he looked a little sad and said, 'But I don't have one.' Following his example, I picked up the pencil and wrote a letter; then, I drew a big heart of love, his heart, and wrapped it carefully.

The session ended in silent satisfaction. He carried the three little gifts to his schoolbag and placed them carefully on top.

The next day, the boy's mother sent me a picture of the dinner table that the boy had set the previous evening. In typical six-year-old style, some of the knives and forks were back to front and the napkins were a little off-centre, but on each plate lay the little gift for each of his family members. It was the best meal they had had for a while, his mother told me, because they were not fed by food but by a six-year-old's love.

---

110   Matt. 13:52.

In this week's gospel reading, the 'Feeding of the Five Thousand', Jesus looks with compassion upon the hungry crowds. When the disciples ask him to send the multitudes away to buy food in the villages, Jesus replies, 'you give them something to eat'. When they say, 'We have nothing here but five loaves and two fish', Jesus says, 'bring what you have to me', and he directs this offering to God—blesses it and breaks it … and all ate and were filled.[111]

Like the story of the six-year-old child, this parable reminds me that we are all called to give, to feed others from the smallest but deepest spaces within.

In our meditation practice, we withdraw for a short while into our own deserted place, a place away from external busyness. We go within, into the poverty of ourselves, sensing how our own anxieties and fears keep us in reactive modes that push others away and guard our self-interests. When we practise letting go of these psychological conflicts, we are surprised to find another, more childlike, space within that can co-join with Christ to make what is meagre a miracle.

In practising meditation, we are really practising the art of bringing to Christ the smallest of who we are, the crumpled piece of paper lovingly wrapped in recycled string, trusting that he will join it to the divine harmony, bless it and make it more than what we could ever imagine, something that could feed and nourish others—a feast!

SUNDAY BETWEEN 7 AND 13 AUGUST (YEAR A)
Matthew 14:22- 36

A Cry from the Heart
BY PAUL WOOD

The story of Peter walking on the water is filled with symbolic and mythic meanings that also serve as a metaphor to teach about the prayer of silent meditation.

First, there is the sea, and the wind and the waves and the fear that all these produce. These are all an echo of the great flood of Noah when the primal waters from the beginning of time collapse back into the Creation the Lord God had made, bringing chaos, destruction and death. The fear of the great deluge is throughout the Bible, which is why in the Book of Revelation it expressly states that there is no sea in paradise. The sea symbolises death.

---

111 Matt. 14:16–21.

Then, tossed about on the wind and waves is the boat, which like the ark, is designed to keep the waters of destruction out. This is like the human ego, which we build, plank by plank, throughout our lives to protect us from sinking into the chaos.

Then, there is the presence of Christ, the Logos, the ordering principle of Creation. Jesus, who had withdrawn from the crowds to be alone and enter into prayer all night, is seen in the early hours of the morning walking on water, untouched by the chaos and destructive energies of the restless sea. A prefiguring of Jesus transcending death. Is it a ghost? Is it an illusion? Peter calls out, 'Lord, if it is you, command me to come to you on the water,' he said, 'Come!'[112] And Peter stepped out of the boat.

Which is not unlike when we first began to meditate—it may all be an illusion, but nonetheless, we step out of our little ego boats in faith. We let go of our usual ego-bound understandings of the world and simply enter the fluidity of the wide-open sea by faith that we will come to the point that holds all things together, the Logos, the Christ.

As Peter steps out and walks on the water towards Jesus, he loses his focus, is distracted by the wind and the waves, and begins to sink. This is similar to being distracted in meditation, when we either wander off or fall into what some meditators call the 'sinking mind'.

In meditation, our intention is to focus the mind on a single point until the wind and waves cease and we discover stillness. However, the reality is that we often lose our focus. We are tossed to and fro by distractions, but once we become aware that we have lost our focus, we must simply let go of the distraction and gently come back to our focal point. It is this act of letting go and coming back that is the essence of meditation. Each letting go of our distraction is a *metanoia*, and each return to our focal point beyond ourselves is a *kenosis* that brings us closer to God.

However, in the story, as fear fills Peter's heart, he cries out 'Lord, save me!' This is interesting because this is not so much about a focused mind as it is a cry from the heart. It is at this point that Jesus reaches out to save Peter. This captures my attention. The moment our hearts reach out beyond ourselves is the moment we are brought into the life of God.

For the grand narration of Christianity is about love, not about our ability to focus. It is about the marriage between the lover and the beloved, the free flow of life from heart to heart. This is the economy of God; this is the Holy Spirit that flows through us and among us, bringing us up into the life of God.

---

[112] Matt. 14:28.

SUNDAY BETWEEN 14 AND 20 AUGUST (YEAR A)
Matthew 15:10–20

Heart as the Centre of Practice
BY MICHELLE WOOD

In this week's gospel, Jesus teaches that our hearts are the centre of our being, and what we do and say proceeds from the heart. The heart is not only the wellspring of our physical life but also the source of our spiritual life. In biblical literature, it is seen as the seat of decision and truth and the place of encounter and covenant. From the great prophets we have beautiful expressions such as 'Set me like a seal on your heart',[113] and 'I will put my law within them, and I will write it on their hearts.'[114]

The Christian path is a path to the heart.

It is not surprising that God incarnate, Jesus, is depicted as one with a sacred heart.

I grew up in the Roman Catholic tradition and was surrounded by depictions of Jesus with long brown hair and a fuzzy beard, opening his flesh like one opens a coat to expose his heart, a heart ricocheting out light that could touch the ends of the earth; a heart ablaze with fire, signalling warmth and the mystery of God; and a heart with a dove, white as snow, descending into it like a dive bomber.

I found it all a bit spooky as a child, but looking back on these images, I can see the significance of these graphics to people throughout the centuries as a way of contemplating the importance of the heart.

St John of Eudes wrote that Jesus gives us his heart, in order to be our heart, so that we might love with his great heart.[115]

To love with a great heart is the Christian path.

The practice of meditation is very much one of coming into the centre of our heart, to be still, to become aware and to stop the noisy thoughts of the mind so that we can be in this other space, this heart space, the seat of relationship with the Triune God. And just as blood and oxygen are pumped through the whole body, so too are we infused and joined with the great lover of all, Christ.

---

113 Song of Sol. 8:6.
114 Jer. 31:33.
115 John Eudes, *The Sacred Heart of Jesus* (Fitzwilliam, NH: Loreto Publications, 2003).

SUNDAY BETWEEN 21 AND 27 AUGUST (YEAR A)
Matthew 16:13–20

The Confession of St Peter and Coming to the Heart of the Matter

BY PAUL WOOD

Last week, Michelle spoke beautifully about the heart as the centre of practice. She said that the practice of meditative prayer brings us into our heart centre. For the heart is the centre of our being; it is the place of our covenant with God; it is core to who we are. Afterwards, we had a wonderful discussion in which Richard pointed out that what we say and what we do reveals our heart, that it is not separate or hidden from the rest of our lives. I would like to build on these notions and present a talk called 'Coming to the Heart of the Matter'.

At the beginning of the gospel story, everyone is asking questions: 'Who is this man?'; 'Where does he get his authority?'; 'By what power does he do and say the things he does?; 'Is he the one we have been waiting for?' There are just as many answers: 'He is the carpenter's son from Nazareth'; 'He is John the Baptist, back from the dead'; 'He is the reincarnation of Elijah'; and so on. In the middle of the gospel story, Peter has a moment of clarity and dares to give voice to it: 'You are Christ the Son of the Living God.' Jesus replies, 'You are right, Peter, and it is on this rock I will build my church. This is the heart of the matter. This is the bedrock.'[116]

In the same way, meditation brings us to clarity and into the heart of the matter. The technique of meditation requires us to still the mind, which is usually very busy. It is, by nature, dualistic and can never rest. It is this, then it is that. For every theory, there is a counter-theory. The mind sees in contrasts. Right is identified by knowing what is wrong, good by knowing bad. It is always moving. It has opinions and makes assumptions; it blames and justifies. The mind is full of smoke and mirrors that keep us eternally speculating while locking us out of our heart centre in the meantime. Meditation teaches us to quieten and still the mind from its mental gymnastics and to simply sit without judgement. This is the heart. The acceptance of who we are and what we are. No avoidance, no excuses, no explanations, no exaggerations, no justifications. Just sitting in the truth of who we really are before the truth of God as God really is. This is the heart of the matter.

We may look at it this way. We have the doctrine that Christ is the Logos, which translates to 'the word' but also means 'the reason' or 'the purpose'

---

[116] Matt. 16:16–18.

or 'the meaning'. Where Christ is the Logos 'through whom all things were made',[117] every rock, every tree, every bumblebee, every rabbit, indeed every plant, animal and human has its 'logoi'. Everything in the network of life has its place, its locus and its logoi within the Logos. As St Paul says, 'He is before all things, and in him all things hold together.'[118] This means that when Peter comes to his confession, he not only comes to the heart of who Jesus is but also to the heart of who Peter is.

This is the heart of the matter.

SUNDAY BETWEEN 28 AUGUST AND 3 SEPTEMBER (YEAR A)
Matthew 16:24–28

Meditation and the Divine Life
BY MICHELLE WOOD

In this week's sacred story, we are called to set our minds not on human things but on divine things. Regular meditation offers a way to do this. In meditation, we let go of the world, still our minds and orient our hearts towards the silent mystery of God, losing our certitude and fixed points of knowing. It is a type of death of the ego self.

We practise the art of losing our attachments to self ('myself', 'my way') so that we may follow the way to life.

Jesus told his disciples, 'If any want to become my followers, let them deny themselves and take up their cross and follow me … those who lose their life for my sake will find it.'[119]

In the fullest divine sense, life is more than our biological functioning. It is an awareness of our aliveness and our pulsating connection to God and all living things. At its deepest level, it is our sense of our ongoing eternal life in God.

The practice of stillness and silent meditation teaches us to dwell attentively in the mystery of our divine lives. However, to do this we need to leave the worldly self behind. The modern psychological name for the worldly self of which Jesus speaks is the 'ego'.

Sometimes our ego can deceptively claim authorship over the divine story, and we become shackled to a lesser version of ourselves, each other and God.

---

117 John 1:3.
118 Col. 1:17.
119 Matt. 16:24–25.

To unshackle from this worldly ego self is to risk losing certainty about who we are and where we are going. Unshackling is a process of becoming conscious of what we are following, what is driving us.

To leave self behind is to risk being vulnerable and letting go to discover how the living word of love dwelling within invites, beckons and quietly calls.

In the world of clambering to get ahead, proving oneself, being better than others, buying more to feel worthy, to feel real, being constantly bombarded by social media posts, it is hard to hear what lies deepest within.

Silent meditation offers a prayerful way of temporarily losing one's worldly self to discover something beyond the cross of this world. In the mystery of silence, one discovers something deep, quiet and life-giving.

SUNDAY BETWEEN 4 AND 10 SEPTEMBER (YEAR A)
Matthew 18:10–20

The Value of the Individual
BY PAUL WOOD

The Parable of the Lost Sheep speaks of the importance of the one lost sheep over the many that are safely in the fold. This is followed by Jesus empowering his disciples to manage any disagreements that arise between them. He says, 'Truly I tell you, whatever you bind on earth will be bound in heaven, and whatever you loose on earth will be loosed in heaven'.[120]

It is disappointing when the Church uses this saying to justify the ordained clergy's exclusive power over others because I suspect that this is the exact opposite of what Jesus is saying here. The powers to bind and to loose, to forbid and to allow, to withhold forgiveness and to forgive belong to all people, not just to a special group that has power over others.

In another story, Jesus tells a paralysed man that his sins are forgiven, thereby 'loosing' him. The authorities are offended and accuse Jesus of blasphemy, but Jesus says that he can prove that he, the Son of Man (that is, all humans), has the power on earth to forgive all sins. He says to the paralysed man, 'Rise, take up your mat and go home.'[121]

Jesus expects everyone to learn to forgive. Each and every individual created in the image of God has the power to forgive. And Jesus says these things because they have to be taught, they have to be learned.

---

120 Matt. 18:18.
121 Matt. 9:6–13.

In her book, Yeonmi Park, a young girl who escaped the dictatorship of North Korea for the democratic West, explains how she had to learn how to be an individual, 'for there was no "I" in North Korea—only "we"'.[122] When asked a simple question such as 'What is your favourite colour?', Yeonmi would panic because she had not yet discovered the idea that she could have a favourite colour. So, these things need to be taught and learned, people need to be empowered. And this, I believe, is what Jesus is doing.

You have the power. Jesus said, 'Whatever you bind on earth will be bound in heaven, and whatever you loose on earth will be loosed in heaven.'[123] That's how significant you are! It is not only the authorities in Jerusalem but also you that has the power.

In Jesus' day, people were not individualists.[124] One's identity was associated with a group—Jew, gentile or Samaritan; slave or free; male or female; Roman or Greek. But Jesus bypassed the identity politics of the day and treated each person as a unique and individual creation. This was a new concept and undermined the old order, leading the authorities to clamp down on the growing gospel.

In the same way, Jesus' teaching on prayer was subversive. He said, 'But whenever you pray, go into your room shut the door and pray to your Father who secret; and your Father who sees in secret will reward you.'[125] In those days, prayer was a public event, spoken aloud in a synagogue. The idea of praying privately or 'in secret' was yet to emerge, much like the concept of the individual.

It is interesting to note that some three centuries later, St Augustine described in *The Confessions of Saint Augustine* the strange phenomenon of St Ambrose reading silently, his eyes scanning the page, but his lips not moving; rather, hearing the words in his own heart: 'But when he was reading, his eye glided over the pages, and his heart searched out the sense, but his voice and tongue were at rest. Ofttimes when we had come (for no man was forbidden to enter, nor was it his wont that any who came should be announced to him), we saw him thus reading to himself, and never otherwise; and having long sat silent (for who durst intrude on one so intent?).'[126]

These skills of silent reading, which we take for granted nowadays, had to be learned.

---

122   Yeonmi Park and Maryanne Vollers, *In Order to Live: A North Korean Girl's Journey to Freedom* (New York: Penguin Press, 2015), 216.
123   Matt. 18:18.
124   Larry Siedentop, *Inventing the Individual: The Origins of Western Liberalism* (Cambridge, MA: Harvard University Press, 2014).
125   Matt. 6:6.
126   Augustine, *The Confessions of Saint Augustine*, trans. E. B. Pusey (London: Global Grey, 2018), 70.

Praying in secret is a pathway to becoming individualised, of stepping into your own unique self. The practice of meditative prayer in the Christian tradition comes directly from Jesus' teachings about praying in secret. The early monks (the word 'monk' comes from the Greek word *monos*, meaning 'one') and nuns went into the wilderness to learn how to pray in secret. These desert mothers and fathers were intrepid explorers of the individual psyche, pioneering the depths of their inner worlds in what Alan Jones describes as a form of 'psychoanalysis in the desert'.[127] They were among the first to discover how to face one's inner self, engage with one's inner demons and work through the layers of fears and attachments that keep one separated from peace and union with Christ.

Part of this inner journey is knowing that *you* have the power to bind and to loose within yourself. It is not a special ordained group in Wangaratta, Jerusalem, Rome or anywhere else that has the power. *You* have the power.

The early Christian explorers in prayer practised stillness and silence using a prayer word or phrase to hold their focus. This is a way to embark on that inner journey of transformation and healing.

SUNDAY BETWEEN 11 AND 17 SEPTEMBER (YEAR A)
Matthew 18:21–35

Forgive from Your Heart Again and Again and Again
BY MICHELLE WOOD

Peter asks Jesus how often one should forgive, suggesting seven times. He probably believed he was being quite spiritually advanced because the common philosophy of the time was 'an eye for an eye and a tooth for a tooth'. However, Jesus bowls him over by suggesting not seven times but seventy-seven times. This is not only a large number, but, even more importantly, Jesus instructs on the *quality* of forgiveness. We are instructed to forgive our brothers and sisters *from the heart*.

How can we do this? How many ways can we say, 'I forgive you from my heart?' Examples include 'I forgive you—let's have a fresh start'; 'You mean more to me than this incident—let's put it behind us'; 'It's okay, we're okay';

---

[127] Alan W. Jones, *Soul Making: The Desert Way of Spirituality* (San Francisco, CA: Harper & Row, 1985), 23.

'I've let go of it—let's move on'; 'Let's get back on track—I love you'; 'Go on with your life. I am alright, I forgive you'.

Why are overt expressions of forgiveness so important? And what happens when we can't let go or forgive, when we get stuck in anger, bitterness and resentment? Someone once wrote that to not forgive is to live in the past. But perhaps it is worse than that; perhaps to not forgive is to not have life and not let another have life. Jesus put forgiveness and love on an equal footing—they are like bookends supporting the whole of a human being.

To forgive from the heart is not the same as settling the score or drawing lines through everything equally or rationalising solutions.

In the ancient Christian writings of the *Philokalia*, the heart is viewed as the spiritual centre, our deepest, truest selves where we can find communion with Christ through prayer. Prayer is described as 'the flower of gentleness and freedom from anger'.[128] And as the 'fruit of joy and thankfulness'.[129] It is more possible to find forgiveness and repair relationships when coming from the heart.

Jesus teaches that it is not seven but seventy-seven times that you need to forgive from the heart. It is a marathon of forgiveness, not a sprint to the finish line. One needs a trained, fit and muscular heart to endure the marathon that Jesus challenges us with.

Meditation is an exercise for strengthening the heart. We practise stillness and surrender, loosening the bonds of anger and bitterness, letting go of the things that tighten the heart, sitting patiently with ourselves. In each moment we attempt to open more to the flow of love in this practice of prayer and deepen in our union with Christ.

SUNDAY BETWEEN 18 AND 24 SEPTEMBER (YEAR A)
Matthew 20:1–16

The Guardians of Silence
BY PAUL WOOD

In the Parable of the Workers in the Vineyard, those who work long hours complain because they receive the same wages as those who work short hours. This parable reminds us to not fall into envy or compare our lot with that of others, for how the Almighty rewards others is not for us to measure. As St

---

128 Nikodimos and Makarios, *Philokalia*, 58.
129 Nikodimos and Makarios, *Philokalia*, 58.

Paul explains, 'It is before their own Lord that they stand or fall.'[130]

In the same way, the discipline of meditation requires us to remain exclusively focused on our own relationship to God. So, it is in this light I wish to speak about distractions, sideways glances, thoughts, images and feelings that prevent us from entering a quiet communion with Christ.

If you visit a place with a strong Hindu culture such as Bali, you may be struck by the monstrous-looking demons located at the entrances and corners of temples. I suspect that these fearful-looking monsters serve as guardians of the sacred. The psychology behind this may be that to enter the sacred place, you must have sufficient maturity to pass the guardians. For the sacred space is not one in which you should simply wander about with childlike naivety. You must prepare yourself before entering.

I suspect that these deeper psychological truths are also the reason for the fearful-looking gargoyles on many Gothic cathedrals and churches in England and Europe. They all face outwards to channel rainwater, but they are also deliberately ugly and demonesque. Perhaps gargoyles also serve as guardians, psychologically and spiritually speaking.

Here at the Holy Trinity Cathedral in Wangaratta, the first stained-glass window that you encounter at the entrance depicts a silly-looking red demon with a pitchfork on the left and the Archangel Michael standing guard with his sword on the right. This may be a modern remnant of these ancient and fearful guardians of sacred places.

Now, I mention these things because they are much like what Robert Sardello describes as 'the guardians of the realm of silence'.[131] He understands this realm to be not just the absence of sound but something real in itself, protected by guardians who are loud, ugly, hateful, envious, lustful, sad, angry, mocking, ridiculing and belittling. They tell you that you are not worthy of entering the sacred silence. Now, rather than seeing these as fleeting feelings and illusions to be brushed aside, we can receive them as opportunities to prepare ourselves to enter the sacred.

It seems to me that this also has parallels with the teachings of Carl Jung, that to grow into our true authentic selves, we must first integrate our shadow selves, those aspects of ourselves that we habitually avoid and hide from others and ourselves out of fear, disgust or embarrassment. The path to wholeness and peace is not by avoiding things that make us uncomfortable but rather by integrating the shadow.

Sometimes Christians can focus on their virtues and goodness so much that they remain wilfully ignorant of their own shadows. This is a great tragedy

---

130   Rom. 14:4.
131   Robert Sardello, *Silence: The Mystery of Wholeness* (Berkely, CA: North Atlantic Books, 2011), 31.

because if we do not acknowledge and own our shadows, we will project them onto others and blame them for things that are legitimately ours to own. This is a source of immense evil.

The Christian path is a path of confession and forgiveness. One cannot come to forgiveness without first coming to confession, and the act of confession means that we must come to know our ugly sinfulness.

In meditation we do not avoid ourselves. We sit with ourselves, with the good and also the bad. With the beautiful and with the ugly. With the saints and with the gargoyles. We sit, we accept, we just are, in stillness, in silence, with our focus and our intentions on God. For remember, 'It is by grace you have been saved through faith, and this is not your own doing; it is the gift of God—not the result of works, so that no one may boast.'[132]

SUNDAY BETWEEN 25 SEPTEMBER AND 1 OCTOBER (YEAR A)

Matthew 21:23–32

Silence, Inner Authority and Uncritical Love

BY MICHELLE WOOD

In this week's sacred story, Jesus is teaching in the temple when the chief priests come and ask him what authority he has to do this.

Jesus radiates a natural authority. The word for this in Greek is *exousia*, which literally means 'out of being'. Jesus is a compelling teacher in the temple out of his own being.

The established authority structures are unnerved by this person Jesus, who appears to be taking it upon himself to speak and teach without being appointed or having the formal credentials or endorsed contacts.

The people who listened to Jesus would have been stepping outside of the normal conventions. They would have had to partly turn away from the conventional chief priests. And, of course, many who listened were already on the outside of these conventions. There is a funny social media post that says something like, 'This year I am going to be more like Jesus—drink wine, hang out with prostitutes, adulterers and sinners and upset religious authorities.'

This sacred story gets me thinking about my own relationship with authoritative religious structures and the development of my own inner authority. I have spent a great deal of my life untangling myself from oppressive

---

132   Eph. 2:8–9.

authority figures and structures but equally throwing myself into them at the same time. I remember telling my adult daughters about being called to the priesthood, and they said, 'Mum, you'll never survive those rigid conservative structures.'

I live in a constant tension of questioning religious authorities and wanting to sincerely submit and humble myself before the wisdoms of the tradition.

I have never been one to blindly accept the authority of others, no matter how well they present. I find it hard to trust people in power. I never believe God has chosen them or that they are infallible. When listening to a religious authority speak, I often ask myself whether I would still listen to this person if they didn't have the uniform, title or pulpit. I am more interested in a convincing life that emulates the values of the gospel, examples of which I often find outside of the Church.

In our spiritual lives, we attempt to reconcile the dilemma of internal versus external authority as we mature and examine things for ourselves. My guess is that people who think about this dilemma are interested in exploring the depths of their own spiritual life and relationship with God rather than being reduced to passive recipients in the pews.

So, how can the daily practice of silent meditation help us discern the way of Christ as the inner authority from the way of human-invented, corrupted spiritual authorities or, as Jesus puts it, the way of heaven or humans?

First, the prayer of silence is intended to purify the mind and cleanse it from psychic irritants such as greed, hatred and jealousy.

Second, meditation brings a state of tranquillity and awareness, a state of concentration and insight.

And third, meditation softens a person from within, through and through.

By looking deeply inside and seeing one's own humanity, one learns to forgive and to love.

It is said that 'an accomplished meditator has achieved a profound understanding of life, and he or she inevitably relates to the world with a deep uncritical love'.[133] Relating to the world with a 'deep uncritical love' must be the ultimate aim of every Christian seeker.

'The kingdom of God is within you,'[134] proclaims Jesus. The practice of silent meditation, along with prayer, reading the Scriptures and engaging in liturgy, the sacraments and loving action, will take us, as they have taken holy men and women in the Christian tradition throughout the centuries, to this reality.

---

133   Henepola Gunaratana, *Mindfulness in Plain English* (Boston, MA: Wisdom, 2011), 9.
134   Luke 17:21.

SUNDAY BETWEEN 2 AND 8 OCTOBER (YEAR A)
Matthew 21:33–42

The Stone
BY PAUL WOOD

How do you crack a joke? Well, you tell a story to set your audience up to a certain way of thinking and expectations. Then, you deliver the punchline, which is like a stone hitting a glass house. Suddenly, the whole meaning of the story collapses, and your audience is pleasantly surprised by seeing the story in a new light. Ha! So, you thought it was this, but it is actually that! Haha, that's funny, and so we laugh.

Now, this is shown in the narratives of the Bible, time and time again, as a divine principle. For example, at the end of the book of Genesis, Joseph says to his brothers, 'Even though you intended to do harm to me, God intended it for good.'[135] So, even evil intentions were made good in the greater narrative of God.

There are many such twists in the Scriptures. And the reason is simple. Our small minds follow our small narratives, which are often ego-bound and limited to our views, but then there is also a greater narrative or a greater mind, which we neither see nor understand, but sometimes it breaks in and makes a mockery of our small world view. Suddenly our little meanings are lost, and we awaken to a greater set of meanings, and we need to adjust, we need to repent.

For example, we have Saul, the great persecutor of Christians, breathing threats and murder and who is on the road to Damascus to persecute even more Christians, when he is confronted by a great light: 'Saul, Saul, why do you persecute me?' Falling on the ground, blinded and disoriented, his meanings are lost, his intentions are confused. But eventually, through healing hands, through talking to others of faith and after three years alone in Arabia, he comes back to become the greatest of all Christian intellects.

Of course, the narratives of the Bible are full of stories of how our small minds are surprised by the greater mind of God. Often, they are humorous, but they are also real and true to our experience of life.

There is a little phrase that is often repeated in the Bible: 'The stone that the builders have rejected has become the cornerstone. This is the Lord's doing, and it is amazing in our eyes.'[136] Dry stone building is all about selecting stones

---

135   Gen. 50:20.
136   Matt. 21:42.

of the right shape to fit in the right place. So, there is this one stone that does not seem to fit anywhere. They keep rejecting it; in fact, it is annoying, they trip over it, stub their toe on it and curse it, but in the end, it is this stone that fits perfectly as the cornerstone that ties the whole building together. This is a divine principle, and Christ is the perfect fulfilment of it. Rejected and cursed, yet the answer we all have been seeking. That's how it works.

Okay, so what has this got to do with meditation? Well, there are many rocks that we meet in life that cause us grief: people, institutions, ourselves. Often in life, our frustrations and sufferings revolve around the same rock that we keep on bumping into. The same bloody block gets in the way. And the more rigid and ego-bound we become, the less our small minds are able to find the right place for it.

But, in the higher narratives of the greater mind it has its proper place. There is a grander narrative in which it all makes sense. There is a bigger landscape and another economy.

So, in meditation, we do not tighten up around our block; we let it be because it has its place in a narrative we cannot yet grasp. We do not harden, we do not fight it, we allow it to be. We relax and let the sun shine on it, let the breeze blow over it. And as our rigid ego begins to soften, as we sit with an open heart and as the waters seep in and around the block, so we may one day discover, to our great surprise, that the very thing that we have been rejecting all our life actually occupies an essential and even a prized place in our building!

This is the mystery.

SUNDAY BETWEEN 9 AND 15 OCTOBER (YEAR A)
Matthew 22:1–14

The Inner Wedding Banquet
BY MICHELLE WOOD

In this week's sacred story, Jesus tells the parable of the kingdom of heaven being like a king who gives his son a wedding banquet, but the invited guests don't turn up, so the king sends the invitation out to everybody.

Traditionally, scholars have interpreted this parable as Jesus challenging the Jewish authorities who are not interested in his teachings or the inclusive nature of the gospel.

I would like to explore how the symbols in this parable relate to the practice of silent meditation. In the practice of silent meditation, we are stepping into an inner wedding banquet. It is an intimate union, expressed beautifully in the poetry of Song of Songs:

> *He brought me to the banqueting house,*
> *and his intention toward me was love.*
> *Sustain me with raisins,*
> *refresh me with apples;*
> *for I am faint with love.*[137]

In stepping into the great wedding hall through the prayer of silence, we bring with us all that we are—the good thoughts and bad, the sluggish and indifferent, the ignorant and brilliant, the dark and shadowy. Our thoughts flood in like the motley crowd in the parable, randomly picked from the streets. But what is important is that we turn up. Turning up is crucial because, in the parable, many don't bother or make light of it or, even worse, kill off the invitation.

The Parable of the Wedding Feast includes three cautionary tales about the things that may stop us from turning up.

First, there are the religious people who are invited but choose not to come because they are too caught up in religiosity and rules. This is like aspects of the self that are overly religious, busily seeing God in the latest guru speak, moral laws, books, churches and structures.

Second are those invitees who make light of the invitation and choose not to come but to go on with their worldly lives. This is like aspects of the self that are too busy for silence and stillness. Our energies are consumed by the home, the farm, the activities of the day, the children, politics, exercise, endlessly scrolling through social media. These grabs for our attention make light of our spiritual life and downplay its importance.

Third is the chap who turns up but does not wear the appropriate wedding garment. He is not interested in the celebration of love and union and has turned up for other reasons. This is like aspects of self that turn up but fail to respect the point of the whole practice—our relationship with God. This may symbolise that which is within us that takes advantage of the invitation to the wedding banquet, using the sacred for our own means, cheapening the divine, exploiting for our personal benefit, failing to respect with appropriate manners, showing up for other reasons than to help celebrate the wedding feast.

Overall, God generously calls every bit of us into intimacy and union—all our good and all our bad—kindly covering our shameful shallowness with a wedding garment of grace.

---

137 Song of Sol. 2:4–5.

Every time Jesus says, 'the kingdom of heaven is like...', he invites us to imagine that there is more than these earthly toils and troubles, political ramblings, religious moralising and inner psychological turmoil and suffering.

Meditation gives us a way of stepping into the great wedding banquet hall, just like the wardrobe gave the characters of Narnia in *The Lion, the Witch and the Wardrobe* a way into another dimension.

With eagerness, God cries out, 'Come, everything is ready, come to the wedding banquet.'

So, let us muster up as much presence as we can to enter the silence and quieten the distractions by allowing every bit of ourselves in. Let us enter in humility, grateful for this invitation, and leave the ordering of things to God.

SUNDAY BETWEEN 16 AND 22 OCTOBER (YEAR A)
Matthew 22:15–22

Be in the World but Not of the World
BY PAUL WOOD

'Give therefore to the emperor the things that are the emperors, and to God the things that are God's.'[138] This statement forms the basis of what we know as the political doctrine of the separation of church and state.

So, I have been thinking about our relationship to the world. The New Testament says a lot about this, which is often summed up the phrase, 'We are in the world, but we are not of the world.' Although we work in the world, participating, paying taxes, forming attachments, loving and grieving, we actually belong somewhere else. Our true citizenship is in heaven. We are just passing through earth for a short while; we are simply sojourners on this land, and our pilgrimage will take us beyond the things of this world to our real home, which is in heaven.

Meditation, particularly those styles that cultivate awareness, help us understand this consciousness of 'being in the world but not of the world'.

When we first learn to meditate, we become aware of our thoughts. And we learn that there are two ways we can relate to our thoughts. The first is to be *in* a thought. When you are in a thought, you do not actually see it because you believe that you are the thought. It is a state of unconsciousness. One is so immersed in thought that one actually inhabits the thought as if it were reality. The second is to stand back from the thought, widen the lens

---

138 Matt. 22:21.

and observe the thought as if from the outside. Then we become conscious of our thoughts; we awaken.

The basic principle of awareness methods of meditation is to cultivate a strong sense of presence, a place from which you observe your thoughts. You may notice that although your mind is always moving from this thought to that, there is a still point from which you can observe the movement of your mind. You would not see this movement if you were moving with it, but there is an observer that can observe the movement. It is this still point that the meditator develops.

Be silent, be still, be attentive. Observe and watch because thoughts will come and go like clouds. Do not follow them like a puppy dog that wants to follow every scent he comes across; rather, let them go and come back to the task of meditation. *Let go* and *come back*.

In my work as a counsellor, I found this useful to teach. For example, I may see someone in deep stress and filled with so much anger towards a particular person that they are unable to get away from it. They react angrily to every thought associated with that person. In the middle of the night, they wake up angry—even though that person is not even there! They are so fused, so attached to the thought of that person that they are unable to get away from it. They live in a permanent state of stress.

How do we navigate this? Well, the therapeutic goal is to defuse the person from the thought. We are able to do this by objectifying the thought, talking about it, setting it within a larger landscape and widening the view, so to speak. We can also do it by learning mindfulness meditation, to develop the technique of being present and still and observing without becoming absorbed.

Finally, the person can say, 'I now understand that I am not my thoughts. Thoughts are things I have, but they are not who I am.' Arriving at this awareness is extremely liberating.

In the same way, we can extend this to 'I am not my feelings. Feelings are things I have, they are not who I am.' Or 'I am not my body. My body is something I have, but it is not who I am.' Well, who am I then? This is the mystery—the unobserved observer cannot be observed by us. This silent witness can only be observed by God.

Once we have developed this awareness, it is like an extra dimension in our lives. We find that at times we are immersed in thought and unconsciousness, and at other times we awaken, we observe and we become conscious. Consciousness moves in and out like breathing—sometimes we are immersed, and at other times we are aware.

This realisation that we are in the world but not of the world liberates us from unhealthy attachments to the world that confuse our relationship to divine love.

SUNDAY BETWEEN 23 AND 29 OCTOBER (YEAR A)
Matthew 22:34–40

The Way of Love and Small Breaths
BY MICHELLE WOOD

In this week's sacred story, Jesus says that the whole of the Law and the teachings of the prophets may be summed up by two things—the love of God and the love of our neighbours.

When we love our neighbour, we are loving the image of God in our neighbour; therefore, we are loving God.[139]

We are made from love and for love. Love is the whole purpose of our lives and the centrality of who we are as human beings.

To have a life of any meaning requires us to participate in the love that flows from God, through us to others and back to God—like the source of a river that flows to the sea. We are like valves that can either be open or closed to this flow of universal love.

When we are open to this flow, love pours from us to others with the directness of a paramedic on the scene of an accident—it is pure response, a pure gift to the other, so strong that the self falls away. Indeed, the falling away of the self is a prerequisite for this universal flow of love, which is why silent prayer and meditation are helpful.

In the silence, stillness and focus of meditation, we train ourselves to let go of the self, and like the deep-sea diver, we leave the surface of things and orient, as best we can, our whole heart, mind and soul to God, opening in humility to the universal gifts of life and love.

In this simple but grace-filled practice, we obtain the sense that, as John Main puts it, 'we are not looking for God but rather God has found us'.[140] The lover and the beloved are united, and the inner wedding feast begins.

By finding an intimate path to the loving God in the simplicity of silence, we can extend this flow of universal love to others.

The two great commandments—the love of God and the love of our neighbour—are alive and contained in the inbreath of our interiority with God and the outbreath of our generous, loving actions in the world.

---

[139] Ian Boxall, 'Matthew', in *The Jerome Biblical Commentary for the Twenty-First Century*, eds. John J. Collins, Gina Hens-Piazza, Barbara E. Reid and Donald Senior (London: T&T Clark, 2020), 1219.
[140] Main, *Inner Christ*, 337.

SUNDAY BETWEEN 30 OCTOBER AND 5 NOVEMBER (YEAR A)
Matthew 23

Immortal, Invisible, God Only Wise
BY PAUL WOOD

We have two possible sets of readings for Sunday. If we keep the Feast of All Saints, we will be standing in the tradition of All Saints' Day, All Souls' Day and Halloween, in which case our Sunday gospel will be the Beatitudes: blessed are the poor in spirit, blessed are the pure in heart, blessed are the meek, blessed are the peacemakers and so on.[141]

Alternatively, if we keep the ordinary Sunday gospel, it is the exact opposite. Rather than blessings, the gospel refers to a series of woes, the criticisms of Jesus against the scribes and the Pharisees, whom he describes as 'hypocrites', 'blind guides', 'a brood of vipers', 'whitewashed tombs', those who 'strain gnats but swallow camels', lead people astray and lock them out of the kingdom of heaven.[142]

Well, I've chosen to go with the woe readings.

Matthew 23 articulates the problems we have with organised religion, and among these 'woes', Jesus gives his teaching about what he expects of his own followers.

On the one hand, religious leaders sit on the seat of Moses, so their existence is legitimate. They hold the tradition; they are the keepers of the oracles of God. However, if they do not practise what they preach, one should not do what they do. Jesus says, do not set yourself up above others as a rabbi, for we are all brothers and sisters. One of the downsides of having strong external religious authorities is that they can do all the thinking for us, so we are kept as children, dependent and disempowered by the so-called experts.

Jesus also says, 'Call no one on earth Father, for you have one Father in heaven.'[143] Of course, we all have earthly fathers when we are young and people who guide us when we are learning, but Jesus expects his disciples to be adults, to let go of earthly authority figures and be guided by the one authority figure in heaven. One of the great evils of religion is that people can sometimes surrender their will, not to God but to a substitute God in the form of religion. This happens in cults, where people bow down to human

---

141 Matt. 5.
142 Matt. 23.
143 Matt. 23:9.

authority figures rather than to the invisible God. In other words, they fall for idols and become beholden to something that is not God.

In the Book of Revelation, St John gives us a vision of the heavenly Jerusalem, where he expressly says that there 'is no temple because the Lord God is the temple'.[144] Religion is never an end in itself; it is only a donkey, not the destination.

Finally, Jesus calls on us to not set ourselves up as examples for others to follow, for we have only one to follow and that is Christ the Messiah.

So, what does all this mean for us meditators? The way of the meditator is to strip away all fake authorities, all those demigods within us that stand between us and God. Silent meditation is a way of cleansing our temple of its idols. Not just the obvious sins, such as greed, anger and self-righteousness but also attachments to dogma, scripted ways of thinking, expectations and fixations, what the old prayer books called 'fond things vainly conceived'. For there are many 'fond things' that get in the way of our relationship to God.

This cleansing is known as the 'apophatic way' in Christian spirituality. The path of stripping away, of unveiling, the journey of unknowing, without images, without words, without dogmas, without expectations. The way of entering the so-called darkness of God that shines so bright. It is the path of silence and emptiness.

Thus, we sit in silence because all our thoughts, words, images and feelings are not the living God; rather, they are just our images of God, reflections of the mind, and so we let them go to become still and silent before the great mystery of the unknowable God. An 1867 hymn by Walter C. Smith goes as follows:

> *Immortal, invisible, God only wise,*
> *In light inaccessible hid from our eyes,*
> *Unresting, unhasting, and silent as light,*
> *Nor wanting, nor wasting, Thou rulest in might.*[145]

SUNDAY BETWEEN 6 AND 12 NOVEMBER (YEAR A)
Matthew 25:1–13

Our Busy Minds – Half In, Half Out
BY MICHELLE WOOD

Reading the gospel stories through the theme of silent meditation is like entering a narrow door. In this week's sacred story, Jesus says, 'Then the

---

144 Rev. 21:22.
145 1 Tim 1:17.

kingdom of heaven will be like ten bridesmaids who took their lamps and went to meet the bridegroom.'[146]

I think that every time we sit to meditate, we are taking our lamps to meet the beloved bridegroom, invited to wed our being to something sacred. In the story of the ten bridesmaids, five are said to be foolish and the other five wise. I think that within ourselves we contain both foolishness and wisdom.

When we meditate, we have five energies within who are wise: alert, open, faithful, attentive and ready. We have another five energies who are foolish: distracted, ill-prepared, fickle, lazy and sloppy.

Half of us in, and half of us out.

The foolish are always trying to steal from the wise. They are too self-seeking to do the work themselves, nagging to be carried, petering out too early, too busy elsewhere to turn up prepared and ready to enter. From these foolish inattentive positions, it is easy to miss what really matters.

Meditation is a prayer practice of attentively waiting in the dark, eyes closed on the lookout.

In the story, the bridegroom is late, and it gets very dark. We begin to see how preparing oneself is important. Through the practice of meditation, we are learning to light the lamp of the mantra or the breath to stay alert and ready.

The bridegroom comes at midnight. In this liminal space between night and day, at the cusp of the new, he comes. As meditators, we sit temporarily in an in-between state, neither caught up in the busyness of the world nor asleep.

We enter the inner chamber of the beloved, and we wait in the dark with our small lamps. We wait patiently, attentively, stretching towards an eternal tipping point between dark and light, noise and quiet, the solitary and communal. We make a bridge between human and God with our inbreath and outbreath.

So, as we prepare to enter this period of silence, let us gather all ten bridesmaids as best we can. Let us give thanks for those bits of wisdom that have got us to this point and prod those who are still on the way, rejoicing in our own weaknesses, as St Benedict puts it, to deal tenderly with the weaknesses of others.

And above all, let us keep awake, for we know neither the day nor the hour that the bridegroom will come.

---

146   Matt. 25:1.

SUNDAY BETWEEN 13 AND 19 NOVEMBER (YEAR A)
Matthew 25:14–30

Life as an Egg
BY PAUL WOOD

If you have ever had psychoanalysis with a Jungian psychotherapist, you'll know that the moment you walk through the door, the therapist makes their first therapeutic judgement of you. They will look at you and assess where you are standing in the arc of your life.

Jungians distinguish between the morning of life and the afternoon of life and suggest that the type of psychology and spirituality needed to navigate the morning of life is very different from that needed to navigate the afternoon of life.

The morning of life is all about growth. Initially, there is a massive expansion of cells and neurons. The child learns at a phenomenal rate, discovering their power and potential in the world. They need to grow a healthy ego or sense of self. They need to establish a persona, an effective mask with which to face the world. As they grow into adulthood, they need to establish themselves both socially and financially. They need meaningful work and to perhaps engage in the noble task of bringing a family into the world. The morning of life is all about growth because what lies ahead of you is the full sun at noonday—the peak of your potential.

But there comes a time when you pass noonday, when you need to accept that the remainder of life is no longer about growth, potential and establishing yourself. Much of this is now past, and that which is ahead is the long afternoon and the gradual setting of the sun. This brings into play an entirely different set of psychological and spiritual skills.

Some people may find that their external circumstances belong to the afternoon, but their internal map still belongs to the morning, bringing a crisis of meaning or a midlife crisis. In fact, Jung noted that those who navigate the afternoon and evening will inevitably need to draw from the wells of religious wisdom.

So, if the morning of life is about growth, ego and persona, then what is needed to successfully navigate the afternoon? Well, allow me to suggest three:

1. Acceptance of things as they are: You cannot go back, change the past, raise your children again or relive your youth. What is done is done, and one must learn to accept things as they are.

2. A sense of the transcendent or the eternal: As one ages, life becomes more translucent. In other words, the eternal light begins to shine through the gradually thinning veil of this world, giving a sense of a greater landscape. Beyond our small ego bubble of awareness, there is a higher order, a meaning beyond just 'me' and 'mine'.
3. The work of consummation: This means to bring everything into completion—the loose ends, the unfinished business—to make things right and create your legacy or what you are leaving behind for future generations. Completing your story is like completing a poem.

The parable this Sunday is a parable of the talents, and its meaning spans both the morning and the afternoon of life. In the morning, we must take the risk to use our talents—this is the stuff of faith. But the parable is also about judgement as we stand in the afternoon—the deeds done and those left undone. These must be reconciled and paid for. For we stand in the shadow of our judgement, which brings all things to their consummation.

And so, life has a shape, the shape of an egg. At first, it is all about growth and expansion, which plateau as we reach middle age. Then, in the afternoon, our options and powers diminish, and finally, the evening is bringing things together and the rounding of the egg to completion.

One of the things that meditation can help us with is the holding of this total consciousness. Life as an egg.

SUNDAY BETWEEN 20 AND 26 NOVEMBER: CHRIST THE KING (YEAR A)

Matthew 25:31–46

Sorting through Ourselves

BY MICHELLE WOOD

This week marks the end of the Church's liturgical calendar. The yearly pilgrimage ends with a feast known as Christ the King. It is heralded with a sacred story about the last judgement, which signifies the end of injustice and a new reality or economy—the kingdom of God—being established through a great sorting and separating. I like to think about this process of sorting and separating as a metaphor to assist us towards loving action in the world.

We are called to be people who are sorting through ourselves all the time, to be awake and to notice how we are going on the scale of alleviating or perpetuating suffering.

The yearlong liturgical cycle gives us a psychological and symbolic map by which to sift and sort through our inner being in relation to the pattern of love displayed by Christ.

At this time, at the end of the liturgical calendar, we can reflect on our spiritual dehiscence—what of ourselves has grown and ripened and fits into this kingdom of love and peace and what needs to be cast out.

The final judgement readings ask a simple question: How well have we loved?

Christ is clear that he is the lover of the whole of humanity, and whatever you do to another person, especially someone who is poor, vulnerable, sick, hungry, isolated or marginalised, is what you do to him.

To love humanity in the way that Christ teaches requires a heart flowing with an abundant, non-discriminatory, universal love, a love that directly fulfils people's basic human needs as they appear in front of you, in the moment, in the here and now.

To do this, we need eyes that see widely and clearly and hearts that flow freely, ready to share with anyone in need.

Silent meditation can help us to stop, see and feel how our heart is flowing. It provides us with a space to see the internal dramas we are caught up in that distract us from noticing the real basic needs of another. In meditation, we sort and separate ourselves from constant distractions by returning our attention to our prayer word or breath.

In meditation, we practise returning to the heart, the centre of our being and the source of love. In this love, our life is everlasting, and our capacity to give is inexhaustible.

YEAR B. THE YEAR OF ST MARK

Advent (Year B)

FIRST SUNDAY OF ADVENT (YEAR B)
Mark 13:24–37

Maranatha – Awake, Alert, Expectant and Full of Hope

BY PAUL WOOD

Last week, Michelle brought us to the consummation of the year in the liturgical calendar with the feast of Christ the King. Her talk was about sorting through ourselves, like dividing the sheep from the goats, as a process of transforming the realm of this existence into the reign of Christ. Now we begin the new cycle of readings in the liturgical calendar, which follows the Gospel of Mark.

We start with the first Sunday of Advent, and surprisingly, it tells of the end of the world. The Old Testament reading begins, 'O that you would tear open the heavens and come down'[147] and the gospel reading says, 'the stars will be falling from heaven and the powers will be shaken. Then, they will see "the Son of Man coming in clouds" in great power and glory.'[148] It is as if the great egg of Creation is cracking open and light from outside is streaming in. The end of the world is also the birth of a new world.

In many ways, this may seem to parallel the state of the world we are in at the moment, with many a public intellectual warning that we're facing a number of existential threats, climate change, nuclear war, runaway technology, pandemics, the break-up of social cohesion, anger, confusion and madness. It is as if the very foundations of our existence are shaking. The signs are all around us. But the important thing to note in the readings is that they are all about something new being born, they are full of hope, they are all about faith and love and they all look to the future and the beyond—their message is keep awake and alert for the day of salvation is coming. Keep awake and alert because you do not know when the master of the house will come, whether in the evening, at midnight, at cock crow or at dawn. Stay awake, be prepared and do not lose hope. Be alert and expectant.

---

147 Isa. 64:1.
148 Mark 13:24–26.

Advent is a word that means 'coming', and the first Sunday of Advent orients our hearts beyond ourselves, beyond this world that is passing away, to God who is coming. This is a particularly good positioning for meditation. We sit, as it were, on the very edge of our consciousness, looking out beyond ourselves, with our back to the things of this world. We are alert and ready with our hearts open to receive new life from God who is coming. It is this positioning of expectation and hope with openness of heart and readiness to receive that is the basic spiritual orientation of the Christian spiritual life. This is the soil in which the Church was born in expectant hopefulness of Christ's return. The prayer phrase *maranatha* means 'Come Lord' in the ancient Aramaic language, the language of Jesus. We find it in many early Christian writings such as in the Didache, but we also find it twice in the New Testament. Once it is retained in the original Aramaic form in the Greek text,[149] which suggests that it was probably already in distinct usage as a saying within the Christian community. The other place it is found is at the very end of the New Testament at the end of the Book of Revelation, which ends with these final words, 'The one who testifies to these things says, "Surely I am coming soon." Amen. Come, Lord Jesus!'[150]

John Main, the founder of the World Community for Christian Meditation, says that '*maranatha*' is not only one of the most ancient Christian prayers in the language that Jesus spoke but also has a harmonic quality in that it helps to bring the mind to silence.[151]

Let's practise silence, stillness and watchfulness with openness of heart to receive the coming of the Lord.

SECOND SUNDAY OF ADVENT (YEAR B)
Mark 1:1–8

Beginnings
BY MICHELLE WOOD

The sacred story this week opens with 'The beginning of the good news of Jesus Christ, the Son of God.'[152]

---

149 1 Cor. 16:22.
150 Rev. 22:20.
151 'John Main: Biography', The School of Meditation, archived from the original 8 May 2012, accessed 5 December 2021, theschoolofmeditation.org.
152 Mark 1:1.

They are the beginning lines of the Gospel of Mark. Beginning lines are especially important. If you ever write a book and attempt to get it published, like me, you will become aware of how crucial these openings are; they are like the curtain going up at the theatre. They create the moment where the reader's imagination is pricked and fired up or where an unsympathetic publisher tosses your manuscript into the recycle bin.

And I must say Mark's beginning is both economical and jam-packed. It says it all.

Beginnings are important in sacred stories, as they are in life.

Bereishit (bear ra sheet) is the first word in the Hebrew scriptures, and it means *in the beginning*. 'In the beginning when God created the heavens and the earth, the earth was a formless void and darkness covered the face of the deep, while a wind from God swept over the face of the waters. Then God said, "Let there be light"; … And God saw that the light was good'.[153]

From this beginning, you get the sense that something magical and transformative is about to happen, not literally but poetically.

The expression '*In the beginning*' gives an ultimate sense of the primacy of God who through wind and breath is the animating force that sets all of life in motion and who proclaims that every bit of Creation is good.

In the opening passages of the Hebrew scriptures and the Gospel of Mark, *beginnings* are tied to ultimate ends and are imbued with goodness: what God creates is good, and what the Son of God brings is good. The 'good news of Jesus Christ, the Son of God'.

The primary task of a Christian is to centre their lives on this original blessing of goodness and be a source of it to others.

A modern example of an individual who engaged in such living is the monk Charles de Foucauld, who wrote, 'I wish to cry the gospel by my whole life.'[154]

His life is described as one that gave witness to the silent, hidden presence of love.[155]

In the practice of silent meditation, we return to our own beginnings—breath and gift of life. Feeling our way, a little more deeply into the hidden presence of love.

We let the wind of God sweep over us, over all that is void and dark within, so that we may open a little wider to receive the good news that the Son of God, the Light of the World, brings.

---

153   Gen. 1:1.
154   Atwell, *Celebrating the Saints*, 500.
155   Atwell, *Celebrating the Saints*, 500.

THIRD SUNDAY OF ADVENT (YEAR B)
John 1:6–8, 19–28

Restoring the Image of God
BY PAUL WOOD

This Sunday, we read about the preaching of John the Baptist. As the crowds flock to John, they are a little like someone who looks at the finger that is pointing at the moon instead of looking at the moon itself. For John is saying: I am not 'the Messiah!' I am 'not the light'—another one who is greater than I is coming, I am not worthy to untie the thong of his sandals; I only baptise with water, but he will baptise with the Holy Spirit. I am not the light; the true light is yet to come.

So how might this preaching be relevant to the inner journey? Well, we note that all forms of sacred psychology differentiate between the self and the true self, or the phenomenal self and the essential self. For how we appear to be and what we know of ourselves is not the truth of ourselves; the true self that is real, authentic, is still waiting to be unveiled and grown into.

For example, we find this in Christian theology with the idea of the image of God. We were created in the image of God, but that image has been lost because of our sin and bad habits, buried beneath layers and layers of guilt and shame. The work of the Christian is to restore the image of God, in oneself and in the whole of Creation.

C. J. Jung spoke of the true self, which he identified as the Christ archetype, that is, the image of God within. But we are locked in our egos and out of touch with our true self. Herein lies the human problem.

The ego, which is our conscious self, is something that we have constructed through negotiation in our social relationships throughout our lives, beginning in infancy where those energies that endeared us to others were brought to the fore, whereas those energies rejected by others soon became hidden and buried within us. The result of this process of growing up is that between our ego and our true selves is a whole lot of underdeveloped and rejected stuff, which Jung called the shadow.

Thus, the journey to recover the truth of ourselves is a journey that must include the shadow. and this means facing a lot of stuff that we have avoided throughout our life, since infancy. This is the hero's journey as in all the great myths. The hero must enter into dark forsaken places and even face the dragon in order to reclaim the treasure or to heal the land. This great journey is what Jung called 'individuation', that is, becoming our individual selves. To do this, we must leave behind the social constructions we have negotiated with the surrounding world, plunge into the depths of who we really are and gradually integrate our shadow elements into our consciousness.

Now, I suggest that the Christian journey is exactly the same, but the language we use is different. The language is of confession and forgiveness. You confess, that is, you acknowledge the truth, no matter how dark and painful it is, your failings, your sin, your shame. To come to a point of confession requires that you enter your shadow, but it is only then, when you confess, that you can be forgiven and find redemption and acceptance of yourself.

Confession—forgiveness, that's how you restore the image. Confession—forgiveness is the golden path. Right foot, left foot, and so we keep on walking even into the shadows.

Confession and forgiveness, like outbreath—inbreath. Confess—forgive. This is the path.

And gradually, as we integrate and accept those elements of ourselves that we have rejected and lost, we slowly begin to reclaim a sense of our original selves as the image of God.

This is the Christian path.

And as we practice meditation, so we let go of our ego and phenomenal selves and sit with openness of heart before the mercy of God to be bathed in endless forgiveness, so that gradually we become more whole people.

Outbreath and inbreath.

FOURTH SUNDAY OF ADVENT (YEAR B)
Luke 1:26–38

Creating a Meditative Womb
BY MICHELLE WOOD

In Canterbury, if you walk the small paths between the rows of wheat and barley, which are as tall as your waist, you may stumble across a church in Wickelhambreaux. And if your curiosity spurs you on past the crumbled headstones and overgrown wildflowers, you will enter an old arched door of a church and be surprised and delighted.

The first thing you will see as you step inside is a dome ceiling painted in Greek blue with thousands of tiny white stars overhead. If you look a little lower down, you will see beautiful angels, as large as adults, painted in simple black ink, flowing like calligraphy letters, encircled and connected by flowers and leaves, their lips painted blood-red as if the words they uttered brought things to life. The angels from on high look downwards into the body of the church as if they are speaking to us. They are poetically painted at the entrance to the sanctuary, which is marked by a large stone arch. The angelic words 'peace, joy, and goodwill to all' are inscribed on the pillars that fall to the floor, rooted like trees.

And then, in the centre of the sanctuary behind the altar, you, the pilgrim, will be bedazzled by prisms of light of every colour of the rainbow. They form a picture of a young woman kneeling on the ground and being greeted by an angel, while all around her everything is erupting in flower, colour and joy.

In the centre of this window, just above the woman's head, is a silver star with shards of light stretching in every direction.

In this most unusual and utterly humble church, you will not see a cross or a crucifixion scene so familiar in its violence and brutality to our eyes.

Instead, you will see fecundity, flowering, renewal, beauty, a mysterious union between the heavens and earth, you will see a human open her heart to incarnate the Word of God and perhaps you will want to, as I did, fall on your knees and give thanks for such a message of total love.

As I think about the sacred story this week, I ask myself: Why are there not more churches depicting a theology of womb, fecundity and the beauty of nature? What has the patriarchal ecclesiastical institution done to it?

I think about the spiritual practices within oneself that are about creating a womb for the Word of God to be received, fed and grown.

I am grateful for the practice of silent meditation, for it is about sitting in the barrenness and yet making fertile the womb of our spiritual being so that we can receive mysteriously something beyond our imaginings. In meditation, we are waiting in openness to say 'yes' to the perplexing, as Mary did.

In the silence, we are seeking the very gift of God incarnating within us and through us.

THE EPIPHANY OF OUR LORD (YEAR B)
Matthew 2:1–12

Journey to the Heart
BY PAUL WOOD

See meditation for Year A on page 13.

FIRST SUNDAY AFTER EPIPHANY (YEAR B)
Mark 1:4–11

The River and the Practice of Silent Meditation
BY MICHELLE WOOD

I have a spiritual practice called the Murray River float. It entails strapping my life jacket onto my bicycle, cycling down to the riverbank, walking a couple of kilometres upstream, plunging into the icy water and floating back downstream. Now, the long wide green river is flowing fast, the waters are high and its dark cold currents look deceptively calm on the surface but pull with such force.

Once you step into a river, you must let go and go with the flow. In a mighty river, like the Murray, you quickly realise that you cannot swim against it and must surrender to something bigger than yourself.

Meditation, like the Murray River float, is best when you let go and surrender to the wider flow of God.

In meditation, one leaves the banks of the world behind and immerses into wider, more powerful, more subtle currents than the paddling pool of one's ego. There is a refreshing release. One opens to another way of relating and being. A heart-centred way.

There are parallels between the experience of the Murray River float and the practice of silent meditation. In both practices, there is a sense of joyous freedom as one tunes into physical sensation and is liberated from the cognitive tussle of thoughts. There is a soulful expansion as one begins to notice the flow of constant change—all is slipping away and yet the new arrives, moment by moment.

Floating on the river, I enjoy seeing things afresh, like the underside of huge gum branches and, in the reeds, the nests of newly hatched dusty moorhens. In meditation, I enjoy sensing the mysterious invisible current of God that moves through all and in all. In both practices, I learn to hold things lightly and feel at one with the clouds floating by. On the river, I experience a sense of playfulness, aliveness and reverence for the beauty of nature. These are qualities that I believe are important for the spiritual life. Through both practices, I get a deep sense of divinity imprinted on nature and the fecundity of life.

This week's sacred story celebrates the baptism of Jesus in River Jordon. A river with deep significance, a river that links the Old Testament and New Testament. Jesus is immersed in the river's waters and like the mythic waters in the Genesis story, he becomes a new creation, a new path for humanity.

When he comes up from the water, the heavens open and the Spirit descends and carries him like a mighty river into the wilderness.

This evening, as we embark on a meditative float into the silence, untangling from the snags of thoughts and surrendering our egos for a short time, may we practice the art of gentle surrender, trusting in the goodness of the flow of life.

SECOND SUNDAY AFTER EPIPHANY (YEAR B)
John 1:43–51

Between Earth and Heaven
BY PAUL WOOD

A fruit of meditation is that we can become more aware of different levels of consciousness. Sometimes, our consciousness is light, free and creative as we become aware of the subtle energies that move within and around us. At other times, our consciousness is heavy, clumsy, mechanical and self-obsessed. Often, we assume that consciousness is a level playing field, but if we think about it, we know that it is very layered. There are higher states of awareness, there are lower states of awareness, and we move up and down between these levels.

There is the mystical and ancient idea of a ladder set up between earth and heaven. We see this first in the Old Testament when the patriarch Jacob had a dream of a ladder and the angels of God ascending and descending upon it. And many a Jewish mystic since has contemplated this ladder and devised many wonderful things about it.

About 1,800 years after Jacob lived, Jesus refers to himself as this ladder: 'Very truly, I tell you, you will see heaven opened and the angels of God ascending and descending upon the Son of Man.'[156]

And so much is made in Christian spirituality of this ladder that reaches all the way to heaven in the person of Jesus. Steps on how to make progress in prayer and get to heaven are the rungs of the ladder. For example, Climacus, in his seventh-century classic 'The Ladder of Divine Ascent',[157] and many others use the ladder idea that connects earth to heaven.

Medieval Christianity came to see the world and society through what is called the 'Great Chain of Being', which is a hierarchical structure with God at the top, followed by the hosts of heaven; the nine orders of angels; and the realm of human beings, with kings at the top, and then bishops and the clergy,

---

156 John 1:51
157 Climacus, 'Ladder of Divine Ascent'.

all the way down to serfs at the bottom. Below the realm of humans is the animal kingdom. Wild animals like the lion are at the top, because a lion is free to do what it wants, and domesticated animals are lower down because they are not free. Then, below the animal kingdom is the plant kingdom—plants are unable to move about, and so, they are even less free. Last is the mineral kingdom consisting of inanimate matter, with gold at the top and slime and gunk at the bottom. Thus, there is this 'Great Chain of Being' that reaches from earth all the way up to heaven, where everything has its God-given place within the orders of Creation.

In our contemporary world, the spiritual teacher Cynthia Bougeault explains a modern rendering of the Great Chain of Being with what she calls 'The Ray of Creation'.[158] Rather than rungs on a ladder, the Ray has different frequencies or vibrations, like a music scale. The Ray begins with the pure love of the unified Godhead, and as it shines, it creates the many levels of consciousness. The higher the level, the freer, more life-giving and more filled with love it is, whereas the lower and denser the level, the more mechanical, unconscious, heavier, physical and lifeless it is, eventually losing coherence and falling into entropy. There is a continuous flow of reciprocal feeding between these realms, like the angels ascending and descending on the ladder.

She writes that the very purpose of our existence is to raise our consciousness up to higher levels where there is greater love, greater freedom and greater coherence. This is what we try to do in the prayer of meditation. She teaches that two things enable us to move up to higher realms of consciousness. One is what she calls 'Conscious Attention'. So, we must not just drift into habitual thinking but rather learn to intentionally use freewill to give our focused attention to something in particular. Become fully aware. For without this ability to focus, we sink into the lower levels of awareness and disintegration. The second is the willingness to carry our suffering without falling into either victimhood or blame. Carry suffering as Jesus did: no blame, no judgement, no avoidance. It is these two things that stop us sinking into the lower levels of consciousness where there is ultimately weeping and the gnashing of teeth. These two things enable us to raise our consciousness to higher levels where there is love and coherence. This is where meditation helps us by raising our consciousness.

---

158   See Cynthia Bourgeault, *Eye of the Heart: A Spiritual Journey into the Imaginal Realm* (Boulder, CO: Shambhala, 2020), 23. Chapter 2, 'Worlds within Worlds', is based on the work of G. I. Gurdjieff.

THIRD SUNDAY AFTER EPIPHANY (YEAR B)
Mark 1:14–20

'Follow Me' and 'I Will Make You'
BY MICHELLE WOOD

In the practice of meditation, one is learning the discipline of following. In our practice, each of us is following something—the breath, a mantra, a prayer word.

To do this, we have to stop following our set ways and the musings of our own minds. But this is hard to do because mental impressions are constant and always come and go. They are like lemonade bubbles rising to the surface of our conscious mind, breaking and disappearing in an effervescent frenzy. These thoughts, feelings and senses are fickle and ever-changing. They are partial, limited renderings of the world.

It is impossible to keep track of all mental impressions as there are so many, which is one of the first things we become aware of when we begin to meditate. How do we respond to this, so that we may get beyond these thought mazes and touch the edges of a deeper, truer reality?

As you know, I have been practising floating down the Murray River and imbuing it with prayerful metaphors, such as surrendering to the wider currents of God. This week, I have also been becoming aware of time. For when I float past people on the banks, park benches and dangling willow arms, and past toddlers sitting on sandbanks and youthful boys scaling great tree heights, I experience time passing and a gentle moving through sensations and thoughts. For you cannot stop when you are in a flow that you must follow. To follow, you must let go, let things pass, no matter how attractive, how interesting or how safe things on the side appear. The art of following is letting go and placing your attention on the greater flow.

I wonder whether this is something like what the first disciples felt when Jesus called them. For immediately, they let go and followed. It was not a decision based on mental cognition. Perhaps it was more like falling in love, for when this happens you have to follow a somewhat more powerful flow.

Jesus says, 'follow me and I will make you…'.

In the context of the sacred story, he is speaking to Simon and Andrew and then to James and John who were all fishermen. He says to them, 'follow me and I will make you fish for people'.[159]

---

[159] Mark 1:17.

I wonder what Jesus may have said had he walked along and met artists painting, …

Follow me and I will make you artists for all people…

… or perhaps women patching cloth …

Follow me and I will make you patch the holes of the entire world…

… or a bunch of buskers at the marketplace.

Follow me and I will make you musicians for the masses …

Whatever the context, I have no doubt that Jesus' call to follow would be linked to both the everydayness of who we are and all that we could become. 'Follow me and I will make you…'; I will make you an ever-expanding expression of love. A love that spills out of self, beyond your everyday labours and travels boundlessly and generously. A love that knows no mental snags or self-enclosed eddies. A love that you are immersed in, that carries you and that through following which you will give water and life to all whom you pass by and who dwell nearby.

So let us in this time of meditation enter that flow of silent love, letting go of all thoughts, and follow the heartbeat of Christ.

FOURTH SUNDAY AFTER EPIPHANY (YEAR B)
Mark 1:21–28

Exousia

BY PAUL WOOD

I had a dream the other night. I was singing a beautiful unknown song. The tune was complex and the lyrics long, and yet, they flowed out of me seamlessly from beginning to the end. I felt each of the guitar strings vibrate under my fingers as I anticipated each progression to a new chord. I was singing with others, and I even managed to sing in harmony. It was beautiful.

The problem is that in reality I cannot do any of these things. So, often, I am made aware of my limitations. Not just the limits of my skill, but the limits of my intellect, the limitations of my character and the limitations of my position in society. I may wish to do something, but often, I cannot do it because I do not have the standing.

I tell you this because in our gospel reading this week Jesus is beginning his public ministry and all are amazed and say, 'Who is this man? He is not like the scribes and Pharisees because he has authority—he does things!'

Now it's this word authority I want to focus on. The Greek word is *exousia*. The root word that it derives from is a word that means 'it is free', in the sense that there is nothing stopping you from acting and there is nothing forcing you to act. So, if you have authority, then you are free, doors will open, nothing stands in your way and you can do as you want. That's *exousia*. It is also translated as 'power'.

But there is also a moral dimension to *exousia* because the root word also means not just 'it is free' but also 'it is right' or 'it is lawful', legitimate, true, authentic. The idea of *exousia* is that it is a power that is both free and right and, in this way, it is like God because ultimately it is only God who is both free and right.

So, in our story, when the demons inside a man rise up and cry out, 'What have you to do with us, Jesus of Nazareth? Have you come to destroy us?', Jesus simply says, 'be silent and come out of him' and the man is healed. And the crowds respond 'What is this? A new teaching! With authority he commands even the unclean spirits, and they obey him.'[160] What *exousia*!

Exousia makes up part of the lexicon of words in the Greek New Testament that describes Jesus in a cosmic battle between good and evil. The gospel story can only be understood properly within the meta-story of a cosmic battle of the principalities and the powers in the heavenly realms, all of which become subject to the authority of Christ, who is above every other authority and every other power.

So how is this applicable to meditation?

Well, in meditation our focus is inward, on that place of our internal world: the place before actions, the place of thoughts and feelings, the place of mind, the place of intent and the place of heart. And in this place, we all have authority. If we choose to think of a pink elephant, we have the authority to do so and immediately a pink elephant will appear. If we choose to banish the pink elephant and think of something else, we can usually do that.

And much of meditation is training the mind to use our authority. That authority that is both free and right.

First, in meditation we use our authority to choose, to focus our attention. Meditation is not about drifting as if you have no 'authority', like a leaf in the wind, but about using our authority over our wandering minds. Engaging our free will to focus. The authority to silence distracting energies in the same way as Jesus silences the demons—no nonsense, be gone. Having authority is to be free. You don't have to do it, but you choose to do it.

And second, meditation is also about finding one's heart for one's heart is one's compass. It brings one into alignment, so that one is right, legitimate, authentic and true—to oneself, to others and to God.

'*Exousia*': Jesus exercised it and so must we in his name.

---

160 Mark 1:24–25.

FIFTH SUNDAY AFTER EPIPHANY (YEAR B)
Mark 1:29–39

Meditation: A Deserted Place

BY MICHELLE WOOD

In the practice of silent meditation, one withdraws from the busyness of life to recentre and find communion with God. There is a beautiful expression: 'For though God be everywhere present, yet God is only present to thee in the deepest, and most central part of the soul.'[161]

So how do we get to the deepest and most central part of the soul, that altar of interface where we consciously bask in the awareness of being with God.

First, we must strip away a lot because so much of life is filled with busyness and action, with important acts of caring for others and contributing to the world.

In this week's sacred story from the Gospel of Mark, Jesus is extremely busy responding to the needs of others, so much so that a whole city of people is gathered around his door.

But we are told that after this intense day and evening of giving, healing and serving, 'In the morning, while it was still very dark, he got up and went out to a deserted place and there he prayed.'[162]

Some translations say, 'a solitary place'. Biblical Greek scholar R. T. France describes it as 'some secluded spot out of the town'.[163]

We do not know what Jesus prayed or how he prayed, but we do know the sort of space he sought. The thoroughly alone, still space. Jesus repeats this pattern of generous serving and withdrawal to be alone with God throughout his life. Mark's short gospel is punctuated by this movement eight times. It is not a one-off but more of a habit, a lifestyle, a going fully into life—enjoying, celebrating and giving all that you can, and then withdrawing into silent, alone spaces so as to return to the centre, to God. An in-among and retreat lifestyle that operates like an inbreath and outbreath. The being in God is essential to being in life. For it is how we come to have a fullness of life.

In meditation, we are making a deserted or solitary place. We seek a time of temporary withdrawal from the world of things, to return to the centre.

---

161 William Law, *The Spirit of Prayer* (n.d., ca. 1750), available at https://ccel.org/ccel/law/prayer/prayer.ii.ii.html.
162 Mark 1:35 (New International Version).
163 R. T. France, *The New International Greek Testament Commentary: The Gospel of Mark* (Grand Rapids, MI: William B. Eerdmans 2002), 112.

We become quiet and seek that feel of how it is early in the morning when it is still dark and no one is up and about. It is the time when the only sound I often hear is the doves cooing and I feel like I have the entire world to myself—cool, peachy and quiet are the mornings.

We close our eyes, still our bodies and focus our minds so that we do not get dragged around by thoughts and feelings that get plenty of airspace during the day.

We descend a little more deeply to the centre, like a sinker on a fishing line.

Remembering that 'though God be everywhere present, yet God is only present to thee in the deepest and most central part of the soul'.[164]

SIXTH SUNDAY AFTER EPIPHANY (YEAR B)
Mark 1:40–45

Touching the Leper
BY PAUL WOOD

Let us picture the world in which Jesus walked, a world that kept a strong divide between the clean and the unclean, the holy and the profane. This divide began with Abraham with the act of circumcision, which marked his descendants as a distinct people among the nations. It was further developed in the Law of Moses, which called the children of Abraham from out of the nations to be 'holy even as I am holy'[165] and gave instructions on what was clean and what unclean and what was holy and what profane. People, things and times were named holy or unclean. Centuries later, the party of the Pharisees arose. The name 'Pharisee' comes from a root meaning 'holy' or 'separated'. The Pharisees emerged at a time, around the Maccabean revolt, when the Jewish nation was being encouraged into syncretism. So, the Pharisees kept very strict rules about what was holy and what was profane. In Jesus' day, they would not touch anything unclean: objects, foods or people. They would not even sit and eat with people deemed unclean and would condemn anyone breaking their strict rules. Into this divided world came Jesus with a heart of compassion. An untouchable leper came to Him, falling on his knees before Him and saying, 'If you will, you can make me clean.'

Now, if Jesus was from God and therefore holy, then by reaching across this great divide between the holy and the profane, between heaven and earth,

---

164 William Law, *Spirit of Prayer*.
165 Exod. 19:6; Lev. 21:8

with just one touch, as if from kryptonite, He could bring the whole Mosaic Law crumbling down, undermining the Law at its very roots.

We might write a piece of fiction about an audacious leper who refused to believe that he was cut off from God—who dared to challenge the Law and, walking up to Jesus the holy man and falling to his knees, called out, 'I dare you to touch me!' We might imagine this leper beginning a revolution that brought Jesus to condemnation and, ultimately, crucifixion. We might picture a revolution that continues through the ages, like yeast in a lump of dough, working away in the world where we now stand with the Universal Declaration of Human Rights and advocacy for diversity, equity and inclusion. These approaches are based on the axiomatic assumption that all human beings are created in the image of God, irrespective of race, religion or conditions. The revolution that began with this audacious leper continues today.

When we meditate, we become conscious of a divided consciousness in ourselves. We sense the holy but also know that our minds are continuously swirling around in the soup of the world's mucky relationships. But what if we could compel the holy to touch us!? Would that not change us at the core? Then, we would no longer be divided and separated from the life of God, who is in all and through all. Rather, we would be connected, redeemed and made whole.

When we meditate, we are the leper, seeking the touch of the holy. The Jesus Prayer is 'Lord Jesus, Son of God, have mercy on me.' It is the cry of the leper, the cry of blind Bartimaeus, the cry of the Syrophoenician woman, the cry of all those sinners on the outside, seeking mercy, seeking wholeness, seeking to belong. This is what we do each time we come to meditation: we stand in those shoes: 'Lord Jesus Christ, Son of God, have mercy on me, a sinner.'

A lovely thing about the Jesus Prayer is its word for mercy: *eleison*. In our liturgies, after the priest has proclaimed absolution, we sing 'Kyrie eleison', which in translation means, 'Lord, have mercy.' Unfortunately, our Western ears do not hear the beauty of this word. Our sense of sin is judicial, but Eastern Orthodox churches hear not a moral failure but rather a sickness. Further, the word *eleison* sounds very much like the word *eleion*, which is the word for olive oil or a healing balm. Thus, the Jesus Prayer, 'Lord Jesus, have mercy', is a cry to receive the soothing healing balm of divine compassion.

In meditation, we sit with open hearts to receive this balm: 'Lord Jesus, have mercy.'

SEVENTH SUNDAY AFTER EPIPHANY (YEAR B)
Mark 2:1–12

Released from Paralysis
BY PAUL WOOD

This story is about a man suffering from paralysis (palsy), a term that may cover conditions ranging from enfeeblement and loss of energy to an inability to move at all. What the condition of this man was or how it related to his sins, we do not know, but we know that he regains his agency when Jesus proclaims the forgiveness of sins. There is a heated debate with the Pharisees about whether Jesus has the authority to forgive sins (this authority is discussed in the meditation for the Fourth Sunday after Epiphany, Year B). Jesus proves he has this authority when he says to the man, 'Pick up your mat and go home.' In one step, the man is set free from his sins and his paralysis.

There will always be parts of our lives that have become paralysed, frozen, immoveable or stuck—or simply enfeebled, depleted or fatigued because of guilt or shame, whether real or imagined. There will always be parts of our lives that need to regain their agency and their vitality through the release of the guilt of sin.

The journey of meditation involves release from our sins, not in any political sense related to the external world, which may or may not declare forgiveness, but internally before God.

Finding personal forgiveness before God is essential if we are to meditate, for we cannot find stillness and silence if we remain in conflict with ourselves or with God.

In meditation, our focus is not on our sins but rather on our prayer word, which keeps our hearts steadily focused towards God. As we sit in silent stillness and relax our normal everyday ego-bound awareness, keeping our attention open and attentive before God, we may find random thoughts or feelings from our lives emerging. If we observe these, we will find that many of them have come from the deep primal level of our consciousness, which is also the place of guilt and shame. Perhaps they relate to unresolved or broken relationships or perhaps personal failings from the past or some unholy feelings of envy or jealousy. All these thoughts and feelings are distractions that interfere with our focus on our prayer word. They should not be wallowed in. Instead, we should simply acknowledge them for what they are and then let them go and return to our prayer word. Each acknowledgement and letting go is a repentance and an acceptance of the grace and mercy of our Heavenly Father. This process may happen many times in a session; it may even go on for years, but it will become less over time and through perseverance. This journey brings us into wholeness and peace, through which we can come to complete, silent stillness before God and regain agency over paralysed aspects of our lives.

Let me give an example. This morning, I was focusing on my prayer word, ma-ra-na-tha. After about five minutes of focus, there came to mind four friends of mine from 20 to 40 years ago, who have all died. I do not know what initiated the memories of them, but they arrived from the depths, one after the other. Three died from alcohol and drug abuse, and the fourth from muscular dystrophy. As I remembered each one, I recalled the essence of their being, which is timeless.

I have come to believe in the idea of the communion of saints—that as we meditate and enter the consciousness of Christ, 'who is before all things and in him, all things hold together',[166] our random memories of those we love are not just isolated and unconnected thoughts in our skulls but a real contact from mind to mind through the universal consciousness of Christ. This understanding gives me an opportunity to say, 'I'm sorry', 'Thank you' and 'Goodbye', knowing that at some level, they have received my sentiments. I can also trust that some sort of paralysis in my own soul has been released, and I have been set free. Having completed this task, I can then return to my practice of focused attention, repeating 'maranatha' for the last five to ten minutes.

EIGHTH SUNDAY AFTER EPIPHANY (YEAR B)
Mark 2:13–22

New Wine in New Wineskins
BY PAUL WOOD

The journey of prayer can be understood in three stages.

1. Verbal prayer

Verbal prayer is the first and most basic level of prayer. Typically, it is what we experience in church: this is our schoolteacher. In a traditional liturgy, we learn to:

---

[166] Col. 1:17.

- come into the presence of God ('Almighty God unto whom all hearts are open')
- confess our sins ('Almighty God, our Maker and our Judge')
- hear the proclamation of forgiveness
- sing Glory to Christ our Saviour
- hear Scripture read and expounded
- pray for each other
- receive consecrated bread and wine
- share communion as one body in Christ.

The liturgy is a complete teacher of our relationship to God through Christ. However, it appears that some people can engage with the liturgy for years but not really move to the next stage of prayer.

In the second stage, we take these external forms, practices and words into ourselves and our private lives through quiet reflection.

2. Reflective and discursive prayer

Many Protestants have a tradition that they refer to as 'quiet time'. Every Christian should have quiet time to reflect and pray. Traditional Anglicans may refer to theirs as morning and evening prayer. This is the staple diet of our personal relationship with God. Learning to pray requires private time to reflect and bring ourselves into the presence of God.

One of the best ways of learning to pray is to use the words of the prayer book. These words are full of scripture, beautifully written and deeply meaningful if we use them intelligently, reflecting on them, chewing on them, reasoning with them and playing with them to personalise them to our contingencies.

My main approach to reflective prayer has always involved going for walks alone—especially in the country, away from others.

Reflective prayer is also called discursive prayer because the mind is always moving from one thing to another. For many, this form of prayer is sufficient for a whole lifetime. However, there is a third stage, which is preceded by a time of spiritual famine, sometimes referred to as the dark night of the soul. At this time, the things that nourished us in the past no longer nourish us; the words have lost their gravity; we have grown tired of explanations, justifications, reasons, ideas, images and all those things that had once captured our imagination. This famine is not because of our lack of faith or our sin, nor is it because of 'not trying hard enough'. Rather, it is the call of the Holy Spirit, which leads us deeper into God, deeper than the level of words, deeper than the light of our intellect, deeper than the light of our understanding, down deeper into the heart of being.

3. Contemplative prayer

Many Christian mystics refer to the importance of bringing the mind into the heart and coming to see things with the 'eyes of the heart'. To achieve this, we must gradually unlearn the habit of seeing with the intellect. Sometimes, this journey into the heart is referred to as the 'journey of unknowing'—a journey into darkness as we leave the light of the intellect behind and, like Moses going up the mountain, enter into the cloud and the darkness to commune with God.

It is dark here because we cannot capture God with the intellect using words and images. God, by definition, is beyond all forms and images—any words, images or ideas about God are mental idols that must be smashed.

However, even though we are unable to apprehend God with our intellect, we can apprehend him fully and totally with our hearts. We can love God even though we cannot see God. We can love God even in the darkness. We can love God's mystery as we love a starlit sky in the still blackness of the night. Thus, the heart, rather than the intellect, becomes our guide.

The difference between discursive prayer and this deeper prayer of the heart—which has been described as pure prayer—is like the difference between the words 'I love you' and a kiss.

The prayer of silence requires learning the way of the heart.

Leave behind the intellect (for a while); leave behind reasonings, justifications, explanations, projections and daydreams. Leave behind that superficial level of operating in the everyday world. Instead, enter into the depths of being itself: enter into the heart of God.

At the level of the heart, all things are connected by love. Here we sit, in silence and stillness, immersed in the waters of divine love.

Each meditation session is like a baptism, in which we are immersed in the waters of God for a time, then brought back to the surface to begin a new life of living the gospel of Christ.

Let us now have twenty minutes of silent prayer.

LAST SUNDAY AFTER EPIPHANY: THE TRANSFIGURATION (YEAR B)
Mark 9:2–9

Gaining Altitude

BY PAUL WOOD

We have often noted that Jesus withdrew to deserted places to be alone. Here, I wish to build on that idea, for our story tells how Jesus climbs a mountain in order to pray. I wish to think about the mountain as a metaphor for prayer, not just a deserted place but also a place on a higher plane.

Remember the roots. In the Old Testament, there is the Holy Mountain of God. It was up there that Moses encountered the burning bush and learned the name of God. It was up the Holy Mountain that Moses went time and again, disappearing into the cloud, and brought down the Ten Commandments. It was also up the Holy Mountain that Elijah went when he was fleeing from Queen Jezebel, and there, he encountered the Lord, not in the wind, not in the earthquake nor in the fire but in the sound of sheer silence. And it was only then, after hearing the sound of sheer silence, that he heard the word of the Lord and found his direction and purpose and returned to the world and changed the course of history.[167]

The Holy Mountain was where both Moses and Elijah had encounters with God, and so, here in our gospel story as Jesus goes up the mountain, we are aware that this is significant.

I suggest that the mountain is a useful symbol because prayer is not just about talking to God on the same level as we talk to people, but also about communion with God on a higher level, above the world so to speak.

Because the kind of mindset that we need to navigate the world is different from the mindset we need to navigate our approach to God.

In the world of everyday consciousness, we need to decide, judge, measure and proceed with caution as we navigate the politics. So, consciousness is full of decisions, concerns, attachments and responsibilities, often filling us with stress.

But our approach to God is very different: Our consciousness is led by faith, devotion and love where we surrender the clutter of this world to rise higher where there is spaciousness and freedom. The view from the

---

[167] The 'sound of sheer silence' is the translation of the New Revised Standard Version. Other translations, such as the King James Bible, translate this as 'a still small voice'. The Hebrew is unclear. I like to use the New Revised Standard Version translation because I think it makes the best sense of the narrative.

mountain top is full of sky. It is limitless: there is peace, bliss and joy. And so, when we pray, we aim to raise our consciousness to a higher level in order to commune with God.

And how? How do we gain altitude?

Well, it happens quite naturally as one surrenders to God. As we sit in meditation before God, thoughts will arise but each thought has a hook on it, and if we become hooked into a thought we will follow it, like we follow a story, as we milk the juice out of it and stoke our own ego—but this keeps us at ground level. The task of meditation is to let go of each thought as it arises and surrender it to God, and this is what the journey is all about, surrendering to God, letting go and letting God. And when one becomes aware that one has got hooked on a thought, or a story or a juicy bone, to simply let it go and surrender it to God.

So how do we gain altitude? Well, it is like ballooning. In order to rise up higher, one must release the hooks, throw out a few sandbags to lighten the load, and in doing this, one gains altitude quite naturally as one becomes more buoyant.

We must remember that it is not just about the twenty minutes of practice but is a life's journey: it may to take decades to let go of something. In life, it seems that we enter into experience, and then we must lift it up to God and eventually let it go. In fact, the last thing we will do in this world is to let go, saying, 'Father, into your hands I commit my spirit.'

The surrender method of meditation is how we gain altitude. So let us now enter into a season of prayer in twenty minutes of silence.

Lent (Year B)

FIRST SUNDAY IN LENT OR ASH WEDNESDAY (YEAR B)
Mark 1:9–15

The Inner Wilderness Pilgrimage
BY MICHELLE WOOD

We enter this session of silent meditation with a story of a dove, a divine voice, demons and angels. We are beginning the inner wilderness pilgrimage of Lent. Lent means forty, and so, for forty days we prepare for the Great Feast of Easter.

Our pilgrimage begins with the story of Jesus' baptism and the Spirit driving him out into the wilderness. What is significant in Mark's account of Jesus' baptism is that the Spirit descends 'into him' (*eis auton*) rather than 'upon him' (*ep auton*) as depicted in Matthew's and Luke's accounts.[168] It is the Holy Spirit 'within' that drives Jesus to that place beyond the comforts of the town and the familiar. Jesus is driven to the wilderness, a place of solitariness, quietude and contemplation. It is here that he is tested.

Similarly, each time we sit in meditation we also enter a type of wilderness. Out of the comforts of conversation, continuous material distractions and the compulsive need to be 'doing something', we are tested. How do we keep our attention focused on God and prayer for twenty minutes? It is hard and we face many inner demons.

What are we modern people to make of the language of demons or Satan and angels? Satan literally means 'adversary', that which opposes the will of God. Demons are those thoughts doing the work of Satan that prevent us from listening to and following God. Angels, on the other hand, are messengers from God—insights, epiphanies and awarenesses—that bring tidings of peace, love, joy and goodwill. When tested in our prayer time of silence, how do we understand the demons of distraction?

The desert mothers and fathers of the fourth century knew this testing landscape well and perhaps are angelic guides for our times. Anyone pursuing a spiritual life of any depth will need to confront their own demons. In the fourth century, Evagrius the Solitary proposed a very helpful map. He wrote

---

168 Collins et al., *Jerome Biblical Commentary*, 124.

that there are three groups of demons—gluttony, avarice and seeking the esteem of other people—and all others follow.[169] He stated that demonic thought is 'acquisitional and ego ridden', whereas angelic thought is 'concerned with the true nature of things and with searching out their spiritual essences'.[170]

In our practice of silent meditation, we can glimpse and perhaps note what sort of demon thoughts pull us off our track. And part of the work to be done in tandem with our practice is to contemplate our being and find ways to further explore and grow psychologically.

John Main OSB had great faith that the practice of silent meditation can help us grow. He wrote, 'As the mantra roots itself in our being it gently but surely draws all the distracted and scattered parts of our being together.'[171]

So, as we sit in the wilderness of our soul, breathing angelic breaths, riding the rooted mantra and persevering in repeating a prayer word, let us remember the words of St Isaiah the Solitary: 'Remain on guard so that the demons do not steal your peace, God dwells peaceably within you.'[172]

SECOND SUNDAY IN LENT (YEAR B)
Mark 8:31–38

The Cross and Transcendence
BY PAUL WOOD

The spiritual journey, that is, our journey to heaven, begins with a break. It begins with a separation when we break away from this world. By this world I mean the world as constructed by human beings. Like the breaking out of bondage in Egypt so that one can journey to the Promised Land. Like the letting go of our fishing nets that entangle us to the domestic so that we are free to follow Jesus. Like the call of Jesus to give away one's possessions and then to 'come, follow me'.[173] These are all calls to break with the world and to begin a journey beyond ourselves and into the transcendence of the divine life. Thus, the breaking away from this world is like a birth: it can be painful and often traumatic and that's how new life begins. This birth can happen to us in one of three ways.

---

169 Nikodimos and Makarios, *Philokalia*, 40.
170 Nikodimos and Makarios, *Philokalia*, 42.
171 Main, *Inner Christ*, 239.
172 Nikodimos and Makarios, *Philokalia*, 24.
173 Mark 10:21.

The first way is through a Damascus-road conversion experience like that of St Paul where you are metaphorically confronted and blinded by a great light, and so you fall down. And then, when your eyes are healed you begin to see all things anew and are no longer breathing threats of violence against Christians but now are one of them and see as they see. You were once like that, but now you're like this. You are converted. A fundamentally dramatic and profound difference. You let go of the old self and you begin a new journey in a new self. These conversions are quite commonplace in evangelical and Pentecostal churches, and a problem with them is that such a sudden conversion comes also with an inversion of one's personality. The personality is suddenly turned upside down and inverted; before, I was a selfish party animal, and my little loving side was unconscious, but now my loving side is visible, and my selfishness is unconscious. The personality has been turned upside down and this is only the beginning. Full conversion is a longer process that takes many years of spiritual work because the new person needs to integrate their suppressed hidden and unconscious world into their consciousness and in this way be healed and made whole.

The second way of letting go of this world is gentler. It happens through lots of small moments scattered throughout one's life where one incrementally awakens to the transcendence and the presence of God. Each small awakening is a little letting go of the things of this world as one journeys deeper into God. These small moments of becoming more aware, maybe through moments of ego loss, are either painful or ecstatic.

The third way of breaking with this world is, of course, the way of all flesh when we are brought, usually kicking and screaming, to the narrow door of death and as we go through the door so we begin our transcendent journey with God.

Whichever way we come to God it begins with the breaking away from this world's total claim over us. Jesus reminds his disciples when he's first teaching them about the Cross, 'for those who want to save their life (in this world) will lose it and those who lose their life for my sake, and for the sake of the gospel, will save it'.[174] Meditation is a gentle way of losing one's life in this world in order to find it in the next. It is about letting go. Letting go of this world, opening ourselves up to transcendence and allowing ourselves to become translucent with eternal light. Allowing the ego of this world to be dissolved in the ever-widening and deepening love of God. This is our journey.

---

174 Mark 8:35.

THIRD SUNDAY IN LENT (YEAR B)
John 2:13–22

Our Body a Temple

BY MICHELLE WOOD

This week's sacred story is set in Jerusalem, at the temple during the time of the Passover.

In the story, Jesus drives out the moneychangers and speaks of his own body as the temple.

The temple of Jerusalem has its origin in the construction of the first tabernacle in a tent of meeting between humans and God. Described in the Book of Exodus, it is where God gives instruction to Moses to build an earthly residence for the divine to reside: 'And have them make me a sanctuary, so that I might dwell among them.'[175]

By the time Jesus came along, the temple was operating in a corrupt manner. It had lost its original purpose. It served other symbolic currencies—money, Pharisaic phobias—it was a social club, run on the exchange of egos and exploiting people.

It was worse than pagan worship because it was blind to itself and claimed superiority.

It operated like a delusional, narcissistic person believing they are a saint.

Jesus takes it to task, firmly.

He calls it away from a confused and lost position of worshipping itself and points to a new type of temple.

Similarly, in the practice of meditation, we make this new temple.

We gather in silence and stillness so that we might reflect our portion of the body of Christ.

Our heart is an altar, an interface between us and the divine.

Each breath is both our gift and offering to God.

Our bread and wine are 'the depths of a soul laid widely open to all the forces which in the moment rise up from every corner of the earth and converge upon the Spirit'.[176]

We drive out thoughts that buy and sell us to a lesser version of ourselves and the world.

Our prayer mantra, a whip, drives them out.

---

175 Exod. 25:8.
176 Pierre Teihard de Chardin, *Hymn of the Universe* (London: Collins Fontana Books, 1974), 19.

In this new temple, one's body will be a house of mercy and one's heart a place of prayer.

For we are, as St Paul puts it, the temple of the living God.

FOURTH SUNDAY IN LENT (YEAR B)
John 3:14–21

The Spectre of the Cross (Snake on a Pole)
BY PAUL WOOD

'And just as Moses lifted up the serpent in the wilderness, so must the Son of Man be lifted up, that whoever believes in him may have eternal life.'[177]

Anthony De Mello told many funny stories about Nasruddin, a character in many Persian folktales, who is like the village fool who reveals deep wisdom through his foolery. Anyway, one day his neighbour finds Nasiruddin crawling about on his knees and asks, 'What are you doing Nasruddin?' 'I am looking for my key', he says. So, his neighbour gets down on the floor and begins looking with him. 'Where did you lose it?', he asks. Nasreddin says, 'I lost it over there.' 'But why are you looking for it here?', he asks. Nasreddin replies, 'It's too dark over there and I can't see, but there's light here, so I can see.'

Ok, a silly story, but it reveals something that we often do. We tread round our familiar and safe thought patterns and knowledge systems, whereas the key that we look for may well be hidden in those dark places we avoid and would rather ignore.

We are like someone with a phobia who is trying to fix it by avoiding what they are afraid of, but the path to healing is to learn to face the very thing we are trying to avoid. Perhaps this is what looking at the bronze serpent to cure the snake problem was all about.[178] As someone once said, 'The answer to the problem is in the problem!' If you want to cure the problem of sin, you need to take a look at the sin!

Now this is the thing about the Cross—it is truly horrifying, truly horrifying. Crucifixion was a torture devised by the Roman Empire to terrify people into submission, to frighten people into compliance. It was a demonstration of the horrendous might of the empire. So, crucifixions were public for all to see, the crucified exposed, stripped naked, mocked, shamed, ridiculed and raised up on a pole for all to see, dying in excruciating pain, a

---

177 John 3:14–15.
178 Num. 21:6–9.

slow agonising death, and then left to rot. Each crucifixion was a horrifying spectre of the might and power of the Roman Empire.

Yet, who would have thought that out of this darkness would come the highest form of love know to humankind! Sacrificial love. Who would have thought that out of this would came the story of redemption of the whole human race? Who would have thought that it was out of these terrifying moments that the highest ethics known to humankind would emerge?

Historian Tom Holland describes in his international bestseller, *Dominion*, how this spectre of the crucified Son of God has gradually transformed the Western world over the centuries. It was like a depth charge that went off in antiquity 2,000 years ago, and although empires seemingly ignored this event on the surface, deep within them, the spectre of 'the Son of God on a cross' was transforming, and is still transforming, the world we live in. Like yeast in dough. If God enters into the worst and darkest and lowest place of human experience and there baptises the dark with divine presence, then nothing is outside of the love of God, nothing is God-forsaken, for all has been immersed in the presence of the divine and all is redeemed.

The spectre of 'the Son of God on a cross' lies at the heart of all the ethics we hold as most sacred and sane in the modern world, where every individual human is of infinite value, no matter how small. No matter what gender, what race, what religion, all human beings are sacred. The Universal Declaration of Human Rights comes directly out of this ethic of the Cross. As do public hospitals, public education, welfare systems and concern for social justice: all this comes out of this ethic.

This is the spectre of the Cross.

So, what has this to do with meditation? Well, meditation is not about avoiding things; rather, it is about paying attention. It can be this, and it can be that. Thus, we could meditate on the spectre of the Cross, not explaining it away but rather gazing at it intentionally, coming to know it. Being attentive. That would be a valid form of meditation. This is what God told Moses to do in the wilderness—put a bronze serpent on a pole and then gaze at it to cure anyone bitten during the serpent infestation.[179]

Perhaps the well-known Jesus Prayer is a prayer that brings us close to the spectre of the Cross. I find that the Jesus Prayer is a gift that keeps on giving.

So, let us meditate, and if you would like to try something different you may try this.

(inbreath) Lord Jesus Christ, Son of God,
(outbreath) have mercy on me, a sinner.

---

179   Num. 21:9.

FIFTH SUNDAY IN LENT (YEAR B)
John 12:20–33

A Seed Knows How to Wait

BY MICHELLE WOOD

Jesus' use of metaphors from the natural world has always interested me. It is as if he knew these to be, like himself, both enduring and universal. Being a rabbi, a teacher, he also perhaps sensed the immediacy and communicative value of natural metaphors, which all people could observe. For instance, 'Very truly, I tell you, unless a grain of wheat falls into the earth and dies, it remains just a single grain; but if it dies, it bears much fruit.'[180]

I have read this passage hundreds of times, but this week, I wondered what it would yield if I really stayed close to the natural world metaphor. Praying it, grounded in the earth, holding seeds in my hands and observing the rising and falling of leaves and seeds in nature all around me.

I found that staying close to the natural world enabled me to hear this overly familiar passage through a gospel voice more interested in ripening and fruits than in bloodshed and sacrifice.

To fall into the earth like a grain of wheat full and ripe is perhaps like falling in love. You get to a point where you can only go one way; you can't go back, and you can't just dash forward and see if it's going to end ok. You have to trust that which is growing within you and the call of the other. Trust that you will land safely on the other side.

Falling into the earth is no more and no less than the fulfilling of one's created purpose, one's calling. One is drawn beyond one's limited and fixed notions of self, to risk, to lose oneself, to trust in the other.

To let go, one has to break the husks of self-containment and self-possession and perhaps lie on the bare earth for a while not knowing what to do but waiting. A seed knows how to wait. A cherry seed can wait alive and internally pulsating for a hundred years before opening.

Often, our own openings occur along our wounds, those cracks of humility that have us leaning a little more into something beyond the self-competent self.

Christ, our pathfinder and way, reassures us that these gestures of letting go and being lifted into a bigger consciousness or landscape will bear fruit. The type of fruit is a drawing in of all people.

---

180   John 12:24.

I most love the line a little further into the story where Jesus says: 'And I, when I am lifted up from the earth, will draw all people to myself.'[181]

One can only draw people to oneself if one is nourishing and plentiful like a laden roadside fruit tree bursting to be harvested by a passer-by.

Christ will fall into God and be lifted up through the love of God.

It is scary and even Christ is troubled in his soul.

But, in meditation, like seeds, we wait in the darkness of the internal world practising the art of letting go into the earth of God.

---

181   John 12:32.

PALM SUNDAY (YEAR B)
Mark 14:1–15:27

Entrance into Holy Week
BY PAUL WOOD

This Sunday, the Church enters into Holy Week, the most sacred week in our calendar. I would like to tell the story of Holy Week through the lens of the reconciliation of opposites.

This is significant for the meditator because we all have opposites within ourselves, good and evil, sacred and profane, which contradict each other, and we have need of reconciliation.

During Holy Week, the sacred unites with the profane but in such a way that the sacred is never compromised. Christ, the highest principle we know, the Logos, through whom the original perfect world was created, the ideal and most perfect human being, the image of God, descends into the bowels of this corrupt world, and there, sort of baptises the place of darkness with the love of God. It is the journey of the reconciliation of opposites.

Let me demonstrate this story through some iconography of the Orthodox Church.

Here is the icon for Palm Sunday: Entry into Jerusalem.

Figure 1: Entry into Jerusalem[182]

Usually, when a king enters through the gates of a walled city, he does so on a war horse, followed by an army, but Jesus comes on a donkey, and it is a joyous occasion. Children sing and remove cloaks and cut branches to make a welcome road to receive Jesus. Singing Hosannah! But there is always a snake in the garden, and you will notice in the foreground a child removing a thorn from his foot. This little detail anticipates the theme of thorns coming in other icons of Holy Week.

---

182   *Icon of the Entry into Jerusalem* (Palm Sunday) - 17th c. Dionysiou Monastery - (11F03)
      "Copyright © Uncut Mountain Supply, Manton, MI, used by permission. All rights reserved."

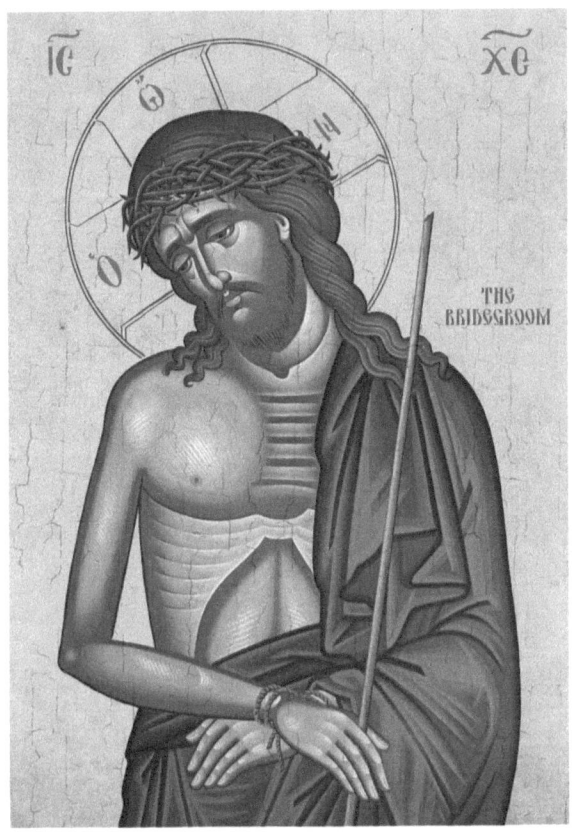

Figure 2: The Bridegroom[183]

This icon is called 'The Bridegroom' because Christ has now entered through the gates of Jerusalem and is in the bridal chamber, ready to win the bride (human hearts) unto himself in divine union.

Christ is dressed as a king, in a red robe and holding a rod, but his crown is made of thorns.

Thorns are the original curse of being cast out of Eden. Thorns are the consequence of sin; the world is full of thorns, which hurt us all the time, but Jesus wears the crown of thorns for us. We note the joining of opposites—the good with the bad, and the high with the low—the pain and the beauty.

---

183   *Icon of Christ the Bridegroom* - (11S28) "Copyright © Uncut Mountain Supply, Manton, MI, used by permission. All rights reserved."

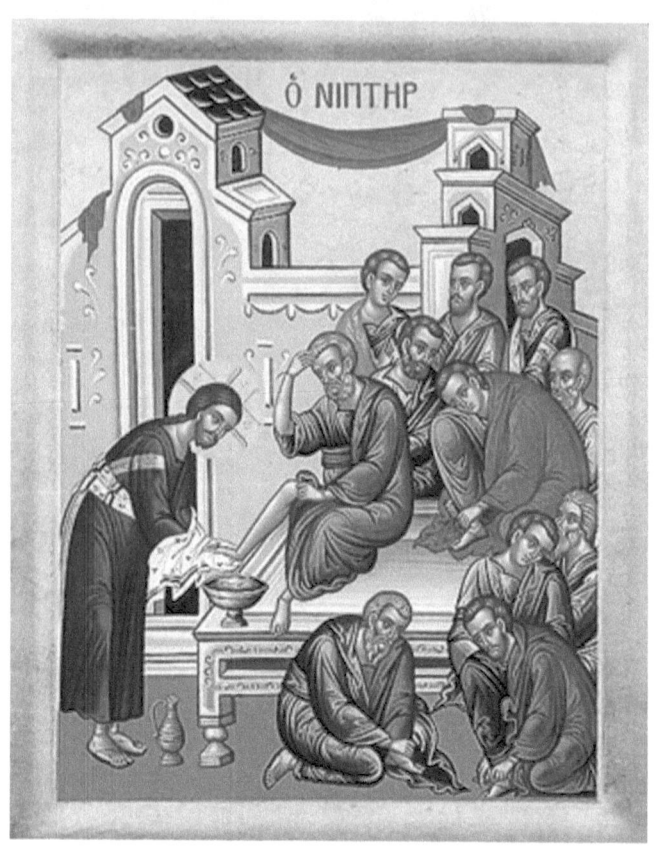

Figure 3: Maundy Thursday – The Washing of Feet[184]

The pose of St Peter putting his hand on his head represents his confusion, as though he is saying, 'You should not be washing my feet; I should be washing yours.' This reversal is part of the journey that unites the sacred with the profane. The first is last and the last is first on the journey towards the union of opposites.

---

184 *Icon of the Washing the Disciples Feet* - 20th c. - (11G30) "Copyright © Uncut Mountain Supply, Manton, MI, used by permission. All rights reserved."

Figure 4: The Mystical Supper[185]

Again, we see the extremes of the high and the low, and the good and the bad, coming together. St John, closest to Jesus' heart, rests his head on his breast, while Judas reaches out for more food.

Christ is the head, the one who is giving food to his disciples, but the real food is himself. The priest and the sacrificial victim are one and the same. This foreshadows the crucifixion.

---

185 *Icon of the Mystical Supper* - (11G06) "Copyright © Uncut Mountain Supply, Manton, MI, used by permission. All rights reserved."

Figure 5: The Crucifixion[186]

This image is where all is fulfilled. The highest and the lowest come together into one. It is the place of consummation. It is where Jesus cries it is finished and breathes his last. The groom is united to his bride. Here is the reconciliation of opposites and the achievement of 'nonduality'.

Some things to note are:

- the notice, 'the King of Glory' or 'The Prince of Peace'
- a stylised phallus: what looks like weakness is actually potentiality and power
- the arms outstretched, in a universal embrace
- the sun and moon and/or angels, which usually give an event cosmic dimensions
- a skull in a cave beneath; Golgotha and also represents the skull of the long-dead Adam.

---

186 *Icon of the Crucifixion* - 20th c. - (11H13) "Copyright © Uncut Mountain Supply, Manton, MI, used bypermission. All rights reserved."

Figure 6: Holy Saturday[187]

On the surface, death looks silent and empty where there is only deep sorrow and lamentations: but it is here that the deep work is happening. As Christ descends into the depths of hell and so baptises the darkest place in the cosmos with his presence, he releases the lost souls there, in what is called 'The Harrowing of Hell'.

On the surface, there is stillness and silence, which veils the deep work of redemption. In the same way, the prayer of silent meditation veils the healing work on a deep level. Thus, Holy Saturday is a good day to mark with silent meditation.

---

187 *Icon of the Lamentation at the Tomb*, 16th c. - (11J17) "Copyright © Uncut Mountain Supply, Manton, MI, used by permission. All rights reserved."

Figure 7: The Resurrection[188]

This image shows Christ emerging from a feminine oval shape like an egg or a vaginal opening. This shape is called a mandorla, and it is the space between two intersecting circles, like the intersection space between two worlds because Christ at this stage is resurrected in this world but has not yet fully ascended into heaven and therefore spans two worlds. However, in many icons of the Ascension (also the Second Coming), the almond shape becomes a self-contained circle representing one complete world.

Beneath the resurrected Christ are the broken doors of hell, where locks and bolts and chains and bones are scattered about. Above this place of destruction, we see Christ standing on the wood of the Cross, raising up two figures, an old man and a young woman.

The old man is Adam, the first man, and the young woman is Eve, the first woman and the mother of all living people. In other words, Christ is setting free from the bondage of death the whole of humanity.

---

[188] *Icon of the Resurrection (11K20)* "Copyright © Uncut Mountain Supply, Manton, MI, used by permission. All rights reserved."

This story of the reconciliation of opposites is an important theme on our journey inwards to the centre of our being. On the surface of things we are full of contradictions; good and evil, right and wrong pull at each other, but if we can come to the heart, to the centre of ourselves, where all things are reconciled and brought into union at the Cross, this is the place of nonduality, this is the place of union and peace.

It is the place we journey towards in meditation and contemplation.

MAUNDY THURSDAY (YEAR B)
John 13:1–7, 31b–35

Love, the Only Thing That Gets Us Through
BY MICHELLE WOOD

I began preparing for Holy Week on Saturday, cutting palms from my garden and arranging them in a vase with autumn leaves of red, amber, yellow and dry crispy twig brown. Each leaf evokes the mystery of the various stages between life and death and represents nature's way of the Cross towards the spring of new life.

I think the only thing that makes the cross or the journey through suffering and death bearable is love. This is why small, meaningful gestures of love carry so much power and strength in times of great pain. For instance, the image of Jacinda Ardern hugging a New Zealander in the aftermath of the terrorist attack in 2019 captured the minds and hearts of all across the world. The tender embrace was projected onto the largest building in the world, in Dubai. A small heartfelt human gesture became such a beacon of light, comfort, strength and peace because in the face of raw, frontline pain, all we have really to offer is love.

Hence, as Christians, our primary spiritual task is to grow a heart capable of great love.

In my counselling work, I see two sisters; the eldest is ten years old and the youngest is seven years old. They live in a very painful home situation. Both of their parents are out of control. It is so stressful that the eldest still wears nappies and wets the bed.

The first time I met her I asked what her biggest worry was, and she answered, 'I worry most about my younger sister seeing my parents yell and how this is affecting her.'

She told me she tries to do all that she can to prevent her sister from seeing and hearing things.

When I met the younger sister, the seven-year-old, and asked her the same question, she answered, 'My biggest worry is my sister, seeing what she cops and how much she does to look after me.'

Over my time of meeting with these two beautiful children, I have heard so many stories of small acts of tenderness and care. I asked them how they managed to learn such love in difficult circumstances, and they replied, 'Well, Michelle, we are teaching each other, we learn from each other.' When I asked how they do that the youngest told me a story.

One day they went shopping for a schoolbag and her elder sister chose one, the last of its kind in the shop. The younger really wanted it.

When they got to the counter, the elder sister looked at her and said, 'Here, you have it.'

She said to me, 'I didn't even have to ask.'

She told me she was so happy in the shop holding that brand-new bag in her hands.

But in bed that night, in among the parents yelling and screaming, she thought of her elder sister and how kind she is, and she was filled with such happiness. The next morning, she got up and put that schoolbag on her elder sister's bed. A small gesture, of such big love.

Suffering and love are intermingled in this human journey.

In everyone's life there is suffering, and no one can escape it.

The only thing that gets us through is love.

Jesus knows this—his whole life on earth has been about this and his mystical life that continues is about this.

Holy Thursday celebrates simple gestures of love—foot washing and sharing bread and wine, a blessing of love for the whole of humankind and Creation.

For it is only through love: God as source of love, Christ as example of love and Spirit as living, moving presence of love that we can overcome all that we need to overcome.

As we enter this time of silent meditation, may we immerse ourselves in this love blessing.

In this sacred time of silent communion, may we practice:

- cleansing from our hearts and minds thoughts other than those of love
- attending to the heartbeat of Christ within us
- slowing down so that we attend to others with more spaciousness and clarity.

Our spiritual practices aim to grow this heart of love so that we can give more freely of our own bodies in small gestures of love to one another and to God.

Easter (Year B)

SECOND SUNDAY OF EASTER (YEAR B)
John 20:19–31

The Locked Room
BY PAUL WOOD

One of the key teachings by Jesus about prayer is that when you pray, go into your room, close the door, that is, close off the outside world, and pray to your father in secret, that is, within yourself, and your Father who sees in secret will reward you.

It is this idea of a secret place, a hidden place, not accessible to the outside world, a place for intimacy with God, uncluttered and uncontaminated by the politics of the world. In meditation, we find a quiet place and close our eyes, like closing the door on the world, and enter into a private intimacy with God.

I suspect that this was a radical teaching in Jesus' day because prayer was generally understood to be public. It was said out loud and was a demonstration to others of one's orthodoxy and conformity. But Jesus taught many times how the true spiritual life is always hidden and secret and is not seen by others.

These days, this idea of a secret place is increasingly important especially because of the technological revolution. Many people say that privacy no longer exists, given the increasing surveillance through artificial intelligence, which is learning all about our conscious and unconscious habits and building profiles of our thought patterns and likely future behaviour. This may result in a surveillance culture where people are monitored constantly, their political/religious/ethical views are observed and recorded, and they become afraid to express themselves and speak their own truths. In such a world, true intimacy will be lost as people lose touch with each other and with themselves, with the centre of who they are.

So, prayer and meditation very much have their place in our modern world. When we withdraw from the world, we enter the secret place and find our centre and intimacy with God.

In our reading this Sunday, we have the story of the frightened disciples in the locked room. They were hiding out of the fear that the angry mobs that had crucified their Lord might be after them next. It is in that locked room, hidden away from the world, that the Risen Christ appears. He did not come in through the door, through the window or down the chimney for he did not come in from the outside. It was as if he was already there on the inside. He just appears before them and says, 'Peace be with you.'

Remember, life always comes from the inside; organic life grows from the inside out—never from the outside in.

This is the nature of the resurrected Jesus; he is no longer simply Jesus of Nazareth, walking the dusty paths of Galilee and bound by the physical laws of space and time, who needs to come in through the door, but has now become the Cosmic Christ who belongs to every time and every place, one who is eternally present to anyone and everyone, even to those locked away and in hiding from the world. He just appears among them and says, 'Peace be with you.'

One of the meditative traditions of Christianity is the saying of the Jesus Prayer, where the repeated saying the name of Jesus invokes his presence.

Bishop Philip Huggins spoke to us recently about how he uses the Jesus Prayer before doing anything public.[189] It gives him a chance to stop, detach from anxieties, invoke the presence of Jesus and centre himself in Christ. This allows peace to arrive and puts him in the right frame of mind to face the public while centred in Christ.

We must remember that our withdrawal from the world is simply so that we can enter into it again and to embody Christ's redeeming love in all the world.

THIRD SUNDAY OF EASTER (YEAR B)
Luke 24:36–48

The Hidden Harmony
MICHELLE WOOD

To live with rationality and yet be open to mystery is complex. Silent meditation is a practice of sitting in the gap. It is a boat to bob about in the wild, dark and unfathomable depths. What it can offer as a prayer practice is openness to that which is beyond all understanding, a sitting with the unknowable and a spirit of not foreclosing on things too soon because we don't fully understand them. At the same time, it sharpens one's judgement so as not to accept things too readily without penetrating them for oneself. Each time we sit, we untangle ourselves from the copious explanations and justifications of this and that,

---

189 Wikipedia, 'Philip Huggins', last modified 21 August 2022, 06:06 (UTC), https://en.wikipedia.org/wiki/Philip_Huggins.

both in the world and ourselves. When I think of a spiritual life that holds rationality and mystery, I think of Etty Hillesum. Etty was taken to Westerbork concentration camp during the Nazi occupation and genocide. She kept a diary during her time at the concentration camp. Eva Hoffman, reflecting on Etty's diaries, wrote, 'By winding her way through her own psyche to the point of self-reconciliation, she had come to a place of where she could feel the hidden harmony of the world.'[190] Increasingly Etty Hillesum's writing reflected this 'hidden harmony'—borders 'where attentiveness to subjectivity meets contemplation, where emotional intuition converges with moral thought'.[191] This ability to delve honestly into one's encounter with reality, even the utterly perplexing and terrifying, is required to find the hidden harmony of the world.

In this week's sacred story, the resurrected Jesus appears, and his disciples are terrified. Nothing about his appearance to them is understandable. He invites them to touch him and asks for something to eat. They understand touch and eating. Just like when we sit to meditate, we understand the materiality of the actions sitting and breathing, but do not perceive fully whatever else is going on in the 'hidden harmony' of the world.

Jesus then opens their minds to understand the Scriptures—the ancient stories and hymns that foretold of a God who would come to bring peace, justice, mercy, forgiveness, love and life. Stories that are signposts of the hidden harmony that is bringing all to reconciliation, perfect completion and joyous fulfilment.

As we come to meditate, we ground ourselves in what we know and open our minds and hearts to the mystery, the hidden harmony beneath the turbulent and often brutal surface of this world.

FOURTH SUNDAY OF EASTER (YEAR B)
John 10:11–18

The Good Shepherd Leading Us up: The Great Resurrection Harvest

BY PAUL WOOD

I wonder what brings you to meditation or the practice of prayer—is it the carrot or the whip? I would hope it has more do with the carrot. That you are responding to a longing in your heart, as if you are being called into

---

190　Etty Hillesum, *An Interrupted Life: The Diaries, 1941-1943 and Letters from Westerbork* (New York: Holt, 1996), x.
191　Hillesum, *Interrupted Life*, x.

something, something more than ordinary, everyday consciousness. This is what I think a calling is, when our hearts say 'Yes!' to venture out beyond our normal everyday self, being called into something higher, called into something different. This is the journey of faith.

And it is not that this is something special, because I think everyone feels this call, to become something more, it belongs to the whole of humanity, to find something other than what we are and have. Why, for example, do human beings aspire for transcendence? Rocks, trees and animals don't seem to do it. A cow does not seem to long to be a better cow! They just accept things as they are, but why cannot we accept things as they are, why do we look to transcend our lot and become something more than what we are?

Some say that the human being was created with a hole in the heart—which they are always trying to fill—but since it's a God-sized hole nothing can fill it except God.

I have heard that C. S. Lewis used to say that this is evidence that we were created for another world because we do not seem to fit in this one.

This is consistent with the Bible narratives that say things like we are citizens of heaven and just sojourners passing through here on earth, and that God in Christ is drawing the whole of humanity up unto himself. Ever since the creation of the world, God has been drawing humanity up into himself, and we are part of that great gathering up called the great resurrection harvest. Christ is the first fruits and we are the rest of the harvest, and this will continue until humanity comes to its completion, its consummation in God.

So that's the big picture, and we, as little human creatures, are simply participating in this grand narrative. Many are doing it unconsciously, but when we pray and when we meditate, we consciously participate in this great resurrection harvest.

So why am I telling you all this? Well, first, because this post-Easter period is called the great fifty days of Easter. It is a time when we learn that Christ is the first fruits of the resurrection, but we are the rest of the harvest—gradually being gathered up. I suggest this is an objective fact that the whole of humanity is being gathered up either consciously or unconsciously.

The second reason is that our sacred story this Sunday is the Good Shepherd: a metaphor for Christ leading us just as a shepherd leads his sheep.

In biblical times, shepherds lived with their sheep and the sheep trusted their shepherds, and wherever the shepherd went the sheep would follow and he would lead them to greener pastures and protect them from danger.

(Unlike Australian sheep who are herded using dogs, motorbikes and whips and kept together by fences).

But our spiritual life is about following, not being herded or controlled. How many times does Jesus say 'Come, follow me'? And as we follow Christ, he becomes our mentor, pattern and model, the one to whom we aspire to become, the one who will lead us from where we are now into a new self, a new consciousness, a new world, a new creation.

So, as we enter into the practice of silence, let us acknowledge that our shepherd is calling and that we are already caught up in this narrative of the great resurrection harvest.

FIFTH SUNDAY OF EASTER (YEAR B)
John 15:1–9

Abiding

BY MICHELLE WOOD

At our final Eucharist during retreat, we had tonight's reading: 'I am the vine, and you are the branches', and 'abide in me as I abide in you.'[192]

Throughout the retreat, in the silence and togetherness, I experienced a type of relational abiding. I became more conscious of the invisible connections between myself, God and others. For example,

- hearing the breath of God moving through the trees and mountain streams
- sensing the presence of another as we sat in silence
- invoking the presence of each one in the group when their name was read aloud, and we held them for a moment in silent prayer every morning and night
- and feeling the presence of Christ through sharing bread and wine together, in the Eucharist, a visible sign of this invisible conjoining.

This experience of being conscious of the interrelationship of things is abiding. Jesus says, 'Abide in me as I abide in you.'

Abiding is a type of tuning into an invisible mystery and intimacy of the bonds between things, so that one perceives how things are in accord with each other.

Abiding, remaining, dwelling, staying in Christ, we come to experience this reality of interrelationship. For, 'All things were created through him and for him: he is before all things and in him all things hold together.'[193]

---

192 John 15:4–5.
193 Col 1:17.

Through Christ's presence and holding us together we are becoming a new humanity. An evolving relational humanity able to hold consciously both diversity and union.

Jesus expresses this vision in his prayer to God where he says, 'I in them and you in me, that they may become completely one, so that the world may know that you have sent me and have loved them even as you have loved me.'[194]

Abiding in Christ is like being connected to the centre of a wheel, the source of love, within us.

It makes possible a sense of affinity and care for all living beings and Creation. A greater capacity to listen and seek harmony for the whole.

Abiding in Christ offers a deep sense of time—for he is the Alpha and the Omega, the beginning and the end.

Perhaps abiding in Christ is a little akin to the Dreamtime in which all time coexists.

Abiding in Christ not only extends our sense of time but also joins us to the depths of love that flows from God and to each other.

When I think about growing my awareness of abiding in Christ and its effects of cojoining me to the whole of humankind and Creation, I imagine that inside of me there is every person whom I have ever encountered; they abide in me; there is an irreducible, non-erasable trace of their presence within me, and mine within them; there is a continuous bond between us through the Holy Spirit that Christ gifts us with, that, like a delicate web, holds all of life and love together.

This awareness brings both a sense of love and responsibility. I am responsible for the health of the body of Christ.

When I think like this, I can take time to remember each person as they arise in my consciousness—in a type of natural prayer without ceasing—asking for all mercy and goodness, healing and love to be poured forth on them abundantly.

Sometimes, this sense of abiding in Christ and becoming knitted to the whole of humanity extends beyond the living to also the communion of saints.

Most mornings, I read about the saint whose feast day it is. I relish those stories because they tell of people who through their everyday lives and struggles cared for the body of Christ and made it visible in their communities.

Remembering people, past and present, saints and loved ones who have passed from this world to the next, holding with love and sorrow the invisible bonds between us, all becomes more possible through abiding in Christ.

Abide in me as I abide in you.[195]

---

194 John 17:22–26.
195 John 15:4–11.

Abiding in Christ is about belonging, a deep sense of belonging to the whole. You cannot abide in Christ and be cut off from the joys and sufferings of the people around you or the wider human family, because abiding in Christ is about being a part of the entire system—vines, leaves, branches, fruits, dead bits, buds ... resurrection ... new life.

The practice of silent meditation allows for this sense of mystical abiding. In the silence and stillness, we quieten our minds so that our heart may rest in his and his in ours, and through this sense of abiding we enter a cosmic connection to the whole.

SIXTH SUNDAY OF EASTER (YEAR B)
John 15:15–17

Inner Guidance
BY PAUL WOOD

In the gospels, the disciples demonstrate two turning points of the spiritual life. The first one is on the shores of Lake Galilee when Jesus first comes to the fishermen Peter, James and John. He says to them, 'Come, follow me', and they let go their fishing nets, livelihoods and domestic concerns and follow him. So, they became disciples, and they walked in the footsteps of their master, and they learned through experience, following the pattern of their mentor, and so, they learned the way of Christ, which takes them through the Cross. Many times, they are sorely tested, and many times they fail, misunderstand and collapse into confusion and fear, but they finally make it through to the second great turning of the spiritual life.

The second great turning point comes when Jesus says to his disciples that he's going away and that the Spirit of Truth, which abides <u>with</u> them, will soon abide <u>in</u> them. It is this change of locus of authority from following an external authority to being ready to follow an internal authority that captures my attention. In fact, I think it is quite remarkable that when Jesus leaves this world he does not give his disciples any external authority to follow; he does not write anything down and then say now you follow that and that'll lead you to all truth, nor does he point to anyone in the group and say now you follow Peter here and he will lead you into all truth. Jesus gives no external authority to follow but instead says when I go away, I'll send to you the Spirit of Truth to indwell you and be with you forever.

At the end of the Gospel of John, the Risen Christ breathes on to his disciples, enacting the way in which the Creator God breathed into the clay image of Adam the breath of life and so Adam became a living soul. In the same way, Jesus breathes into his disciples the breath of life and says, 'Receive the Holy Spirit',[196] and so transfers his Spirit into them through this symbolic act and thereby creates a new humanity. Now this is remarkable in that Jesus entrusts all his teachings to the wind of the spirit, not to a written form but to the wind of the spirit, which will morph and change throughout the lives of each person between the hearing and the speaking. What an amazing act of faith in humanity by Jesus!

I wonder whether it was contrary to the expectations of Jesus that within a generation his disciples would have written down all what they remembered about his life and teachings, and so, the Church became a monolith of unchangeable truth but a truth that is secondary. The primary source before the books and before the set doctrines is the Spirit of Jesus. This indwelling Holy Spirit continues to live in the lives of all those who truly hear the gospel, allowing it to transform their lives and then, in turn, passing it on.

We, who have been formed by the external authority of the Church, and also the external authority of the Scriptures, find ourselves to be contemplatives where our discipline is to listen to the internal witness of the spirit within us.

Such guidance as suggested above may seem radical and contrary to how we have been taught, and yet, it is quite common sense when we realise that the Spirit of Truth is not about ideas of the mind but rather about love from the heart.

When we meditate, we become silent; we close our eyes and we become more aware of our own internal world as we strive to go beneath our thoughts and our restlessness, so that we can come to the centre of our being, to the primal source, the heart, and here, we sit and we listen, we wait open and receptive.

ASCENSION DAY (YEAR B)
Acts of the Apostles 1:1–14

The Great Silence of God
BY PAUL WOOD

Ascension Day is forty days after Easter, and for the past forty days, we have been reflecting on the resurrected Christ, but now that story is over; he has been gathered up into heaven, to be seen no more, until the *parousia* at the end of time.

---

[196] John 20:22.

The story that St Luke tells is that the disciples are told to wait in the city until they receive power from on high. It is in this period of waiting, between the Ascension and the day of Pentecost, that we get a glimpse of the 'great silence' of God.

Waiting for God to act, waiting for God to fulfil the promise, waiting for God to send us a new guide to be with us forever.

And so, they enter into the great silence of God for ten days.

There are many 'great silences' throughout the narrative of the Scriptures; many of them are tiny, but some are expansive.

The first great silence is in the opening verses of Genesis: 'The earth was a formless void and darkness covered the face of the deep, while a wind from God swept over the face of the waters.'[197]

When we meditate, we are entering into that great, deep silence, before the first word 'Let there be light'. This silence is full of potential, for the Spirit of God is brooding over the deep. It is into this place, before the first word, that we enter when we enter into silent meditation. This is our practice. And, of course, the Hebrew tradition celebrates this practice every seven days by keeping the Sabbath, which is like the silence before the new working week.

The next great silence of God is on Holy Saturday, after the high drama of Good Friday and immediately before the pristine newness of resurrection at Easter. Here is the silence of the tomb. Here, there is nothing. When we meditate, we also enter into the silence of the tomb, believing that the same God who created the world, and who raised Jesus from the dead, will also refresh and renew us.

There is a sense in which each time we meditate, it is like a baptism, as we are united with Christ in his death, buried with him under the waters and then raised up that we might also walk in newness of life.[198]

The third great silence of God is in the space between the Ascension and the day of Pentecost. Here God is silent. All that remained with the disciples was a promise, but a relationship with the divine was no more. They were temporally orphaned. This gap of ten days of waiting for the promise. Ten days of the silence of God.

Jesus had told them that it is to their advantage that he goes away for it is only then that the Holy Spirit, the advocate, the strengthener, will come and be with them forever. But first, they must wait.

Of course, we all know about this 'in-between' space in our own lives, and in terms of the grand map of life, this, the silence of living between the resurrection and the *parousia*, when Christ will come again.

---

197 Gen. 1:2.
198 Rom. 6:3–4.

These are in-between moments.
So, with these themes in the air, let us now enter into silent meditation as we also wait for the gift of the Holy Spirit to come and renew our lives.

Pentecost (Year B)

DAY OF PENTECOST (YEAR B)
Acts of the Apostles 2:1–11

Blow Our Minds
BY MICHELLE WOOD

The themes in the sacred story of Pentecost are somewhat magical.

The disciples of Jesus are all gathered in Jerusalem. They are told to wait for a promise—a gift, that Jesus called the Holy Spirit—the advocate, comforter, strengthener.

The gift comes not like a post parcel but in a violent wind.

We are told, in Acts, that something like flames of fire settle over each person's head, and there is a miracle of speech and understanding between people of different languages and cultures.

I guess in the beginning of any relationship this is always the first miracle. Another understands me, they get where I am coming from, I can be myself with them.

There is something so deeply human and gratifying about feeling like another understands us from our own lexicon of language. Language is a complex thing—it is so easy to be misunderstood or have our words misappropriated. Between speaker and hearer there is always a gap. To navigate this gap and build a bridge of understanding requires a continual humility, openness and patient curiosity to really hear the other.

In counselling, people will express the importance of language in sentiments such as 'Finally, someone has listened and understood me; and with that there is relief, healing and the beginnings of peace.'

Real understanding by another is marked by an experience of knowing that they are not just slotting us into their prefabricated versions of things but are taking the time to understand our particular meanings of words, our particular facial expressions or tones, without assumptions and judgements.

Imagine if this language miracle of understanding could happen between the people of Palestine and Israel. Imagine what it would take to clear the minds, reset the ears with an openness, to really hear the pain, humanity and needs of the other. What kind of mighty wind would blow away and clear the minds of anger, intergenerational pain and trauma?

Come Holy Spirit, Holy Wind, Holy Breath.

All conflict, it could be said, is a conflict of language. For in language, both verbal and non-verbal, we meet the other. It is how we come closest to another or what we use to draw up the battle lines. Each word is a step towards or away from another.

Once, an engineer and a philosopher were looking at a cathedral in awe. The engineer looked up and said, 'I wonder how many stones it took to create this?', but the philosopher said, 'I wonder how many words?'

Pentecost is a feast to celebrate words that build understandings in places unimaginable and previously unattainable.

I so much like to believe in this Pentecost miracle as I sit with fighting couples in the counselling room or read the world news.

The great French psychoanalyst Jacques Lacan asked this question:
What are the relationships that make thought think the way it does?

It is a good question because it helps us consider that it is through relationships, through language, through communication, through communion with others that our thinking develops.

The story of Pentecost is that of new relationships and subsequently new thinking being possible.

This mighty wind, the Holy Spirit, literally blows their minds and they can speak to the other in a way that the other understands. With this language intimacy, human heart connects to human heart. A bigger sense of belonging to the human family is experienced.

Through this bestowing of the breath of God humanity is re-created just like in the beginning when the Spirit moved over the waters.

The old thinking orders that people carry in their heads crumble just as the veil in the temple was torn in two.

The heavens opened and the Spirit that descended like a dove on Jesus now descends and fills the new humanity.

Pentecost celebrates this universal blessing of connection and communion offered by God to the whole of humanity.

The final word is that God loves all and will remain with us until every tear is dried and all suffering has ended.

This Holy Spirit, like yeast in the dough, will fill the lives of people and we will see it in those acts both small and huge where people communicate peace, joy, healing, light and love, transforming us all towards the good or God.

As we move into our practice of silence, may we open our minds to the cleansing of the Spirit, with each breath letting it blow away all divisive thoughts so that we can come into that space of encountering the universal language of just being, just being human, just being human in relation to other humans, being loved and held in communion with one another and God.

TRINITY SUNDAY (YEAR B)
Romans 8:14–17

The Holy Trinity
BY PAUL WOOD

It took the early Church something like three hundred years to cobble together a theology to make sense of the Christ event, the gospel experience, which was something like a bombshell in the middle of a monotheistic religion. Boom! How do you make sense of Jesus saying things such as 'I and the Father are one'? What does this mean in a monotheistic religion? Does it mean that Jesus is God, uncreated and eternal and, if so, then how is he part of this world? What happened on the Cross? Did God die, and if God died, then why did not the whole universe collapse? And what of the Holy Spirit? In one sense, it is the Spirit of Jesus, and so, the gospel event continues through us, but if Jesus is God, then it is also the same Spirit that moved over the face of the waters at the beginning of Creation.

How do you make sense of all this in a world mixed up in Judaism, pagan polytheism, Greek philosophy, Roman law and emperor worship?

It was a bombshell in the middle of Old Testament religion.

And the early Church muddled through making sense of all this, often in serious conflict with each other until they came to an agreement about AD 325, when they cobbled together, at the Council of Nicaea, a statement we know as the Nicene Creed, which is said every Sunday during our usual liturgy. This statement of belief managed to hold most of these exploding fragments together into the bonds of an orthodoxy.

'God is one, three in one and one in three'.

And each of the metaphors used in the Creed, such as 'Light from light' and 'begotten not made', are deeply reasoned theological statements.

Perhaps one of the problems with the doctrine of the Trinity is that it can simply remain an abstracted notion, like a triangle in the sky, so much so that one forgets that it comes directly out of lived relational experience—the experience of the gospel in the lives of the Apostles.

So, how does the practice of meditation relate to the gospel experience?

We are told by St Paul that when we pray, it is the God's Spirit bearing witness with our spirits that we are children of God (i.e., we belong to God). So, the prayer we pray does not originate with us but is prompted by the Spirit of God, which is then prayed through us to God the Creator.

What this means is that as we pray, we are participating in the conversation of the Trinity.

And when we practice silent meditation, we are participating in the life of the Trinity in a non-verbal way.

Sure, we can pray in words to ask for help and to explain to our God all our problems: all this is important. Life is a struggle, and by articulating our struggle we can begin to make sense of it. We pray because we cannot help but pray and reach out in words, sometimes in lamentation and sometimes in praise, sometimes in confession and sometimes in thanksgiving, and so we muddle through making sense of things.

But when we meditate, we are not doing any of those wordy things; rather, we are simply participating in that part of God, who is silent and unknown.

Wordless love.

And here let us be still, let us become empty and let us witness the silence and the mystery. Let us be awake to that side of God that is totally other than all that we know.

Wordless love

For twenty minutes, if we put aside all thoughts, requests, explanations, ideas, stories, excuses and apologies and instead, for twenty minutes, if we focus on that side of God that is beyond words, beyond explanations, we will simply enter the deep mystery of God. Stop and wonder, and sense the awe of the invisible God in wordless love.

And let us remember that we do not bring ourselves to meditation; rather, we are prompted by God working within us to bring us into union with God's own being.

SUNDAY BETWEEN 5 AND 11 JUNE (YEAR B)
Mark 3:20–35

Binding the Strong Man

BY PAUL WOOD

Do you have a body memory of being restrained as a child? Of being held down by an adult, perhaps during a tantrum, or perhaps being bound, either physically or morally, by those more powerful than you? This passage is about restraint. Clearly, in life, there is the proper use of restraint, for example, when one is filled with rage, and the improper use of restraint, such as when one is stopped from doing something good and life-giving.

In this passage, Jesus' family are coming to restrain him following a report that 'He has gone out of his mind.'[199] But Jesus does not allow himself to be restrained by his family and points out that his true family are those 'Whoever does the will of God is my brother and sister and mother.'[200] This immediately brings the narrative from an earthly everyday level to a spiritual and cosmic level.

Others also try to morally restrain him, like the scribes who came down from Jerusalem saying, 'He has Beelzebul, and by the ruler of the demons he casts out demons'.[201] Jesus is not restrained by the absurdity of their logic and asks, 'How can Satan cast out Satan?'[202] If Jesus is healing people, then clearly something other than Satan is operative here. The healing power has a higher and deeper origin. In this way, Jesus does not allow himself to be restrained by the Jerusalem scribes either.

Restraint may have a proper place, but to try and restrain the work of the life-giving gospel and the work of the Holy Spirit is blasphemy. This sin is unforgivable.

Meditation has an interesting relationship to the use of restraint. The discipline requires one to sit still and not fidget. This requires self-restraint and in this state the mind begins to roam about unconsciously without direction, purpose or ethics. The strong man of the ego, which is unruly and roams as it wills, is restrained by giving it a single repetitive task, such as repeating a prayer phrase. Learning to bind the unruly, strong man is the task of meditation.

Once the strong man is bound by a single simple task, then one can begin to notice other things—things that are usually overshadowed by the strong man and his loud presence, things of the shadows, things of the margins, small things, soft things and beautiful things. One will notice that something else is happening from the deeper and more primal waters of the soul. The creative Spirit of Life, which we read about in Genesis and also in the gospels.

In meditation, we bind the strong man for the release of the Spirit.

---

199 Mark 3:21.
200 Mark 3:35.
201 Mark 3:23.
202 Mark 3:24.

SUNDAY BETWEEN 12 AND 18 JUNE (YEAR B)
Mark 4:26–34

Love Keeps Breaking Through
BY MICHELLE WOOD

Jesus tells us that the kingdom of God is within us and has a slow, organic growth like a seed.

Recently, a young woman came to counselling and explained to me all these little breadcrumb signs that her 'dream boy' was scattering for her. He did not talk much, and so, a lot of how he felt was hidden and was communicated in these tiny almost indecipherable signs—walking her to her car after a football game, sitting a little close at a party, catching her eye and staring for an extra second too long that pushed it from glance to gaze.

These little signs grew day by day, night by night, until the heart swelled enough to create a relationship. Neither of them knew where it was going, but bit by bit love is born, the harvest comes.

She had come to counselling because she had regrettably broken his heart and they had parted company. She was very tight-lipped and controlled and tried to tell me in a matter-of-fact way—that that was that! I could see her trying to shake it off her mind as a gardener rubs soil off his hands after a day's work. But when I asked what was dream boy's name and she spoke it aloud, she began to well up and tears rolled down her face. 'I'm not sure why I am crying,' she said, 'it's over, it happened a while ago now.' Her head was saying one thing, but the mystery of the body was saying another. That which was hidden was coming to the surface like the stalk that breaks through the earth.

We live out of so many mysterious currents, mostly unconscious. Life proceeds quickly and before we know it, we are spontaneously reminiscing about our youth, parents and childhood, wondering how we ended up here and not there.

The great psychoanalyst Freud believed that the truth would always seek to find a way out.

When people come to therapy, it is because this flickering of truth has been lost because of hurts and pain. It is buried, and so, it is the therapist job to listen deeply and create spaces for the invisible and hidden to come into integrated relationship with the whole person.

When people come to therapy, they are seeking transformation, new life.

But what about us when we come to meditation: Are we seeking transformation?

I certainly was some twenty-odd years ago, when I first stumbled into a little meditation group led by Richard and Anamaya.

I was seeking depth and wisdom and most of all a way of transforming myself. I had read a lot about Buddhism and yearned for a Christian practice that would tune me into a deeper reality and help transform my mind and heart. Although I knew the gospel values well since these were drilled into me in childhood—love God and love your neighbour—I was looking for a way to transform myself so that I could live out of these more authentically.

Before I learned about Christian meditation, I was reading about the Buddhist's way of transforming the raw condition of ill-will (which we would call sin). To deal with ill-will and its expressions such as anger, jealousy and hate, Buddhist teachings speak of four inner rooms that one could go into: the rooms of loving kindness, compassion, empathetic joy and equanimity. I read that these four rooms are like a well-equipped kitchen with a good pantry, somewhere that you could go into to transform the raw condition of ill-will into something good. The Buddhists think of these as rooms of divine abiding.

When we meditate, we also enter a room of divine abiding. We abide in Christ. By abiding in Christ, we abide in love, and we open to the seeds of gospel within us. These seeds will always outwardly manifest love—love of God and love of our neighbours. Love of God and love of others are the bricks and mortar of the kingdom of God.

And it's not all a love-and-bubbles type of love: it's sometimes dark, deeply sacrificial and painful. It is especially then that we need our inner room of meditation to nourish and strengthen the seeds of the gospel within so that this gift of God sprouts and produces that which shelters, heals, serves and strengthens others.

SUNDAY BETWEEN 19 AND 25 JUNE (YEAR B)
Mark 4:35–41

Crossing over the Sea
BY PAUL WOOD

Jesus says to his disciples, 'Let us go across to the other side'.[203] Now I want to talk about crossing over on a mythic level because this is what I think this story demands. Let me retell you the story of the sea.

---

203   Luke 8:22.

In the beginning when God created the heavens and the earth, the Spirit of God moved over the face of the waters. Those primal waters are there in the very beginning. The Creation story tells us that God separated the waters by creating a dome in the midst of the waters so that there were waters above the dome and waters under the dome, and then, the Lord God gathered the waters under the dome together and dry land appeared. And thus, the world as we have it is surrounded by these primal waters, above, beneath and on all sides. And this is obvious. The rain comes down from above; beneath the earth there is water, as evidenced by springs and wells; and if you travel to the ends of the earth, you will find the sea, where the breakers roar but only so far because the Spirit of God holds them in check and says, stay where you are. So, all of life is surrounded by these primal waters that are held at bay by the Spirit of God.

And it is in this dry land the Lord God made the Garden of Eden. We know the story about how sin creeps into this beautiful garden paradise, and eventually, by the time we get to Genesis Chapter 6, the wickedness of humans becomes so severe that the Lord God says, 'My spirit shall not abide in mortals forever'.[204] And the Lord God was sorry that he had created humans and as he withdraws his Spirit, the great deluge of Noah's time begins. This great flood that destroys the whole world is actually the collapse of God's Creation; it is uncreation, as the primal waters come flooding back. If you read the narrative, you will see that it does not just rain down from above, but 'all the fountains of the great deep burst forth'[205] and water comes welling up and rushing in on all sides. The great deluge is the collapse of God's good Creation!

This is the mythic background through which the Bible sees and interprets reality. The Hebrews were land people, and they had a great fear of the sea; it was both terrifying and destructive. The monsters you read about in the Bible are all water creatures—the great Leviathan and the Behemoth, not to mention the big fish that saves Jonah as he is thrown into the sea for destruction. So, when the Hebrew mind saw the sea, with all the mythic background of the destruction of the great flood, what they saw was something they feared; it was a place where life is destroyed, where all meanings are dissolved and broken down. This is the very reason that in the Book of Revelation, in the description of heavenly paradise, it is expressly said that 'the sea was no more';[206] the sea is banished from heaven, together with death, separation and fear.

Now, with that as the mythic background, it may give new meaning to the gospel story when:

---

204 Gen. 6:3.
205 Gen. 7:11.
206 Rev. 21:1.

- Jesus chooses daring fishermen as disciples
- Jesus walks on the water—for he does not sink into the place of destruction
- this story begins with the invitation, 'Let us go across to the other side'.

'Let us go across the sea to the other side' is a journey we all must make when we die. Across the sea to the other side, and if we know Jesus is in our boat, that the resurrected and immortal One is within us, then we will have no fear.

'Let us go across the sea to the other side' is also something like meditation. We have built for ourselves a little boat, a structure, a method, a discipline to keep us sinking into watery chaos. One's discipline may involve a prayer word or mantra, or it may involve following one's breath, or one may practice the surrender technique. This is our little boat: this is the structure, the discipline that keeps us afloat as we abandon ourselves to the ways of the sea.

And as we leave the solid land of physical objectivity and certainties, we abandon ourselves to the currents and winds of the spirit. Where will it take us?

Stories are told of the 'white martyrdom' of early Celtic Christians who left their homes and their families to cross the Irish sea in little boats, abandoning themselves to the currents and winds of the spirit. Wherever they landed, they called it 'the land of their Resurrection' and it is there they built an altar, claimed the land for Christ and so evangelised the British Isles.

'Let us go across the sea to the other side.'

SUNDAY BETWEEN 26 JUNE AND 2 JULY (YEAR B)
Mark 5:24–34

Touching the Holy
BY MICHELLE WOOD

Meditation is about pushing through our crowded mind to touch the hem of the holy.

In this week's sacred story, a woman who endured a terrible illness, haemorrhaging for twelve years, reaches out to touch the hem of Jesus in a desperate but confident act to be healed. 'If I but touch his clothes, I will be made well,' she proclaims.[207]

---

207   Mark 5:28.

Bleeding was not just any run-of-the-mill illness in the ancient world but held severe consequences.

Women's lives were governed by tightly prescribed laws that separated the so-called pure and holy from the 'impure and profane'. In the Book of Leviticus, it is written that when a woman is discharging blood, she is impure/unclean for seven days and anyone who touches her or even sits where she has sat is unclean and must wash and stay away from the community for seven days.[208]

Given these understandings of blood, imagine the life of ostracisation this woman bleeding for twelve years experienced in this community.

When the woman haemorrhaging reaches out to touch Jesus, she knows she is transgressing the Law, but she risks and reaches.

What inspired such a bold gesture?

She had a type of mantra, 'If I but touch his clothes, I will be made well.'

She is desperate, yes, she has nothing, yes, she is getting worse, yes, but is she also batting for a different type of holy?

A holy that transcends 'man-made' laws.

She must have yearned so deeply in her heart for change.

Perhaps in her journey of solitariness, surrender and suffering, she prayed like Hildegard:

> *O, comforting fire of Spirit,*
> *Life, within the very life of all Creation.*
> *Holy you are giving life to All.*
> *Holy you are anointing,*
> *Those who are not whole.*
> *Holy you are cleansing,*
> *A festering wound.*[209]

She touches the holy with her festering wound. She risks all. The power of it provokes such tenderness from Jesus that he listens to her story and calls her 'Daughter'.[210]

This action of touching restores not only the health of her body but, most importantly, her freedom to form relationships and belong again in her community. She will no longer have to wander alone. She is blessed with peace at last—and one can only speculate how that went on to shape her life and what she was enabled to give to others.

John Main wrote that the first step when we come to meditate is to be restored to ourselves: 'we have to find, expand and experience our own capacity

---

208 Lev. 15:19.
209 Dan Clendenin, 'O Comforting Fire of Spirit', *Journey with Jesus*, https://www.journeywithjesus.net/poemsandprayers/590-hildegard-of-bingen-o-comforting-fire-of-spirit.
210 Mark 5:34.

for peace, for serenity, and for harmony before we can begin to appreciate our God who is the author of all harmony and serenity.'[211]

The practice of meditation is one of quiet boldness; like the woman, we come with all that is a bloody mess within us. Our sitting is akin to that intentional gesture of reaching beyond self to touch the holy.

SUNDAY BETWEEN 3 AND 9 JULY (YEAR B)
Mark 6:6b–13

Authority over Unclean Spirits
BY PAUL WOOD

What does it mean when Jesus gives his disciples authority over unclean spirits? And by unclean spirits, we are not just talking about unclean spirits in others out there, but rather, we are concerned about the unclean spirits within ourselves because, as meditators and contemplatives, we are concerned with our inward journey.

Perhaps an unclean spirit or an impure spirit within ourselves is any spirit that contaminates that which is holy, destroys peace, fragments our being, destroys our sense of wholeness and erodes our sense of salvation and hence is a distraction that takes us away from God.

These negative energies may be seen as fearful, hateful and nasty, and when Jesus gives his disciples authority over unclean spirits it is to ensure that they should not fall under the control of unclean spirits and become subject to their influence. If you have authority over unclean spirits, then you are able to take charge of yourself and not succumb to them, become their vassal or bow down to any powers that are less than God—for that is idolatry.

During our time of silent meditation, many spirits may come to tempt us away from our path and they are not all holy.

Remember, in the first letter of St John he instructs us to not believe every spirit that comes but to test spirits to see if they come from God. In the end, there are only two spirits: unclean spirits, and the Holy Spirit. Identifying them requires discernment.

And so, I find that I am faced with many unclean spirits every time I meditate! These are not quite as dramatic as the demons that St Anthony of the Desert fought off in his cave all night long. They came to him as devouring beasts and then as beautiful women dancing around his being, trying to tear

---

211 Main, *Inner Christ*, 13.

him away from his focus on God. But he did not fall under their influence because his love for God and the salvation of his soul was paramount. Thus, he exercised his authority over unclean spirits.

It seems to me that the New Testament gives us clear instruction about how to deal with these temptations, which is not to negotiate with them. As St James says, 'Resist the devil and he will flee from you'[212] and 'Draw near to God and he will draw near to you.'[213] And this is what we do with distractions during meditation: we reject them, and we also seek refuge by drawing near to God.

Remember that the primary requirement of the Christian is to worship God, and this orients our hearts Godward and all else follows from this. But in meditation, we talk about paying attention rather than worship, but perhaps these two things are the same. When we worship, we give our attention to God, and when we meditate, we give our attention to God. Our attention is our basic orientation, like a compass that points Godward, so we meditate.

In meditation, we do this by a repeating a prayer word or phrase to keep our attention in one place—Godward. For example, we repeat the prayer word '*maranatha*', which means 'Come Lord'.

We may use the Jesus Prayer by continually coming to the Lord Jesus in surrender: 'Lord Jesus, have mercy'.

The process of surrendering may also be towards God Almighty, by surrendering continually every thought, every idea, every feeling, every attachment, surrendering to that which is beyond ourselves to the transcendent invisible Creator of all.

Whatever our method of meditation, we orient ourselves towards God in meditation just as we do in worship.

SUNDAY BETWEEN 10 AND 16 JULY (YEAR B)
Mark 6:14–29

Silent Meditation and Sweetness of Heart
BY MICHELLE WOOD

This is a very sad and violent story to reflect upon. Herod knows John the Baptist to be a holy and righteous man, and yet he has him arrested and killed in accordance with his wife Herodias' desire for vengeance. Her anger has been aroused because John has been pointing out to Herod that it was wrong for him to take and marry his brother's wife.

---

212 James 4:7.
213 James 4:8.

Herod, supposedly a ruler, is more like a spinning top—confused and unable to trust his own discernment of what is holy and righteous. His lack of discernment, conceit and weakness leave him controlled by the whims of others and cause him to commit a horrendous act that haunts him with guilt.

So, I would like to ask a highly imaginative question: what if Herod had been a meditator? What if he had practised twenty minutes of silent meditation, coming before God each morning and evening for prayer, settled, still, centred, attentive and humbly listening to the presence of the Holy?

It's the type of question I contemplate about leaders, particularly when I look at the politics of the world, the levels of corruption and the speed with which people resort to and execute unbearable levels of violence. Do these leaders not feel guilt at their murderous decisions and actions? What conditions allow leaders to be at such a distance from the ones they harm that they do not even experience guilt? Is guilt helpful in reorienting the heart?

Inwardly, I ask: in what ways does guilt prompt me to examine my own states of corruption, conceit and weakness? The space of silent meditation takes me gently into the heartland of the holy. This prayerful stillness, composure and humility help me to build a centre of stability for wise reflection.

Recently, I have been contemplating my life in relation to moral integrity. Like everybody, I know there are things that I have done that I wished I hadn't and things I left undone that I wished I had done. So, how do we meet and reckon with these things in ways that produce healing and wholesomeness?

In Buddhism, moral integrity is called *sila*. It is seen as the foundation of practice and is represented as the lotus flower that you see the Buddha sit on. The Buddhist will speak of not being able to progress spiritually without *sila*. To develop it, one must follow the five moral precepts: abstain from killing living beings, stealing, sexual misconduct, lying and intoxication. Similarly, for Christians, moral integrity or purity of heart is founded on keeping the commandments and developing a heart sweet enough to fulfil the greatest commandment of love.

Loving thought and action are the foundation on which our faith develops. And this is not the same as being scared into keeping rules; this is more like honestly trying to understand ourselves, our weaknesses, our shadow, our unhelpful patterns or conditions and our blockages. Perhaps we all have a little bit of Herod inside—following others' whims, going against our conscience and making deals we wish we hadn't.

It takes time and space to come to know these things. If we don't take the time to notice and feel the pricks of conscience or heart pain, it is difficult to make amends and not repeat the same actions.

Attention to our inner psychological worlds and attention to God are paramount in the evolution of our capacities to live the love commandment.

Silent meditation is a prayer practice to train our attention to develop a humble, attentive, listening approach: a prayerful centre. By cultivating stability, peace and collectedness rooted in God, we can more wisely reflect on our lives.

The desert father St Isaiah the Solitary described this approach as 'a sweetness of heart' and 'a posture of receiving God's illumination' (spiritual knowledge).[214]

SUNDAY BETWEEN 17 AND 23 JULY (YEAR B)
Mark 6:30–34, 53–56

A Little Cove of One's Own
BY MICHELLE WOOD

Long ago, I had this cassette tape of Italian children aged about ten years retelling the gospel stories in their own words. It was very funny. One little boy named Luigi spoke about Jesus and his disciples being so busy that everywhere they went they were hassled by people. People were always at them saying, 'Jesus, my mother is sick', 'Jesus, my brother Lazarus is dead and really smelly', 'Jesus, we have no wine', 'Jesus, I can't stop bleeding', 'Jesus, I can't walk', 'Jesus, I can't see', 'Jesus, my dog only has two legs', etc. Luigi reported that everywhere Jesus went he was met with complaint, complaint, complaint from sun-up to sundown. He offered a rendition of Jesus huffing and puffing along like a ten-year-old nagged endlessly to clean their room. I cannot do justice to his unique retelling, but it was both hilarious and somewhat accurate in capturing the feel of people's overwhelming cries for help.

Today's gospel opens with the disciples returning after being out and about in the villages healing, helping and teaching and crowds of people keep pouring in.

Jesus' response to this relentless sense of pressure on him and his faithful workers is 'Come away to a deserted place all by yourselves and rest a while.'[215]

Just as Jesus called the disciples to follow him—to follow his example of bringing healing, justice and good news to people—he equally called them to seclusion, nature and rest.

A fuller invite might have read: Come away to a deserted place, a little bay, on a rocky shore by the Sea of Galilee, where the sound of the wind shakes the green succulents that poke and prickle their way to the sky and time is measured by sea splashes upon ancient stones. Climb rocky boulders,

---

214   Nikodimos and Makarios, *Philokalia*, 24.
215   Mark 6:31.

roll up your tunics, let your hair down, paddle in the clear blue sea—balm for the feet—breathe in the salt, cast off the demands of all that you have just been doing and find the child within; take a pebble shimmery and speckled in your hand, study it like the Torah, marvel at the free beauty feast, reignite your sense of awe and mystery as we watch the sun rise and set, rise and set, and sleep under the stars, with the sea breeze our blanket. Sit perched on a hill in the long sea grasses, feel them swish on your skin and in silence open your mind and heart to whatever comes, cast off whatever is weighing you down … listen deeply, you are free.

The spirituality of rest or Sabbath is as important as the spirituality of action, comparable to how listening is as important (if not more) than speaking. Imagine living in a world where people just spoke at one another all the time, and no one was silent, still and listening to receive the message.

The modern world feels ever busy, and noise fills every crack of ear space—mechanical, computerised, beeping noises; the noise of cars, lawnmowers and phones; the music pumped out of every shopping, health and sports building; and the noise from churches. TV screens, like gargoyles, appear out of every crevice, contributing to the noise.

Rest, seclusion, quiet and nature are vital to our spirit. And I am not talking about a protected calmness and unnatural detachment but about having sufficient freedom to look clearly at what's there, inside and outside. There is a need to resist some of the imprisoning models pushed at us, to resist some of the systems of power in which we live. By being more deeply open and receptive to the true and the real, we become more genuinely active, capable of living from an active centre of our being, not the periphery, and not just reactive.

Keeping busy like little rats on wheels—looking industrious, important and successful—can keep us living on the surface and although it can look good, it is often filled with anxiety—like shallow breathing, surface living does not fully nourish us. You only have to look at the data on anxiety disorders in the Western world to see that.

Perhaps we need more tranquillity rather than tranquillisers.

There is a beautiful definition of tranquillity in *The Way of Chuang Tzu*—tranquillity is that state where one does not divide between activity and contemplation but enters into union with the nameless, invisible Tao.[216]

I suspect this is something like what Jesus is inviting his faithful workers into.

Come away to a deserted, secluded, solitary, quiet place all by yourselves and rest a while.

---

216   Thomas Merton, *The Way of Chuang Tzu* (New York: New Directions, 1996), 26.

Rest a while in God, come to see things in union, not division.

In fact, coming to rest in God will help you to see and respond to the whole.

The eyes of compassion will be restored. Jesus had a continual life pattern of solitary retreat and service—like inbreath and outbreath.

The practice of silent meditation is a way of going to a deserted, secluded, solitary place by ourselves to be with God. For twenty minutes, we let go of all the jobs, the busyness of being with people, and we enter a sanctuary of silence.

Of course, one finds that one's own head is full of lists, daydreams and conflicts, but in time, with focus on our breathing and a prayer word, that internal noise fades and we find spots and spaces of tranquillity, little coves of beauty and union, our own little piece of Galilee.

SUNDAY BETWEEN 24 AND 30 JULY (YEAR B)
John 6:1–21

Withdrawal into the Mountains
BY PAUL WOOD

On Sunday, we have two big stories, 'Feeding the Five Thousand' and 'Jesus Walks on the Water', and both are full of rich mythic symbolism. However, I would like to say something about one verse that is snuggled in between these two great big mythic stories. Like a gem in a valley, the verse simply says, 'When Jesus realized that they were about to come and take him by force to make him king, he withdrew again to the mountain by himself.'[217]

Now we know that Jesus had this rhythmic habit of going off by himself to deserted places to pray. He does this many times, and part of the agenda, in this instance at least, is getting away from the ego projections of the crowd who wanted to force him to be their king.

We all get tangled up in the world of projections and opinions but getting away from them is a process. Physically removing oneself is only the first step, but then one needs to disentangle oneself from all the mental and emotional baggage that one carries, which come from the world's projections, and this takes time (perhaps even a lifetime). Climbing up a mountain, in and among rocks, under an open sky, where there is a fresh sea breeze and no one to watch except the stars that are gradually awakening—and here Jesus remains all night long up to the early hours of the morning.

---

217   John 6:15.

Perhaps the mountain is a good illustration of prayer because it not just separates you from the world but also takes you up to a higher plane—a higher plane of consciousness, a place more spacious and full of sky, a place of timelessness and open universals, a place closer to the eternal nature of God—that is quite unlike the clamour of the crowds.

And I would hope that in our silent meditation we first disentangle ourselves from all the entanglements and ego-clutter of the world, the stuff that fills our normal everyday consciousness, and that we gradually find a higher plane of openness where we sit.

Our intention is to pray to God, and the Bible shows us that God is the Creator of the universe, the ruler of history, the mighty eternal One, but Jesus teaches us to approach God as Abba, which is a word that a child uses for their father, and so, it is about intimacy—but also a title of respect for our elders.

And this is what I suspect Jesus was doing; he was coming into respectful intimacy with his Heavenly Father in order to reorient himself as the Son of God and to recentre himself in 'who he is': not a popular king but the child of God.

And in the same way, as we come to silent prayer we seek respectful intimacy, where there is a simple openness before our Creator—and that's it. Just this will help to orient ourselves when we return to the world, amid all its ego projections, clutter and busyness.

Now if finding intimacy with God as Father does not work for you, may I suggest you approach God as Spirit, as Holy Spirit, for the Spirit of God has feminine qualities identified with giving life, nurture, guidance and wisdom. But metaphors are only human projections, lenses through which to look, and God is not any of them because God is God, and eventually, we must move beyond the limitations of words and metaphors and sit with the great life-giving mystery. Once again, this is a process, and it takes time.

One final thing:

After Jesus fed the crowds in the wilderness, he withdrew to the mountain by himself and there he stayed all night long. When he comes down, he comes down not with the Law of God written in stone, as Moses did, but with his victory over death, made visible by his walking on the sea.

The sea, the very stuff that brings to mind the trauma of the great flood of Noah's time, the sea, the place of chaos and destruction, and Jesus does not sink into it but walks over it.

Perhaps we too, if we are able to find intimacy with God, will be able to return to the world without sinking into our existential fears of chaos—and perhaps, in this way we too can walk on water!

SUNDAY BETWEEN 31 JULY AND 6 AUGUST (YEAR B)
John 6:32–35

Being Living Bread

BY MICHELLE WOOD

I recently saw a poster with a picture of Jesus sitting on grass with a group of followers around him, with a caption that read,

> *And Jesus said unto the theologians,*
> *'Who do you say that I am?'*
> *They replied,*
> *'You are the eschatological manifestation of the ground of our being, the kerygma of which we find the ultimate meaning in interpersonal relationships.'*
> *And Jesus said 'What?'*

In this week's sacred story, Jesus answers his own question. He says, 'I am the bread of life, … the living bread.'[218]

I imagine an elaboration of this as, 'I bring the gift of nourishment, the good news, the warmth, and the light of God into all the suffering and transform it through living a human life of love.'

Living a human life of love as though we are nourishing the staple food of bread for another, living bread, is to follow the example of Christ.

We are naturally fed by the gospel stories and indeed any story that reveals the mystery of living bread. A way of being, whereby whatever little we have we break it open, multiply to its fullest and offer to whoever needs. Whether this be love, forgiveness, peace, joy, generosity, justice, inspiration—unexpected gifts of living bread.

Recently, I read a story, 'Poor People' by Dostoyevsky, set in 1845 in winter in Russia.[219] The people in the story live in incredible poverty and in shanty boarding conditions. Within the squalor of sickness and these desperate conditions, there is a young woman named Vavara. Her father is dead and her mother seriously ill. Vavara sits by her mother's bedside day and night, in the bitter dark cold, in grief and unbearable pain. One night, the door of their tiny room opens and a young man, who is her tutor, enters. He says, 'It must be lonely sitting here all by yourself. I have bought you a book; it will help you pass the time.'

---

218 John 6:35.
219 Fyodor Dostoyevsky, 'Poor People', in *Fyodor Dostoyevsky Stories*, trans. Andrei Goncharov (Moscow: Progress Publishers Moscow, 1977), 29–148.

Vavara reflects that she cannot remember whether she opened the book that he placed in her hands but could remember the pleasant warmth within her from this act of kindness.

Each night from then onwards, he visited in the evening with a book. And often, they talked during those anxious nights by the flickering candle.

Her mother eventually grew well, and Vavara wanted to express her thanks to the young tutor as his birthday was approaching.

She counted out all the money she possessed, which was not much, and decided to buy her faithful friend a second-hand copy of the collected works of Pushkin for his birthday.

She did not have quite enough money to buy the collection of six books but, at the bookstore, ran into the tutor's father by chance. The tutor's father lived a destitute life, and the tutor was ashamed of him.

The father too was trying to scrape money together to buy a book for his son, but he had only half a rubble and a twenty-kopek piece, which meant he could not afford even one page of a book.

Vavara suggested that he give his money to her so that she would have enough to buy the collection of six books and they could then give the gift together. The poor old man was wild with joy and poured all the money he had into the hands of the bookseller.

When it came to the birthday and working out how to give the present, the father was so ashamed that he had not even contributed to the cost of one page of a book that he could barely look at the girl to come to some arrangement.

The young woman was overcome by his loss of dignity and decided that he should give the whole present. He pointed out that he could not do this because then she would have nothing to give. She said that she would have two gifts—of seeing the father's pleasure in giving and his connection to his son strengthening—and that anyway, her friend, the tutor, would receive the book, which was all that mattered. This young woman was being the living bread. She was willing to lay down her own interest to give more life. It is a beautiful story. By giving so much with so little, Vavara illustrates a real loaves and fishes miracle.

Deep within all of us, we have been gifted with living bread and the choice to receive and to give. To pass on life through the energies of goodness or close it down. We can starve another (or ourselves, for that matter) or lay out a feast.

Living bread never runs out because it flows from the source.

'We receive from God, in the Spirit, and in the same Spirit we return love to God through loving another.'[220] The more centred in God we can become, the more bottomless or eternal is the capacity for giving.

The Western world is full of junk-food thinking. Empty thoughts, like empty calories, sustain for such short periods and clever ideas evaporate like the morning dew, but we subject ourselves to copious amounts of mindless consumption of social media and screens, and so, it is not a wonder that we suffer from a diarrhoea of thoughts.

The practice of silent meditation and contemplative prayer help us to return to that which is truly nourishing—living bread, that which sustains all life.

SUNDAY BETWEEN 7 AND 13 AUGUST (YEAR B)
John 6:35, 41–51

The Basics of Meditation
BY PAUL WOOD

When we first come to meditation, we might notice a number of things happen in the silence. Feelings of pointlessness, a sense of wasting time and perhaps boredom, impatience and anger—all sorts of things are there in the silence. It's a busy time. These energies are part of us, and so, just learning to sit in the silence with these energies and to become aware of them is a good first lesson. But if we continue to observe our consciousness, we will also notice that in order to avoid the emptiness of silence we begin to daydream and analyse ideas. You might notice, if you observe your behaviour, that your mind moves about from one thing to the next, creating stories, analysing problems, remembering issues and worrying about this and that, and most of it is worthless roughage. Some people call this the monkey mind, which jumps from one tree to another, swinging from one mental drama to the next, and there seems to be nothing we can do to stop it. It is with us 24/7. It is what minds do. And there is no escape. Or is there?

You might notice that during normal everyday consciousness, as you walk about, there are times when you do stop thinking. Little moments when your internal world stops its endless restless moving about and instead falls into perfect quietude. These moments are so fleeting and private that we forget them within seconds of experiencing them. These are moments that happen when our mind switches from the thinking mode to the paying attention

---

220 Thomas Merton, *Seeds of Contemplation* (Wheathampstead, Hertfordshire: Anthony Clarke Books 1961), 124.

mode, before slipping back into thinking mode again. For example, when you stop and you smell a flower, in that very moment that the scent reaches your nostrils you will notice that your thinking has completely stopped. In that moment, you are silent inside because you are attentive to the sense of the fragrance.

Now, attentiveness is what we are interested in as meditators. This is the skill of meditation: learning to pay attention and staying with it. We must recognise that paying attention is different from thinking—when we are attentive, we are not thinking, and when we are thinking, we are not attentive. Meditation is the skill of learning to pay attention. Here is another example: when we become aware of the bluishness of the blue sky we may experience a short moment of ecstasy, but we cannot hold onto that experience for long before the thinking mind comes and takes over to give an explanation of it. It is as if we catch a glimpse of heaven, and immediately, it closes over again and we return to the endless chatter of thoughts, back to the busy mind.

Now, there are many ways of being attentive and staying with it, and this is why many people are into sports. It's what Rupert Sheldrake calls the yoga of the West.[221]

For example, take motorcycle racing. Going around the racetrack at 150 miles an hour means that you're one hundred per cent focused. Your attention is absolute, and this is exhilarating because you've left behind that endless mental chatter while you are transfixed in focused attention. When we are attentive, we are in the moment, we are open and receptive, but when we're thinking, we are closed within the bubble of our own ego awareness. When we meditate, we seek to train our minds in the ways of paying attention, which is part of worship. Paying attention not in a dramatic way like in sport, but in a gentle disciplined way, which is about the flow of love, the flow of life.

Christian Silent Meditation has a number of incarnations, and it has a long history. In the present contemporary world, there are basically five movements that I can identify.

The first is the World Community for Christian Meditation, and it's this group that we belong to. It uses *maranatha* as its word of focus. It is a good word. It is an Aramaic word that means 'Come Lord', and because it's Aramaic, the language that Jesus spoke, it has a universal appeal. It is also a word that can easily be said as a mantra divided up into four syllables: *ma-ra-na-tha*.

The second movement is the Centering Prayer movement. This is more prominent in the United States, and it focuses on the surrender method of meditation or the self-emptying method. Here, as thoughts come you simply

---

221 Rupert Sheldrake, 'Friedi Kühne', https://www.sheldrake.org/videos/friedi-kuhne.

surrender them to the Godhead. Its focus is less on attention than on intention, the orientation of heart.

The next movement is the Orthodox Jesus Prayer. The Jesus Prayer has a long, rich history and is also referred to as the prayer of the heart. The prayer phrase 'Lord Jesus Christ, Son of God, have mercy on me, a sinner' is repeated over and over. Shorter versions are also used sometimes, with the shortest being simply 'Jesus have mercy'. The prayer begins as words in the mind, but through practice will move into the heart as humility and divine presence.

Another group in our contemporary world are the Quakers. From what I gather about them, they are not prescriptive about what they do in their silence, except that they wait together until one is moved to speak. Silence is about waiting and listening to the spirit, until one quakes with a message for the whole group.

The last category of practice among Christians that I am aware of is Breath Meditation. It is very rich because of the rich resources of what the word breath means in the Scriptures. Apart from being rich with biblical meanings, breath meditation is also a way of hacking the parasympathetic nervous system, which will change one's consciousness and indeed, as some people say, will change one's life.

SUNDAY BETWEEN 14 AND 20 AUGUST (YEAR B)
John 6:52–59

Union with Christ

BY PAUL WOOD

Jesus says, 'Unless you eat the flesh of the Son of Man and drink his blood, you have no life in you' and 'Those who eat my flesh and drink my blood abide in me and I in them.'

What is this about? Well, it is about union—two becoming one. This is reflected in the Prayer of Humble Access from the *Book of Common Prayer*, recited just before the reception of Holy Communion:[222]

> *Grant us, therefore, gracious Lord,*
> *so to eat the flesh of your dear Son Jesus Christ,*
> *and to drink his blood,*
> *that our sinful bodies may be made clean by his body,*

---

222 *The Book of Common Prayer* (Cambridge: Cambridge University Press, first published in 1662), 274.

and our souls washed through his most precious blood,
and that we may evermore dwell in him, and he in us. Amen.

It is about union. It is about two becoming one.

Here, we are interested in the prayer of meditation. So, let's just think of meditation tonight in terms of finding our union with Christ and bringing our consciousness into union with God.

The journey of meditation is a journey of becoming one with the Cosmic Christ, 'who is before all things and in him all things hold together':[223] the eternal Logos of God. But we can only become one with Christ if we can take in and inwardly digest his life of sacrificial love.

Those who think they can come to meditation and use its techniques to bypass the long history of their sins or avoid the painful journey of confession and forgiveness are deluded. We must be at peace with ourselves before we can become still before the great mystery of God.

In Buddhism, the Buddha is often depicted as serene and sitting on a lotus flower. The lotus flower symbolises the flowering of moral integrity, which is a sound platform on which to sit and meditate. One cannot find serenity if one is sitting on a lot of bad stuff. In the same way, if Christians are to find silent stillness before God, they must have a good platform, but this is not their own righteousness. Rather, it is the righteousness imputed to us by God, for 'By grace you have been saved through faith. And this is not of your own doing; it is the gift of God, not the result of works so no one may boast.'[224]

This grace is discovered through confession, acknowledgement of our failings and finding our peace with God, just as we are. Dietrich Bonhoeffer famously coined the phrase 'cheap grace' in reference to those who expect forgiveness without the corresponding repentance. Indeed, to become one with Christ is to pass through a painful journey, as reflected by the phrase 'unless you eat the flesh and drink my blood'. Only after we experience true participation in the sacrifice of Christ, which means acknowledgement of our own wretched state and what it cost God—the scandal of the Cross—only then do we discover the abundance of grace.

The journey of meditation does not mean bypassing ourselves and avoiding acknowledgement of our sins. Rather, it is an opportunity to sit in silent stillness before God and, if memories and thoughts resurface, simply acknowledge them and then let them go. This is the practice of confession and forgiveness. It is the right and left foot of the journey. Acknowledge and let go; acknowledge and let go. Eventually, as fewer thoughts intrude

---

223 Col. 1:17.
224 Eph. 2:8–9.

into our silent stillness, we discover more and more the immense grace and forgiveness of God.

'Unless you eat the flesh of the Son of Man and drink his blood, you have no life in you', and 'Those who eat my flesh and drink my blood abide in me and I in them.'

This is how we journey to become one with Christ, 'who is before all things and in him all things hold together'.

SUNDAY BETWEEN 21 AND 27 AUGUST (YEAR B)
John 6:56–69

Meditation and Eternal Life
BY MICHELLE WOOD

'Jesus asked the twelve, 'Do you also wish to go away?' Simon Peter answered him, "Lord to whom can we go? You have the words of eternal life".[225]

The path of Christian transformation is one of meeting Christ in the flesh, opening our hearts to feed on his example of love and going with him on a journey through the Cross.

It is a journey whereby we gradually learn to leave self-interest behind, dying to the limited, fixed, material notions of self, so that we may receive the gift of eternal life.

The spiritual journey is from our body, our flesh and our incarnate ways of living love, from self-centred preoccupation to mystical expansion of consciousness, into union with God beyond and yet mysteriously inclusive of the body.

The practice of silent meditation is training in this expansion of consciousness. It involves expanding one's frame of vision from the obvious on-the-ground things that one can perceive to the highest, most difficult mysteries.

To do this, we have to go beyond what we know. Meditation is a practice of taking us beyond what we know.

It is like when one goes to catch a flight. At the airport, there is busyness: a hustle and bustle, beeping machines, shops, flashing lights, guns, guards and crowds of people. Some airports like Singapore are so huge that one has to ride in an electric cart to get from one side to another.

---

[225] John 6:68.

But when you are seated on the plane and it begins to ascend and you look out the window, as the plane ascends, what once seemed like a whole busy cosmopolitan place becomes smaller and smaller. Before you know it, you can see beyond its walls; you see the roads and houses that were always there but you couldn't see them; you rise higher and then they begin to look like ants. Then you begin to see mountains and the sea, and they too were always there but you just couldn't see them. And you ascend higher and higher until all you can see are the clouds, and then just endless sky.

The practice of meditation is a practice of ascending so that we can feel a little further into the mystery of Jesus' teachings and sense them for ourselves.

By quietening our minds, we have lift-off, leaving the ground of the busy day. We begin to detach from our framed material view, gradually letting go of self: of our preoccupations, our stressors and worries, even our delights, casting them out of our basket like sandbags out of a hot air balloon.

We ascend. And when thoughts come and go, there is no self-attachment to them, for we abide in Christ.

When the bells go at the end of meditation, we re-enter this world, hopefully a little less caught up in its stuff that pulls our attention away from our primary purpose to love and serve others, not counting the cost because we are free, expanded in awareness and participators in the grand narrative of eternal life.

SUNDAY BETWEEN 28 AUGUST AND 3 SEPTEMBER (YEAR B)
Mark 7:1–8, 14–21

The Light of the Gospel
BY PAUL WOOD

As meditators, we sit in silence together once a week and the fruits of this discipline are, one hopes, that we are gradually becoming more aware of silence and emptiness within our everyday lives. The effect of this decluttering enables us to become gradually more aware of other things, things that we are usually not aware of. Things forgotten, things sidelined, things rejected, things lost and those things that are over the horizon of one's ego awareness.

And so, one of the fruits of meditation is the expansion of consciousness, particularly into those areas that are sometimes called the shadows.

And this, it seems to me, is what Jesus is doing. He is bringing light into shadow places, bringing the gospel to the poor rejected and lost. Shining a light and exposing the truth of what is hidden in darkness, things of shame, things of fear, things of hurt, things that hide behind a veneer of righteousness.

Jesus is our great champion, whose name means God saves, for Jesus is our great liberator who enters into our darkness and frees us from the bondage that keeps us less than what God created us to be—so that we may be free to expand into the fullness of who God created us to be—and thereby serve the world with greater goodness.

In Sunday's gospel, some Pharisees who had come down from Jerusalem to check on this Jesus phenomena criticised the disciples because they ate with unwashed hands, these backward grubby, dirty, uncouth hillbillies from Galilee.

And Jesus brings to light what is hidden in the shadows, exposing those things that hide behind the façade of legalistic righteousness, and points out that a person is not morally defiled by what they eat, for that goes into the stomach and passes out, but they are morally defiled by what comes out of their hearts—their behaviour.

And so, once again Jesus brings light into the darkness and baptises the darkness in the light of his presence so that people become more aware.

Part of what we are doing by meditating is bringing the light of our consciousness, our Christ consciousness, into the dark and hidden places of our psyche, into what Jung called the shadow.

We all have our shadow. Bits of us that we hide from others and from ourselves, those things that we reject; it began way back in our infancy, and we continue to do it even to this day.

Meditation helps because as we create more empty spaces within our lives, so we are more able to welcome and observe rejected bits of ourselves, unwashed memories, the uncouth feelings and thoughts, things that are normally outside the bubble of our awareness. We can observe them and integrate them back into our lives through the gospel of grace.

And as we gradually become more whole, so the kingdom of light slowly expands.

And remember, what is in the darkness is not all bad. Often it is said it is ninety per cent pure gold, and ten per cent pure evil. We must navigate with care.

To evangelise is not just to take the light of the gospel to the ends of the earth but also to bring the light of the gospel of grace into the depths of ourselves.

And this is our life's journey, and it is the journey of salvation.

SUNDAY BETWEEN 4 AND 10 SEPTEMBER (YEAR B)
Mark 7:24–37

Take Off Your Rhinoceros Head, Smell the Spring Blossoms and Offer Healing Wherever You Can!
BY MICHELLE WOOD

I sit under a shower of snow-white spring blossoms. They are blowing in wind breaths off the branches onto the concrete floor. They land softly like parachutes and twirl over and over the concrete like tumbling clowns. I sit partaking in this spring circus, leaning against a white wall with the warm morning sun on my face and sipping lemon tea with a sprig of rosemary. I watch spring blossoms being captured in a spider web, like fish in a net. It is Wednesday.

I am thinking about each of the meditators in our group and about the talk that I must give. I am thinking about the spring blossoms and the Syrophoenician woman kneeling at Jesus' feet, begging him to heal her little daughter. I am thinking about his insulting response about feeding the children before you feed the dogs and her courageous response that even the dogs are allowed to eat the crumbs under the master's table. These exchanges tumble in my mind like the blossoms that are now beginning to look like the gift of crumbs on the concrete floor.

The practice of silence and the spring blossoms open me to deep listening, listening to nature and the gospel.

I usually hear the voice of Jesus, in the gospel stories, as the voice of love, but today, I grapple with his short and gruff exchange with the Syrophoenician woman. Is this gruff voice like the voice of a tired overloaded mother, I ponder.

My day flows from silent meditation and prayer into some contemplative reading.

I have been re-reading Thomas Merton's 'Raids on the Unspeakable'. I have read this collection of essays many times. The first essay is *Rain and the Rhinoceros*, and it is about living the solitary life and being alive to the natural world.

It begins with Merton walking in the dark of night back to his little solitary hut through the woods in the pouring rain. He describes listening to the talk that the rain makes over the ridges and the talk of the water courses everywhere in the hollows. He cannot resist listening, experiencing, sensing, smelling and feeling the wet. At home, he listens to the rain on his roof with the attention of someone trying to crack the Enigma code.

In his little hut, he is reading Ionesco's play *The Rhinoceros*.

The Rhinoceros is about people losing their humanity and being caught up in this machine of the world. The plot of the play is that all the humans in the world are turned into rhinoceroses except for one, and that one is made to feel like a monster. That man goes about trying to find a photograph of the last human being before they were all turned into rhinoceroses so that someone will believe him, but this is an impossible task and he is ridiculed.

We all have this challenge of living in a mechanistic world that that sidelines nature, a capitalistic world that sidelines our humanness and can ruthlessly demand us to put on a rhinoceros head and live out of its mechanistic unnatural agendas.

And this is at the heart of tonight's sacred story.

The Syrophoenician woman by her natural flow of love breaks into Jesus' human heart.

She calls him out of his busy world of the mission, and the machine of agendas, which might privilege some over others, back to the reality of the human encounter in the moment.

The real human encounter of healing at your feet or in front of you cannot be left or put on hold while you organise the rest of your timetable.

The real human encounter of healing involves giving what you can in the living present moment of need.

Denying this real living encounter is like telling the spring blossoms not to fall or ignoring the sound of rain.

The rain, the white spring blossoms, the Syrophoenician woman and silent meditation remind us to be in the living, the present, nursing the needs of the world before us, in the festival of now.

So, let us prepare for our time of silent meditation. Using this time of practice as an opportunity to open our conscious awareness. Helped by our prayer word, breath counting and or mantra to still our minds of all those prefabricated thoughts and compulsive agendas, letting them all go lightly. Let us begin to pay attention to the living pulsating beat of life all around us.

And let us like the Syrophoenician woman throw our whole self at the feet of the divine one and see what happens.

SUNDAY BETWEEN 11 AND 17 SEPTEMBER (YEAR B)
Mark 8:27–38

The Cross: In This Place and At This Time
BY PAUL WOOD

I have been thinking this week about the symbol of the Cross. A symbol that I am finding to be deeply profound. It is basically a pole and a beam, which are two lines that intersect each other.

Some people have tried to suggest alternatives to the symbol of the Cross because of all the negative associations with it resulting from the horrifying torture of crucifixion. They also say that the symbol itself is visually disruptive and violent to the eye because it has no gentle curves, looks like a sword and is associated with crusades and persecutions. They point out that the early Church was reticent about using the symbol and instead used the symbol of a fish—which, of course, is understandable in that they were a church under persecution and crucifixion was still legal then, and so, why encourage your persecutors by giving them ideas!

Some contemporary Christians, promoting a Creation spirituality, have suggested an incomplete circle illustrating the open tomb as a preferred symbol.

So, I would like to acknowledge these problems and then put them aside and look with fresh eyes on the symbol of the Cross.

Two lines that intersect. The vertical line can be extended up into the heights of infinity and also down into its depths. And the horizontal line can be extended infinitely in both directions, left and right. And the Cross is like where infinity meets at this particular point in the middle. Like the story of the incarnation, the story of the divine and the human meeting, at a particular time, at a particular place, in a particular person.

Just as each person is a particular and unique creation of God, where spirit and matter meet, in this particular person, in this particular time and this particular place. And this cannot be blurred. Often, you might wish it otherwise; for example, when you have a sick child you would do anything to swap places with them but you cannot! You are you and I am me—we are each our particular creation. However, there are times when two lives do intersect, connect and influence each other.

In Sunday's gospel, two destinies meet in the story of Peter's confession. Peter comes to the truth of who Jesus is, 'You are the Christ, the Son of the living God.'[226] And this meeting of two destinies has consequences, and so,

---

226 Matt. 16:16.

Jesus says, 'If any want to become my followers, let them deny themselves and take up their cross and follow me.'[227] The crossing over of two lines—the vertical meets the horizontal, the divine meets the human.

Further, it is interesting in that this meeting point of the Cross also involves suffering. A crucifix will depict a man torn between the heavens and the earth, with arms spread wide open in both directions as if embracing the world.

It is not just a picture of Jesus but is also a picture of our reality, where our consciousness is being torn between the human and the divine, and our humanness with other humans is also being torn.

Some assume that suffering is an intrusion into our consciousness and should not be there, but there is always that suffering that is legitimately ours to suffer, which only we must suffer. This is our cross. For if we do not carry our own cross, the suffering that is legitimately ours to suffer, then we will be forcing some other innocent person to carry it for us, which is both wrong and destructive.

The discipline of meditation is to pay attention to whatever you are observing; and to pay attention is to meet it. One cannot meet the other without paying attention. Paying attention is differs from thinking. When one is attentive, one is open and receptive to the other, but when one is thinking, one is caught up in oneself and one is not open, not receptive and not meeting the other. The small self needs to be sacrificed in order to open into the big self and be free, open, receptive, expectant, to meet whatever God brings your way. It is this state of awareness we try to establish and sustain during our twenty minutes of silence in this place at this time.

SUNDAY BETWEEN 18 AND 24 SEPTEMBER (YEAR B)
Mark 9:30–37

The Poetry of Smallness
BY MICHELLE WOOD

It is now early spring. I meditate. Prayer books arranged beside me, eyes closed, bells ringing. The cool morning air carries the very faint, subtle smell of magnolias flowering. A smell mix of fruity, honey champagne.

My ears catch the early morning sounds of doves cooing. One of the few blessings of the COVID-19 pandemic was the shushing of cars.

---

227   Matt. 16:24.

Bells ring, and eyes open to the curly-whirly arches of willow branches doing acrobatic backbends. They are shaped like rainbows and twist and turn in the gentle breeze. There is so much beauty to enjoy in every moment. When I think about what takes us away from enjoying beauty and being in the present, I conclude it is conflict. I ponder: What is at the root of conflict?

And this takes me to the theme of this week's sacred story in which Jesus is walking from Galilee to Capernaum with his friends. When they arrive at Capernaum, he asks them what they have been arguing about, and they all look down and go silent.

The story goes that they were arguing about who is the greatest of them.

I began thinking about how much human conflict comes out of these arrogant relationships of power. I stumbled across an article titled, 'The Greatest Most Successful Visionary Leader in the 21st century', who has 'been driving our cultural conversation for more than thirty years'.[228] With a synchronistic snap, the gospel question 'Who is the greatest?' came immediately to mind.

I thought curiously, 'Who is that, and what makes them the greatest?'

Well, the leader whom the article was about is Anna Wintour, and even if you have not heard of her, you will no doubt know of the magazine that she produces. She is the Editor-in-Chief of the magazine *Vogue*. The magazine that flaunts the gala of the avant-garde, art and colour, costume and celebrity, ritz & glitz, heels and lipsticks: *Vogue* has it all. If one gets on its front cover, one joins a lengthy list of greats, ranging from the Royal family to Hollywood stars and US politicians.

In this article, Anna Wintour gives seven tips on how to be the greatest leader:

As I began to read, I wondered about leadership and whether these tips relate in any way to the type of leader Jesus is as he tries to sort out the squabbles in his team.

The tips are as follows:

Tip 1. A great leader is someone who can push you forward, who isn't pulling you back.

Jesus is definitely a pushing forward type of leader.

He is pushing us into a new vision of leadership, a leader who is a servant of all.

By his conversation and questions and his use of metaphor, he enlivens the disciples' imaginations and hearts to see beyond petty rivalries.

Tip 2. Great leaders don't micromanage but empower those who they are working with because they know they are nothing without the team.

Jesus teaches primarily by showing, not telling, and then sets people free.

---

228 https://www.masterclass.com/classes/anna-wintour-teaches-creativity-and-leadership

He doesn't micromanage with a book of rules and laws, like the Pharisees. His leadership is all about genuine relationship.

Tip 3. Great leaders surround themselves with a team whose opinions they can trust and who are not afraid to disagree with them.

Think about the Syrophoenician woman and her capacity to disagree with Jesus. And how he responds to her by opening to her larger world view. He is a leader interested in dialogue and transformation.

Tip 4. Great leaders know there is a time that you must break the rules because it's about being part of the conversation of the day.

Jesus is particularly good at this one, right from healing on the Sabbath, to not fasting, to talking to women and healing people who are considered gentiles.

Tip 5. A great leader remembers that they are leading not following and that is an important lesson to keep in mind.

Jesus key words time and time again are 'follow me …'.

Tip 6. A great leader is driven by their heart, their talent and their instinct. This is important because if you start to question and look at what other people are doing to the left or the right, you will lose your clarity of thought.

Jesus must have been a compelling person to have attracted such devoted followers.

Jesus never looks to others for confirmation or needy ego attention.

Rather, Jesus returns to God in prayer, quietness and solitude when looking for direction.

He never looks sideways but always to God.

Tip 7. A great leader looks to the information at hand, but in the end, a decision must come from who you are; you have to own your decisions and who you are without apology.

Jesus engages afresh with the Hebrew scriptures, to articulate the good news.

He emanates an exousia, a power that comes from within him, a charism.

He will not apologise for who he is and what he is about even when standing before Pilate who will order his death.

Jesus is the greatest teacher of smallness in leadership. His tip in today's story is about paying attention to the smallest, so one can learn the way of being the least, a way free of puffed-upness so that one can be the greatest leader of love.

Outside my window now, the sunlight, like the silence and the gospel, begins to illuminate the beauty of this new day. Blossoms on the white blossom tree have now dropped to the floor, and only the stem and a flower head remain like a skeleton. Each small flower head has a dozen stamens like arm bones that stretch up to the sky, and tiny dots of pollen at their ends act like full stops. My period of meditation and contemplation concludes, and I prepare for work!

SUNDAY BETWEEN 25 SEPTEMBER AND 1 OCTOBER (YEAR B)

The Feast Day of St Michael and All Angels
Revelation 12:7–12

The Winds of Change
BY PAUL WOOD

The equinox! Huge swaying gum branches against a racy blue sky. I love this time of year when the wind is gusty. This is the time of year when the powers of the air are caught up in the equinoxal battle between light and darkness. For the powers of darkness that have ruled over the land for the past six months have now met their match in the awakening forces of the kingdom of light. One will be vanquished and the other will reign supreme—but just for six months.

It is always at this time of year, the time of the equinox, that we traditionally celebrate St. Michael and All Angels. In our prayerbook, it is one of the significant Holy Days, which we used to call Michaelmas.

So, who is Saint Michael?

Well, Michael is not a person but an archangel. The leader of the angels of light who threw Satan and his legions out of heaven. We read about Michael in a number of places in the Bible, principally in the Book of Revelation, but also elsewhere in both the New Testament and the Old Testament. In tradition, Michael is a guardian angel, and as an archangel, he is the chief guardian angel and defender of God's people.

So these days, I am barracking for St Michael because we live in a time of great change, and one might gaze in curious horror as the invisible forces that influence human affairs are turning the 'great wheel of destiny' on Western civilisation, and within this change, at its heart, is the decline of the Western Church. Many have lost touch with their religion and despise it, and many are asking 'Are we about to enter into another Dark Age?'

So, this time of year with all the turbulence of the equinox, its associations with angels, destinies and the changing of balances in nature, reminds us that the summer–winter–summer–winter rhythm is an endless cycle, and that there are many cycles and rhythms and rhythms within rhythms, for the whole of nature is alive with the pulse and the oscillation of numerous different frequencies.

One curious rhythm is the sleep–wake cycle. We sleep and so does every animal. Sometimes we are conscious and sometimes we are not—how curious! Where do we go when we are not here?

Here is another rhythm. Every living person has a heartbeat, the pulse of life, 24/7, and whether we are awake or asleep, conscious or unconscious, the steady pulse is always there keeping us alive. Da-bomf, da-bomf.

And in the same way, every living creature breathes in and then out, not just humans and animals but also plants. To breathe is to be alive. The whole of life is breathing a rhythm, in and then out, in and then out.

As meditators we may become more conscious of our breathing, and this can change our life, especially if we live under stress, because consciously learning to breathe properly is to hack into our unconscious parasympathetic nervous system and so lead ourselves from stress into peace.

But here is another awareness that meditators develop and that is to notice the cycles of their consciousness.

Attention–thinking–attention–thinking. It is almost like an external/internal rhythm. You will notice that this goes on throughout the day, but many of us are more caught up in thinking than in paying attention. Meditation will help us become aware of this cycle and also to balance it, by becoming more attentive.

Here is another awareness that perhaps only a meditator might notice. When the outbreath turns into the inbreath, what of the in-between moment? The moment of transition from one form to the other. This is a great mystery, like the mystery of Holy Saturday, which is in between Good Friday and Easter Day and turns the end into the beginning.

Perhaps at this time of the equinox, it is good to notice these moments of change, these turnings.

Let us now meditate.

SUNDAY BETWEEN 2 AND 8 OCTOBER (YEAR B)
Mark 10:13–16

Receive as a Child
BY MICHELLE WOOD

On Sunday morning, I meditated and in between the breeze, the birdsong and the breath, she came to me as a three-year-old with wispy hair and smooth olive skin.

She wore what we used to call her funny face, navy gumboots and a floral spring dress with ruffled sleeves. She came to me so vividly that I could almost receive her in my arms. I could almost feel her soft little puffy warm cheek against mine and hear her whispering in my ear. She came to me from I do not know where or how, but for a moment I was flooded with love as I remembered her who is now twenty-six years old, my daughter.

We often speak of silent meditation as a way of cutting off all thoughts and focusing on breath and mantra as if aspiring to a steely, cold space of nothingness, a blank Zen wall.

But my own experience does not resonate with that. The practice of silent meditation takes me to a deeper, stiller place where I notice and receive more, perhaps a taste of the kingdom of God where peace, love and beauty reign.

In the practice of silent meditation, for a brief time, my mind is not captured by polemics and emotions are not distortedly pulling me this way or that (once I settle and find that point of stillness). My body is still, in one place, just breathing, and as I recite my prayer word, I experience an opening, a waiting, an attentiveness. While I sit like this, my inside posture is more like an *orans* position or that of a whirling dervish, with one hand upstretched to heaven and the other to the earth as if I could channel a link between them.

This morning, for whatever reason, during the silence and stillness I received a love vision of my daughter as a small child. It was perhaps because of my contemplations of this week's sacred story, where Jesus says, 'whoever does not receive the kingdom of God as a little child will never enter it'.[229]

I did not dwell on the vision or cling or attach to it or wonder what she is having for breakfast and follow it like a puppy dog following a smell.

I received it as a mysterious gift and let it go as I have had to receive the gift of her as a three-year-old and let it go.

Receiving and relinquishing, rejoicing and mourning, the mystery and beauty of things coming and going, time passing, time present and time eternal.

The regular practice of meditation stabilises us in this grand flow for through Christ we are held in a constant union.

As Julian of Norwich put it:

> *He is our clothing,*
> *That for love wraps around us,*
> *And winds around us,*
> *Embraces us*
> *And encloses us,*
> *Drapes around us for tender love,*
> *That he may never leave us.*[230]

---

229 Mark 10:15.
230 Manton and Muir, *Julian of Norwich*, 118.

In this time of meditation, may you feel surrounded—not cotton-wooled but rather, opened profoundly to that which only the path of silence, stillness and receptivity can teach.

SUNDAY BETWEEN 9 AND 15 OCTOBER (YEAR B)
Mark 10:17–31

The Narrow Way

BY PAUL WOOD

The gospel story this Sunday is from Chapter 10 in the Gospel of Mark and is about the rich young man who wanted to follow Jesus but was unable to because he could not leave behind his riches. He could not detach himself from his possessions, to be free enough to follow Jesus, as discipleship demands.

When Jesus sees the rich young man's internal struggle and his disappointment and grief at not being able to let go of his stuff, he says to his disciples that 'it is easier for a camel to go through the eye of a needle than for someone who is rich to enter the kingdom of God'.[231] You cannot go through the narrow door and take everything with you. You need to slim down to just your slippery self—and that's it!

Now we frequently find this same story in meditation. Beginners often start with good intentions and even great enthusiasm, but the moment they commit to the task to leave everything behind (even if it is only for twenty minutes), to sit in stillness and, in silence, focus on just one small thing—because this is what silent meditation demands, a time of fidelity and focus—the moment they do that, they suddenly remember all sorts of other concerns, pressing issues, nagging responsibilities and bright ideas. Suddenly, they feel that they do not have time to waste, and so, they say things like:

'I never found the time'.

Or 'I have more important things to do!'

And so, many would-be meditators walk away from practising meditation just like the rich young man who walks away—and his walking away reveals the truth, that he did not own his possession: his possessions owned him and he was imprisoned.

Learning to meditate has to do with untangling oneself. We may talk about detachment or about defusing ourselves from our thoughts and feelings.

---

231 Matt. 19:24.

All this is about letting go and beginning the journey along the narrow path that leads to life.

Remember, in the beginning of the gospel story, Jesus calls to the fishermen, 'Come, follow me', and they immediately leave their nets and their entanglements with the world, leave their livelihoods and families, and follow him. This is the basis of discipleship: letting go and beginning the journey.

And one might ask: Why did they give up everything to follow him? What is the motivation? Why would anyone want to leave all to follow Jesus?

And, of course, the answer is love. I suspect the fishermen were waiting for some big story, looking for adventure, and along comes Jesus offering a grand vision of the kingdom of God, which they fell in love with.

And, as we know, love makes us do some crazy things; love requires us to take risks, such as casting everything else aside for your love:

In the words of Bob Dylan:

> *Oh, but if I had the stars from the darkest night*
> *And the diamonds from the deepest ocean*
> *I'd forsake them all for your sweet kiss*
> *For that's all I'm wishin' to be ownin'*[232]

What will you forsake in order to have this one thing? The pearl of great price? In the last analysis, love is the only reason we do anything that takes us beyond ourselves.

I like to think that my twenty minutes of silent meditation is like going to the gym to train my mind and heart in the ways of letting go of all things and practising fidelity so that I may walk that narrow path that leads to life. Like when passing a thread through the eye of a needle, it requires complete focus, and each time I wander off, which I do many times a session, the discipline is to come back to the narrow path, and each time I return, I am strengthening that muscle of my ability to focus and pay attention.

This is the essence of silent meditation.

---

[232] Bob Dylan, 'Boots of Spanish Leather', The Official Bob Dylan Site, accessed 7 November 2023, https://www.bobdylan.com/songs/boots-spanish-leather/.

SUNDAY BETWEEN 16 AND 22 OCTOBER (YEAR B)
Mark 10:35–45

Making a Throne of Humility and Peace
BY MICHELLE WOOD

There is a story of a small group of six who left the city lights of the now champagne-growing capital, Rheims in northwest France, and headed into the deserted mountains of Chartreuse to live a life of quiet contemplation, scholarship and prayer. Their idiom was 'The Cross is steady while the world is turning.' Their leader was a man called St Bruno who was fifty-two years old at the time of their departure in AD 1084.

They were following the ideals of the Christian desert mothers and fathers of the fourth century and making it their own. The monastery they founded still stands today. The world indeed has kept turning, but nearly a thousand years later, monks and nuns are still there in the mountains, sitting still.

For people like us who look for little spots of silence and stillness, there is much that we can glean from listening to the tradition of Christian monastics.

One such writer is Guigo II, who was the ninth Pryor (or leader) of this monastery. He wrote: 'The one who is mounted on pride does not know how to sit still, let your throne be humility and peace.'[233]

This week, I contemplated this teaching each time I sat in meditation. It became a bit of a doorway to think about this week's sacred story.

Guigo II proposed that once you have attained some humility and peace, you would be able to sit alone and be silent.[234]

It makes sense because often what stops the silence and listening deeply is an intoxication with our own thoughts. On the importance of silence, he teaches that the one who cannot be alone cannot be silent. And the one who cannot be silent cannot hear God.

He composed a beautiful prayer: 'Let all my world be silent in your presence, Lord, so that I may hear what the Lord God may say in my heart. Your words are so softly spoken that no one can hear them except in a deep silence.'[235]

Humility and peace are the throne. Aloneness and silence are the practice.

Perhaps if we could do this, we would hear the word of God in the flap of a butterfly's wing.

---

233   Atwell, *Celebrating the Saints*, 392.
234   Atwell, *Celebrating the Saints*, 392.
235   Atwell, *Celebrating the Saints*, 392.

We would hear in nuanced ways the words of the sacred stories as they land in our heart, watering it like rain. Perhaps we too would discover that centre within, the cross that is steady, although the world keeps turning.

As we enter this time of meditation, in our little group, like the six that went into the mountains, we support one another.

May the prayer of Guigo be our prayer: 'Let all my world be silent in your presence, Lord, so that I may hear what the Lord God may say in my heart. Your words are so softly spoken that no one can hear them except in a deep silence.'[236]

SUNDAY BETWEEN 23 AND 29 OCTOBER (YEAR B)
Mark 10:46–52

The Practice of Emptiness
BY PAUL WOOD

The beggar sits in the dust at the side of the road; he sits in darkness because he is blind, and yet, he is expectant and hopeful, his hands held out, palms facing up, forming a beggar's bowl, hopeful that someone will drop a morsel of food into his empty hands.

Tonight, I wish to reflect on 'the practice of emptiness'. For such is the posture of a meditator, maybe not in terms of physically holding their hands out with palms facing up but in terms of the orientation of heart—this is the posture. Simply being receptive and sitting in poverty and emptiness.

I try and practice emptiness when I remember. I might be in intense thought throughout the day. I may be messaging frantically on my smartphone or thinking about what to cook when suddenly I remember to practice emptiness.

Stop, enter into the poverty of emptiness and become receptive like a beggar beside the road.

One way of practising emptiness is to stop thinking and start listening to ordinary things, the wind, one's footsteps, a far-off aircraft hum, the scuffle, clink and clash and jazz while washing up, the splashing against the sound of distant traffic, or the hum of electricity, the tap of an insect against the window pane, and sometimes, in special moments, the screaming sound of sheer silence. Just listen, just receive, just be attentive, without reflection,

---

236   Atwell, *Celebrating the Saints*, 392.

without words, without meanings, without explanations, without judging—just listen, just receive.

Such is the practice of emptiness.

It has been a long time, perhaps three years, since I have been able to receive communion in my preferred manner, which is to kneel at the altar rail, close my eyes, put my empty hands out and to simply wait, in silence, eyes closed, ready and attentive to receive the sacred mystery. Some early Church fathers taught that one should place the right hand, on top of the left hand, palms up, so as to make, not a beggar's bowl, but rather, a throne to receive the king.

I liked it best when the priest moved slowly along the line, mindful of this sacred act of giving and receiving, so that I could hold this posture for as long as possible before I had to leave the sanctuary.

Such is the posture of the meditator—they may not be physically holding their hands out, but their heart is receptive, open, empty and ready to receive the presence of Christ.

Perhaps opposite to this posture is that of the priest who stands at the altar, also holding their hands out, palms facing up, but they are doing so to give offering to God. The priests' hands are not empty; they are full of the prayers and offerings of people and ultimately of the whole world. It is this posture of sacrificial giving that the priest may have, but it is not the same posture of the beggar sitting in poverty with an expectant receiving heart.

Yet, both actions are important.

Sometimes, being full of ourselves we need to cry out to God in thanksgiving or intercession, but at other times, being empty within ourselves, we need to simply receive like a blind beggar.

This is what we do in meditation. Often, meditators have a word to help them focus their attention. Without a word, we would wander off daydreaming about this and then that. The World Community for Christian Meditation uses the prayer word *maranatha*, an Aramaic word that means 'Come Lord'.

But there is also a long history of using the name of Jesus as our word of focus, as in the hymn 'How sweet the name of Jesus sounds'. This hymn is a devotion, not to the person of Jesus, but to the name of Jesus and the sound.

Now in our story this Sunday, the blind beggar Bartimaeus cries out, 'Jesus, Son of David, have mercy on me',[237] just as many others do in the Bible. This cry for salvation—'Jesus have mercy', 'Lord have mercy'—which is said many times in the gospels, has been captured by the Orthodox Tradition in the Jesus Prayer.

'Lord Jesus / have mercy.'

---

237   Mark 10:47.

Repeat this over and over in meditation as a way to focus.

The Jesus Prayer makes you sit in dust with those who are unsaved and who cry out for salvation.

This is very different from the Lord's Prayer where we pray 'Our Father who art in heaven', standing as a child of God and as a member of the body of Christ. You belong!

Whereas those who pray the Jesus Prayer find that they sit with the unsaved. Lord Jesus / have mercy.

In this way, the Jesus Prayer is intercessory in nature as we sit in the dust among all those who are in darkness, including ourselves, unhealed in body or mind, lame, blind, paralysed or sick and outcasts and sinners who wait patiently for salvation. 'Lord Jesus have mercy.'

Let us now enter into a time of emptiness.

ALL SAINTS' DAY (YEAR B)
Revelation 21:1–6a

The Saints: Mystics, Monastics, Artists and Poets
BY MICHELLE WOOD

The gospel given to us by Jesus is a message of love and peace rising like the sun across the whole of humanity, gradually transforming us with its light. *See, I am making all things new* is the catchcry of our reading this week.

And although Jesus is the pioneer and perfecter of our faith, we see this warm luminous divine light in human lives—sometimes flickering like a candle, sometimes ablaze and sometimes erupting on the scene of history like fireworks. These people lighten humanity's darkness with hearts that burn with a love that is transformative. A Holy Love. The Church has called these people saints, which means holy, and this week we celebrate them.

As a child, I thought a saint was someone who did charity work like Mother Teresa or St Vincent DePaul. As an adolescent, I thought a saint was someone who risked their life to bring about justice, to make a stand for what is right like Oscar Romero. These two threads of Christian saintliness have inspired and shaped my life.

But as I have gotten older, a third strand of saints has appeared. One that was not easy to find. I did not come across these saints in all my years of sitting in pews or of listening to various priests and teachers, for it is a rare thing to find someone who can convey this type of Christian saintliness and one has to look for it in the unexpected.

What I am talking about is the saint whose primary expression of Christian love is prayer as a monastic, a mystic, an artist, a recluse, a nature lover, a scholar, a poet. A saint who is rooted in prayer, solitude and silence.

These saints are holy men and women who have found weird, off-the-beaten-track ways to find intimacy with God. They have lived in caves or in the desert sometimes or built monasteries in the mountains and have even created prayer cells and spots in their own homes sometimes, like us.

In every decade, there have been these holy men and women, and I rejoice in their example.

So let me tell you about a few quirky saints from the Christian tradition who have gifted us with the path of meditation and contemplative prayer.

A favourite of mine is St Evagrius the Solitary.

Evagrius lived in the Kellia desert in the fourth century. He is said to have had exceptional gifts of psychological insights and the ability to make vivid descriptions; here's one: 'we should watch our thoughts like a shepherd watches his sheep.'[238]

He knew a thing or two about mindfulness.

Or what about the obscure Celtic saint, Canice, Bishop and Abbott in the seventh century, who founded many monasteries in Ireland and was much loved in Wales and Scotland.

St Canice was a poet, a quieter, gentler type who liked to escape into the solitude of the woods and islands, where the birds chirruped at tidemark or the deer moved slowly between the trees to the lake shore to drink.

He has been described as a lonely figure with an attractive personality, who copied the Scriptures and was a fine preacher.

And also, we have St Julian of Norwich in the fourteenth century. She lived as a recluse in a little homely cell on the church grounds, but she always had a window out to the street and all sorts of people would come and seek her counsel. She wrote from a rich feminine poetic voice with keen theological insight things such as, 'God is nearer to us than our own soul, for our soul is naturally embedded in God in endless love'.[239]

The path of silence, solitude, loving attention and prayer is a well-trodden Christian path. Think about Simone Weil, Thomas Merton, John Main, Rowan Williams, Laurence Freeman, Evelyn Underhill and Mary Oliver, to name but a few.

And although this mystic form of saintliness is not as well seen perhaps as the louder, more bureaucratic forms or the media-snatching fundamentalist

---

238   Nikodimos and Makarios, *Philokalia*, 48.
239   Manton and Muir, *Julian of Norwich*, 86.

forms of Christianity, it is nevertheless a quiet stream from the spring of Christ and his example of solitary prayer in the depths of the wilderness.

Even though considered fringe in the Christian world today, it may ultimately be the saving grace of gospel transmission. For as the theologian Karl Rahner blatantly put it, 'the Christian of the future will be a mystic or he or she will not exist at all'.[240]

As we come to our own time of meditation may we sense that inner light, across all time, that is making all things anew.

SUNDAY BETWEEN 6 AND 12 NOVEMBER (YEAR B)
Mark 12:41–44

The Widow's Mite
BY PAUL WOOD

The gospel story this Sunday is that about the widow's mite and the two little copper coins she dropped into the temple treasury, and our task at Quiet Communion is to ask, 'What does this story say about silent meditation, if anything?'

And perhaps here is a connection.

One of the effects of silent meditation is a gradual change in consciousness, where one becomes more aware of the small things, the incidental things, things previously overlooked and usually lost to one's attention because of all the other big concerns, the loud demands of the world and the needy response of one's ego, which easily dominates the landscape, and so, one does not notice the small things unless one stops intentionally to become attentive.

In the 1970s, I was very taken with the book *Small Is Beautiful: A Study of Economics as if People Mattered*.[241] Its author, E. F. Schumacher, was an economist who fought against what he called the economics of giantism and automation, like that of the huge multinational corporations that moved into third-world countries, and so, he promoted small industries, small systems, which were close to nature and where people and relationships mattered. Village industries and village technologies. He worked for a new orientation for science and technology towards the organic, the gentle, the elegant and the beautiful.

---

240 Karl Rahner, *The Practice of Faith* (London: SCM Press, 1985), 22.
241 Ernst Friedrich Schumacher, *Small Is Beautiful*: A Study of Economics as if People Mattered (London: Blond & Briggs, 1973).

For me, this little book was full of wisdom and had a great influence on my life, and it spoke directly into the gospel narrative, for almost everything Jesus teaches seems small, personal and intimate. Here are some examples:

- The Widow's Mite (Mark 12:41–44)
- The Parable of the Mustard Seed (Mark 4:30–32)
- Whoever is faithful in a very little is faithful also in much (Luke 16:10)
- A little leaven leavens the whole lump (Matthew 13:33)
- Blessed are the poor (Matthew 5:3)
- Blessed are the meek (Matthew 5:5)
- Are not five sparrows sold for two pennies? Yet not one of them is forgotten in God's sight. … You are of more value than many sparrows. (Luke 12:6–7)

And so it is with the widow's mite. No matter how small her charity—two small copper coins—she gave it out of her poverty, and therefore, her giving is very, very great relative to her means. If we just measure by the laws of the material world, a mite is not really helpful for it is too small. We need philanthropists like Bill Gates to donate and really make a difference. But this poor widow opened her heart in costly charity. And it is the opening of heart that is the significant factor here, not how much one gives.

In the economy of life, we give and we receive. The physical economy that uses money is a crude parody of the real economy, which is about love and the giving and receiving of life.

We receive gifts and we give gifts. Freely we have received, so let us freely give. We breathe in and we breathe out. This is the eternal economy, it is the economy of God, it is the economy of grace, it is the economy of love and at the heart of this economy is the sacrifice of the Cross—and this widow is very much a part of that eternal economy.

Now when we meditate, we are dealing with small things, tiny incremental changes in consciousness, and it is easy to think it is not important or that it is insignificant and will not change the world. But a compass that is out by a tiny fraction of a degree puts you in a completely different landscape once you have walked a hundred miles. If we change our heart, transform our consciousness, we can, through time, make huge differences in ourselves, in our relationships, in our world and to future generations.

As the song says, 'Let there be peace on earth and let it begin with me'.[242]

---

242 Jill Jackson and Sy Miller, 1955. *Let There Be Peace On Earth*. Jan-Lee Music, https://hymnary.org/text/let_there_be_peace_on_earth.

SUNDAY BETWEEN 13 AND 19 NOVEMBER (YEAR B)
Mark 13:1–8

Birth Pangs

BY MICHELLE WOOD

I worked with a child in counselling twenty years ago who used to hide under tables in the classroom, hit other children and swear at teachers. He had no friends and was never invited to class parties. I saw him every week for about five years. And each week, I tried to create a simple, stable and gentle counselling space for him. A space just to be. To be himself, however he was, a space of listening with loving attention to his top concerns, trying to understand what the tantrums were saying, what he needed and what I could do.

Over time, he learned to express with words and pictures what life was like for him and how he felt about school and home, his foster home. For this child was in and out of foster care and the child protection system.

If you asked the school principal about my work at that time, they would have said, 'useless.'

My worked ended when this child was placed in fulltime care with another family member in another town.

But some ten years later, one day at work I received an email from a young man who wanted to come and meet with me.

And he came. A lovely, tall, polite, nineteen-year-old man. He came to thank me and to tell me what a difference I had made to his life and how this had helped get him through. He came to tell me that he was alright now and that he had finished Year 12 and was going to university to study psychology. He had a girlfriend, who was an interior decorator, and they had their own place that they had made a home together. He was keen to show me some photos. A new life born out of such travail.

The birth of the new is not comfortable or predictable.

Sometimes you must wait a long time in the birth pangs—stretching, opening, thinning, repeating, ripping, tearing, room making, crying, groaning for the next.

This is true in my own life, and I am sure in yours too. Times when what we put our securities in, what we thought were grand structures that would not let us down, crumble into dust.

The loss of job, a relationship, a physical or mental illness, a traumatic accident … the death of someone we love—these are apocalyptic moments where the rug is well and truly pulled out from under our feet.

Where we lament, despair and scratch around in the dust thinking it's the end.

At this time of year, the Church calendar is drawing to the end. Only a few more weeks until December, and the new Christian year begins; we enter Advent and prepare for the great celebration of the birth of Jesus at Christmas.

We are at a point in the cycle of gospel readings where we are reflecting on the end of old orders and Jesus is orienting us towards the new Creation that God is birthing in humanity.

Last week, Jesus sat opposite the temple treasury and commented on the widow's generosity from her poverty. He valued her spiritual wealth and contrasted her offering with that of others who gave from pure monetary wealth.

This week, he sits opposite the temple, the jewel of the Jewish religion, and while one disciple is waxing lyrically about the grand structure, Jesus tells him not a stone will be left standing...

Jesus teaches that the Christian path is not to be found through monetary means, prestigious positions, birthright, grand church structures, fundamentalist laws or Pharisees in fancy fringes.

All these high-status securities are crumbling ... even the security of Jesus himself as a physical body that the disciples can reliably wake up next to each morning is going to pass... he keeps telling them.

What will be left when all is gone, according to Jesus, is the birth pangs of the new. And he reassures us not to be alarmed.

As I contemplate the dynamics of the apocalyptic moments in my life and the birth pangs of the new, I'm aware that one thing that silent meditation has gifted me is an interior stability.

When things fall apart, I can go into this inner room, this well-lit chapel of peace. Where my spirit resides in union with Christ. I experience in this space a taste of that which is eternal—eternally good, eternally loving and eternally healing, holding me tenderly like a midwife through the birth pangs into the new.

SUNDAY BETWEEN 20 AND 26 NOVEMBER (YEAR B)
John 18:33–38

The Feast of Christ the King
BY PAUL WOOD

This weekend is the last Sunday in the Church's calendar, and so, we celebrate the great feast of 'Christ the King' to complete the year. And so, I would like to reflect on the idea of kingship.

When we think of kings, we tend to have in our mind's eye something like a hierarchy at the top of which is 'The King', the most powerful man in the hierarchy. This was the standard model of all the great empires of antiquity, such as those of the Egyptians, Babylonians, Medes, Assyrians, Persians, Greeks and Romans. To be a king, one had to have might, power and the will to crush opponents. So, this is the first image of a king.

But when Jesus arrives, he reverses the assumption that might is right and inverts the hierarchy on its head so that the first becomes the last and Christ the King comes to the lowest place in the hierarchy, among the poor and the outcasts, and suffers a shameful sinner's death. This reversal of hierarchy is called 'the folly of the Cross', something that was considered a complete nonsense at the time but yet gives grace and dignity to the meek, the rejected and lost and blesses them with divine significance.

Historian Tom Holland and theologian N. T. Wright, when talking about this event of the crucifixion, say that it was something like a depth charge that went off in antiquity, largely unnoticed on the surface by the great powers of the world, but slowly over the centuries, it is been shaping and changing the course of things, like yeast in the dough, so much so that now all our modern ethics about the value of the human life, like the Universal Declaration of Human Rights, are all organically connected back to this one event.[243] A king with a crown of thorns, the image of the Son of God hanging on a cross—the upside-down hierarchy. So that's the second image: an upside-down triangle.

But here is another shape, perhaps more palatable to the modern mind, the shape of a wheel revolving around a central point. The King is the one at the centre, the place where all the spokes come together and meet in one place. Perhaps we see this shape best in the biblical idea that a king is like a shepherd; they live with the flock, and their welfare is dependent upon each other. In this context, Jesus give us the image of the Good Shepherd standing among the flock, protecting and leading to green pastures. The Shepherd King is at the centre.

The last shape I suggest for kingship is far more diffuse for it is like a cloud. Sometimes, when you see or read a whodunit story, you cannot make sense of it, for there are all these clues along the way but since you do not know which are significant, which are true and which are false, you cannot be sure you have got the narrative right. It could be this or it could be that, but then, when you finally get to the end, the whole narrative begins to make sense, everything falls into place because now you have got the meaning principle that interprets the whole.

---

243 Premier Unbelievable? 'Tom Holland Tells NT Wright: Why I Changed My Mind about Christianity', 17 July 2018, video, https://www.youtube.com/watch?v=AIJ9gK47Ogw&t=5s.

Or the key that unlocks the door. Perhaps this is this what St Paul means when he writes of 'the mystery that has been hidden throughout the ages and generations but has now been revealed to his saints. To them God chose to make known how great among the gentiles are the riches of the glory of this mystery, which is Christ in you, the hope of glory'.[244] So, he goes on to say, 'Christ is all and in all'.[245]

Perhaps this is why St John refers to Christ as the Logos, which is the ordering principle of all Creation: 'All things came into being through him'.[246]

To conclude, one might look at the kingship of Christ in a variety of ways, namely:

1. the top of a hierarchy of authority
2. an inverted hierarchy = selflessness
3. the centre of a wheel = relational
4. a diffused presence throughout the whole, holding all things together = mystical

So, how might these images speak to the practice of silent meditation? Well, I am not sure.

Perhaps a king is simply an ordering principle that brings diverse elements into harmony and peace. And when we meditate, we too must bring to order our restless thoughts and unruly passions into a harmonic whole. Perhaps we will find each of these models has its place within our own practice.

---

244   Col 1:26–27.
245   Col. 3:11.
246   John 1:3.

YEAR C. THE YEAR OF ST LUKE

Advent (Year C)

FIRST SUNDAY OF ADVENT (YEAR C)
Luke 21:25–38

A Way to a Light Heart
BY MICHELLE WOOD

Advent begins this week with a sacred story that tells of the symbolic end of the world: cosmic orders collapsing, nations in distress and people fearful. But Jesus reassures that the kingdom of God—a kingdom where love and peace will finally reign—is coming.

The end and the beginning are one in this prophetic narrative.

And on this grand stage of transformation, we are given some advice: 'Be on guard so that your hearts are not weighed down with dissipation and drunkenness and the worries of this life, and that day does not catch you unexpectedly, like a trap.'[247]

Could this season of Advent be a time of heart unburdening, balancing and lightening? Can we cast out or aside the things that weigh us down?

And what part, if any, could the practice of silent meditation play in helping us have a stripped back, spacious, simpler, slimmer Christmas?

While we contemplate what we are guarding our heart from, maybe we could also be curious about what we could be attentive to.

How could we be more attentive to the mystical Bethlehem star that is rising? How could we sense new beginnings in among the turbulence of this world? Could this Advent be a time of attentive attuning?

An Advent where we notice signs of the life–death dance all around us, such as a backyard tree laden with orange, heart-shaped apricots. Perhaps we could take a moment to smell their ripening sweetness each day. Knowing that they will drop to the ground or be picked and relinquish their life to feed us.

This simple practice could tune us into the landscape of endings and beginnings, metaphors that are prevalent in our sacred readings at this time.

Or perhaps we need to wake up our drunken hearts by taking a dip into the cool sea or not yet warm enough rivers.

---

247 Luke 21:34.

A light heart that is not weighed down is one that is present, alert, unhurried, spacious and able to sense the story that is unfolding underneath the seemingly chaotic world. It is a heart not troubled.

Do not let your hearts be troubled, says Jesus.

In Christian literature, the heart (*kardia*) is the spiritual centre of being, it is the space in which the mystery of the union between divine and human is consummated.

If our lives are full of clutter, attachments or lazily off in la-la land escapism, we will be available to meet neither the child of poverty born in a stable nor the King of Glory riding on a cloud … neither the small things nor the grand things.

The practice of silent meditation is a practice of stripping back and letting go of all that is weighing down our hearts.

Letting go for a short piece of time our desires. Desires for sex, another glass of wine, buying another thing, another clever thought; letting go of all thoughts, letting go of conflict or fear, letting go of worries about ourselves or others, letting go of anger, letting go of all the lies we tell ourselves and others, letting go of all the politics of fighting and forces that surround us, letting go, unwrapping our hearts from all these superficial, passing things like we unwrap the layers of paper in the game of pass the parcel to find the gift.

In the practice of silent meditation, we close our physical eyes so that we can return to the gift of our heart, our inner altar, and wait patiently for the humble Christ Child and the glorious Christ the King. The beginning and the end.

Remembering the words of the Beatitude, 'Blessed are the pure in heart, for they will see God.'[248]

SECOND SUNDAY OF ADVENT (YEAR C)
Luke 3:1–6

The Spirituality of the Wilderness
BY PAUL WOOD

'The voice of one crying out in the wilderness.'[249]

Wilderness: there is a lot of it out there in the Great Dividing Range of Eastern Australia. Endless eucalypt forests and mountains, valleys and streams—one could walk for days and never see any sign of humanity, and

---

248   Matt. 5:8.
249   John 1:23.

this is just a few miles from here where we are on the Murray River. I was amazed when flying from Melbourne to Singapore that we flew for six hours over a vast empty red centre of Australia. Six hours! before we came to the top end of Australia, and then, it was endless sea. There is a lot of wilderness down there. A lot of emptiness.

Sometimes I look at pictures of the places of wilderness in the Bible lands, Syria, Jordan, Iraq, Saudi Arabia and the Egyptian deserts. The wilderness can be very rugged with huge mountain ranges and is often very harsh, rocky and dry. Who would live there? And what do they do? One thing is for sure: no one is wearing high heels or fine raiment in the wilderness!

Cities are great cultural centres of the world, and they produce many good things—culture, fashion, art, philosophy, learning, science, technology and many amazing, wonderful things.

But what does the wilderness produce?

Besides thorns and thistles?

What good comes out of the wilderness?

When you are alone in the wilderness, you face the harsh fact of Creation without artificial stuff diluting the experience and getting in the way. You experience raw Creation. You may experience fear, wonder, might, beauty, majesty, awe and a sense of the holy. And if you have problems within yourself, like sadness, boredom, anxiety or guilt, well, there is nowhere to escape to, no entertainment, no TV: just yourself as you are before the truth of God as God is.

The wilderness has long been understood to be a crucible for the soul and a place of prayer and transformation. Haute cuisine and fast-food belong to the cities, but the wilderness is something about emptiness, nakedness and raw encounter with the holiness of God.

Christian meditation has its roots in the wilderness. We can trace our history back through Christian saints, mystics and monasteries always outside of the mainstream, back to the teachings on prayer by the desert mothers and fathers, back before them to the prayer habits of Jesus, who withdrew time and again into the wilderness to pray, and back before Jesus to John the Baptist, the wilderness man who ate locusts and wild honey and cried out 'Prepare the way of the Lord'![250] And back before him to the Old Testament prophets and further all the way back to the ancient times of Moses and his encounter with God in the wilderness on the Holy Mountain, and back further still to the patriarchs and to Abraham, the father of the faith, who left his father's house in ancient times, and went out into the wilderness, to the land that God would show him, and there made a covenant with God under the starry sky.

---

[250] Isa. 40:3.

The biblical tradition of wilderness is about raw encounter with a holy God, away from the artificial everyday world. You can hear the wilderness breeze whispering, 'Prepare the way of the Lord!'

There is a sense that when we meditate, we are returning to the wilderness. To our raw basic self. No frills, just as we are. Stripped of the clutter and worldly fluff, back to the basics of the naked self, as we are before the truth of God as God is. And the message is 'Prepare the way of the Lord!'

In the practice of meditation, we are preparing the way by becoming still, attentive, open and receptive. Smoothing out the extremes of our mind, the high mountains and the deep valleys, making a smooth highway to receive the Lord. When we focus our attention in meditation, we are straightening out the deceptive mind and the crooked heart that want to avoid this and avoid that and to go over there instead of simply going straight. Meditation is immediate, and it is simple.

THIRD SUNDAY OF ADVENT (YEAR C)
Luke 3:7- 18

The Amour of Light
BY PAUL WOOD

Advent is our preparation to meet Christ not just as the nascent child in the stable of Bethlehem, but also as the glorious being at the end of time who comes to judge the whole world. To meet such a being one can do none other than to approach not only with expectation and joy but also with great humility, awe, and a holy fear.

It is in this frame that we prepare to meet Christ by reading, in this week's gospel, the fiery preaching of John the Baptist who comes from out of the wilderness. His message is like thunder, "you brood of vipers! Who warned you to flee from the wrath to come?" for "the one who is coming will baptize you with the Holy Spirit and fire." "His winnowing fork is in his hand .... and the chaff he will burn with unquenchable fire."

This is a clear call to repent and be baptised in preparation to meet Christ.

Perhaps on a gentler sounding note, 'The Collect for Advent' in the *Book of Common Prayer* says: "*Almighty God, give us grace that we may cast away the works of darkness, and put upon us the armour of light.*"

I would like to explore silent meditation as the practice of casting away the works of darkness and receiving the "armour of light."

When we meditate, and if we pay attention to our breathing, we can understand the outbreath is getting rid of the stale air filled with carbon dioxide, as something similar to casting away the works of darkness. Getting rid of all that is hidden in darkness, unacknowledged sin, bad memories, falsehoods, shameful deeds, and foolish wrongs. As these are brought to light so we breathe them out and let them go.

As we meditate we focus on our prayer word or our breathing and as thoughts arise that take us away from our focus, we become aware of them, so we let them go, offering them up as a sacrifice, like a burnt offering before God – gone, transformed into smoke – gone away. Each time we do this we refocus our attention back to our prayer word. If one does not offer it up and let it go one will continue to be kept captive to the same old narratives of the unredeemed self. So, we do not keep it in, but we cast it out.

Our expiring breath is only half the story, because in meditation we also 'breathe in,' fresh air, new life, and new beginnings.

"Almighty God, give us grace that we may cast away the works of darkness, and put upon us the armour of light."

The armour of light is given to us as we breathe in forgiveness, and we start again. The pure oxygen of the grace of God, is freely given, it is unearned, it is pure gift, and it sustains us every second of our lives. Breathing in new life is unearned and freely given to all living beings. Fresh, new, uncontaminated, clean, and pristine. The gift of life, the gift of breath, the gift of fresh oxygen.

A person who has not learnt how to breathe in the depths of their soul, who has not learnt to bring to light things hidden in darkness and then confess them is like someone holding their breath, too afraid to breathe. But it is only when we 'breathe out' can we 'breathe in' the freely given grace of new life.

So, our hope is that our meditation will teach us spiritual breathing in the depths of our soul.

Let us learn how to breathe. Let us learn the ways of confession and forgiveness so that when we meet our Lord Jesus Christ we may do so with truth and with humility.

FOURTH SUNDAY OF ADVENT (YEAR C)
Luke 1:39-55

The Visitation

BY PAUL WOOD

Every week, we come together and sit still and quiet, not to daydream passively, but rather, to be actively attentive and receptive before the great mystery of God. When we make an empty and silent space, we are creating a womb, as it were, to receive and nurture the Spirit of Christ within ourselves.

Now this Sunday, the Sunday before Christmas, we are brought to the story of Mary who is already pregnant. As you probably know, in the Greek Orthodox Church Mary is called the *Theotokos*, that is, the God-bearer, the one who bears the life of God within her womb. In today's part of the story the pregnant Mary visits her cousin Elizabeth, who is also pregnant, and when Elizabeth hears Mary's greeting, the baby within her, who is the future John the Baptist, leaps with joy for being in the presence of the Christ, who is as yet unborn and inside Mary. The two unborn babies meet, as it were. This is a special moment, which is called 'The Visitation', when the two women meet, but also that which is within them is also part of the meeting. There are four of them! Mary, Elizabeth, the baby prophet John the Baptist and the baby Jesus inside Mary.

The Visitation is interesting and full of wonder and joy. It is in this context that Mary says her famous words, which are full of joy and praise, 'My soul magnifies the Lord, and my spirit rejoices in God my Saviour': this is Mary's song of praise, which we know as 'The Magnificat'.[251]

I often think that the womb is a useful metaphor for the unconscious, that there is always stuff within us, hidden from others and mostly hidden from ourselves, waiting to come out, and that when we meet another person, it is not just the meeting of two conscious people, but there is also a whole lot more going on; the conscious meets the unconscious and the unconscious meets the unconscious—it's complex.

When we meet with other people, we bring with us all the hidden stuff brewing within us; much of it is not divine, but when the prophet inside me meets the Christ inside you, it is like 'The Visitation' and an occasion for a song of joy and praise.

So, for meditation tonight I would like to try something different, an imaginary thinking meditation that you may choose to do or not to do. I invite you to stand in the shoes of Elizabeth: bring to mind each member of your

---

251 Luke 1:46–55.

family or each one of your friends, allow the prophet within you to recognise the Christ in them and then give a prayer of thanks and praise.

It is a spiritual exercise to recognise Christ, yet unborn and hidden in the other. It is a way of praying, and it may well be a good preparation for Christmas.

CHRISTMAS DAY (YEAR C)
Luke 2:8–20

Drawing Near to the Centre of Existence
BY MICHELLE WOOD

Something profound happened in that little stable in Bethlehem. And sometimes, we ordinary folk, like the shepherds, stumble into scenes of holiness.

Each time we practice silent meditation, we sit in a type of interior Bethlehem stable.

We sit in the Emmanuel reality: God with us.

And our response is to move a little nearer to the one whose name is love, who is the Word made flesh. Breath by breath, we turn our attention.

Downing the tools of everyday labours, like the shepherds, we draw towards the light.

Sometimes sensing we are approaching something holy, precious, small, vulnerable, wrapped in swaddling, one whose light is filling every pore on the planet.

Drawing onwards, drawing nearer, breath by breath to the heart of universal love, the Christ.

When nearer to Christ, one is nearer to all people and all living things because he is the centre of all existence. There is greater capacity from this centre to love more and be attentive to the suffering of others—from the person who wept in the counselling room, to the manic tattooed man crying obscenities in Dean Street, to the children who lost their lives tragically in Tasmania.

Feeling from the centre of our being is different from feeling from the mind or the crowd or the political.

In the practice of meditation, we go inwards to the centre of our creation to be with Christ who is at the centre of all Creation so that we can go outwards enlightened by love.

In the spiritual poverty of our stable, may we move just a little nearer to the light of God with us, the centre of all existence.

THE EPIPHANY OF OUR LORD (YEAR C)
Matthew 2:1-12

Journey to the Heart

See meditation for Year A on page 13.

FIRST SUNDAY AFTER EPIPHANY (YEAR C)
Luke 3:15–22

Prayer
BY MICHELLE WOOD

'Now when all the people were baptized, and when Jesus also had been baptized and was praying, the heaven was opened'.[252]

When Jesus had been baptised and was praying, the heaven was opened. I would like to reflect with you upon praying and heaven opening.

Let me tell you a story.

Long ago, I had a moment where it felt like the heaven opened. I was in a space betwixt and between, finishing an old life and not yet launched into the new.

Often at these times of crossroads, when we are a little lost, where things aren't so clear-cut, when we are not sure of our next step, there is space and room to sense God.

We wrestle and ask questions, look beyond, outwards and upwards and ponder how our own small life is in tune with a grander narrative—what is our purpose? What are we really called to do? How should we live?

Somehow at these junctures, when we haven't got everything stitched up into certainties, or are overwhelmed by busyness, and stagnant by routines ... there is some slack, and we are more available to the heaven opening.

The early Celtic Church called the meeting points between heaven and earth *thin spaces*.

---

[252] Luke 3:21.

And contemporary Anglo-Irish Poet David Whyte writes:

> *Sometimes everything*
> *has to be inscribed*
> *across the heavens*
> *so you can find*
> *the one line*
> *already written within you.*
> *Sometimes it takes*
> *a great sky*
> *to find that*
> *first, bright,*
> *and indescribable*
> *wedge of freedom*
> *in your own heart.*[253]

At this time of my life, I was looking for that which is 'inscribed across the heavens'. And one evening, I was sitting by the banks of Lake Nillahacootie as the sun was setting. I'd finished a time of silent meditation and prayer.

And I was waiting.

Paul came and sat quietly next to me, and we watched two large pelicans begin to circle over the lake. It felt unusual and I had not seen them before. I remember thinking of all the artworks in which Jesus is depicted as a pelican.

In medieval Europe, the pelican was thought to be particularly attentive to her young, to the point of providing her own blood by wounding her breast when no other food was available. As a result, the pelican became a symbol of Jesus. You can see this image depicted in the stained-glass windows of many churches, often behind the altar.

Watching the pelicans circle, my eyes raised to the sky, I saw those magnificent birds making large and invisible circles, never-ending circles.

At this time in our life, Paul and I were exploring questions of marriage. Were we ready? Was this right?

Under the rising moon and the circling pelicans, we had a sundowner. When we put our glasses down on the earthy bank and started to talk about our wedding, immediately the strangest thing happened. One of the glasses made a loud ping sound and when we looked at the ground before us, we saw that its rim had popped off and was shaped in a perfect glass circle, like a wedding ring.

We were amazed. It really felt like a mystical experience. Like the heaven had opened, and there was a sense of this marriage being blessed by God. In

---

[253] David Whyte, *House of Belonging* (Langley, WA: Many Rivers Press, 2002), 37.

that moment, it felt like there was a connection between our small lives and the story of God's goodness and love.

We both laughed in amazement.

Biblical literature is full of these wonderous moments, thin spaces, signs, where the heaven opens. In the New Testament, we get some beautiful accounts of these: from the star in the sky over the stable where Jesus was born, to the baptism celebrated today and the dove, to the transfiguration on the Holy Mountain of Sinai, and the temple curtain being torn in two … spaces where we get glimpses of the glory of God…

And as we cycle through these mystical stories each year in our liturgical calendar, we are invited to see how our own lives join with the God story, the great love story.

As the poet recounts:

> *Sometimes everything*
> *has to be inscribed*
> *across the heavens*
> *so you can find*
> *the one line*
> *already written within you.*

In today's gospel, after being baptised, Jesus was praying, and the heaven opened.

Prayer, in fact, is this wonderful poetic turning towards the reality of the heaven opening.

It is making space to be with God who is already with us. It is joining our small and seemingly insignificant story to God's glorious and miraculous transformative story, which involves the healing of the whole world by love.

When we move nearer to God, the heavens open and our hearts expand just a little more with love for in the divine presence, the one whose name is love, we can't but help bring all whom we care about.

Prayer isn't a shopping list to a man with a white beard in the sky.

Rather, prayer is being on the lookout for heaven opening like a farmer looks out for rain.

Prayer is grateful acknowledgement for each inbreath and outbreath that we receive from God.

In the quiet prayer of silent meditation, one reaches into the peace and stillness of God's eternity; in intercession prayer, one reaches into the rough-and-tumble of the world.

The Greek word that we habitually translate as *intercession* is more accurately rendered as 'encounter', to be with someone on behalf of or in relation to others.[254] Former archbishop of Canterbury Michael Ramsey said that prayer is being with God so that we can be with people. He suggests that prayer is not about piety but rather, naked sincerity. Prayer is the human yearning to be transformed by heaven opening and the Spirit of God descending into our hearts, blessing our lives with purpose, meaning and love.

If we contemplate how Jesus prays throughout his life, we will see that at every significant moment he prays. Often by himself, seeking a quiet but heaven opening space—at his baptism, before appointing the twelve, on the mountain before the transfiguration, at the Last Supper, in the Garden of Gethsemane and in those last hours on Calvary.

As we sit to practice silent meditation, may we, following his example, be receptive to the heavens opening. Alert to mysterious, thin spaces. Attentive to the edge where the heavens and earth momentarily touch.

SECOND SUNDAY AFTER EPIPHANY (YEAR C)
John 2:1–11

Water into Wine and the Transformation of Consciousness
BY PAUL WOOD

One of the effects of practising meditation is that we become more aware of different states of consciousness. Sometimes we are so caught up in our thoughts that we are not conscious of the present moment at all. Other times we are focused upon the present, but we are rigid, uptight and uncomfortable with ourselves and our surroundings. At other times, we may find ourselves more integrated and at peace, and so, we find a centre of stillness and silence.

Achieving an altered state of consciousness is a preoccupation of humanity, which has discovered all sorts of ways to change consciousness—from religious practices, stories, films and sports to various drugs.

The drug of choice in Christianity is wine. If you do a word search in the Bible, you will find about 250 references to wine. Wine brings a change of consciousness—it is the stuff of mirth, and excess and joy and fun and laughter and is even called a divine blessing[255] (but yes, wine also has a shadow side, and the Bible refers to that also, and so, the New Testament tells us not to be drunk with wine but rather to be filled with the Holy Spirit!).

---

254 Michael Ramsey. *The Christian Priest Today*. (Eugene: Wipf and Stock, 1982), 14.
255 Gen. 27:28.

Today's reading is about Jesus transforming water into wine. Water, the ordinary stuff of this world, is turned into the special stuff of celebration! Just as Jesus transforms the old age and brings in the new age. The old age was about the Law, but the new age is about grace. The old age was based upon tablets of stone, but the new age is about the age of the Spirit. The old age was about the absence of Christ—the new age is about the presence of Christ!

This idea of 'transformation into the new' is important to the Christian. The spiritual life begins with a *metanoia*, seeing things in a new way, beginning again, with a new consciousness and a transformation into a new life.

Alan Jones, in writing about the desert tradition, refers to spiritual transformation as 'Soul Making'.[256] This is our work on earth—to become better souls, which means growing in our capacity to love. This is what the spiritual life is about. It's about learning to love. And this is the hard stuff in life. Learning to love with the wide-open generosity of God, learning to come out from our self-protective shells, learning to give life, to love generously and wastefully after the image of Christ, the Son of God. To grow is to grow in love.

When Jesus transforms water into wine, he does it at a wedding! This is the umbrella story within which water is transformed into wine. There are stories within stories. There is my story and there is your story, but then, there is also our story, maybe our family story or our national story, but then, there is 'the big story' in which we all live, the highest story of all, the umbrella story, under which all other stories are contained. It is what we might call the 'grand narrative'. This story is about God for it talks about our creation and also our redemption and our purpose and the consummation of history.

The transformation of our souls can only happen because we live within the grand narrative, which is about the Great Love of God. Let us remember that the New Testament speaks of Christ as the bridegroom.[257] He has come to woo our souls and win over our hearts in devotion and commitment so that he may bring his bride, at the consummation of all things, to the great wedding feast in heaven. Here, finally, the bride stands at the altar with her beloved groom and there they are united forever. That is the grand narrative—it is the story of union, where bride and groom become one at the consummation of history.

The umbrella story is the story of the Great Love of God. Our own spiritual transformation is about growing in our capacity to love. When we meditate, we sit still, we open our hearts and so allow our consciousness to be transformed by the Great Love of God. Like water being transformed into wine.

---

256 Jones, *Soul Making*, 23.
257 John 3:29.

THIRD SUNDAY AFTER EPIPHANY (YEAR C)
Luke 4:16–19

Christ's Manifesto and Meditation

BY MICHELLE WOOD

In 1991, when I was eighteen years old, I went on my first ever overseas trip. Now being the way that I am, I chose to go to that place that nobody goes to. Back then, it was Pakistan. Naively, I didn't know much about the situation there or the impending Gulf War, although the physiotherapist I was living with did ask, 'Is it really safe to go there at this time?'

I did, however, have some sense of the country—its beauty, poverty and conflict—through my correspondence with my former school principal, Br Walter Smith, who at the ripe age of seventy years set off from Adelaide to build a school in a poor village 180 kilometres west of Lahore in a town called Sargodha.

When I read the sacred story this week, I found myself thinking of that mysterious place, a little village in Sargodha. Its mucky dirt roads lined with litter and open drains, which were full of men (but no women), chooks, trucks, donkeys, bicycles, plastic bags blown around and children playing and living in *bustis* or rubbish heaps.

In this week's sacred story, at the very beginning of his ministry, at around the age 30 years, Jesus reads his great message of liberation aloud to the folk of his hometown, Nazareth. He proclaims: 'The Spirit of the Lord is upon me, because he has anointed me to bring good news to the poor. He has sent me to proclaim release to the captives and recovery of sight to the blind, to let the oppressed go free, to proclaim the year of the Lord's favor.'[258]

In biblical literature, this year of God's favour is called the Jubilee.

First prescribed in the Book of Leviticus, it occurs every forty-nine years; the fiftieth year was a Jubilee when Hebrew slaves and prisoners would be freed, debts would be forgiven, care would be extended to the outcast and the mercies of Yahweh would be particularly manifest.

The Jubilee is that clean slate, the levelling of the playing field, the chance to begin again; it is a redistribution of wealth, of property; it is the interruption of the status quo. It is the dismantling of the things that keep people from being human. It is the freedom to return to your family, and the joy of resting in the givenness of God.

---

258 Luke 4:18–19.

I struggled this week to think about how all this fits into a practice of meditation because my heart kept going to Sargodha and wondering whether anything had changed, whether they had any sort of Jubilee. A great reset, so that all the children could enjoy the basics.

Instead of making links with meditation, I found myself Googling maps and images of those little roads and places, hoping to see some good news.

I read some good news stories of hope here and there, but there was still so much poverty and violence.

I thought about Br Walter, a human being who has inspired me, and how the little school he helped start has grown and continues to give an education to the poorest of poor, both Muslim and Christian, in that place.

I read about one young woman, Meerba, who went to that school and was about to enter a medical college. She spends her evenings tutoring over 200 children a week in basic literacy and numeracy. I felt some jubilation reading her story and sensed the Christlikeness of her heart.

So, what has this all to do with meditation?

Well, perhaps a possible way of viewing the practice of meditation is as a time of inner reset. An inner reset that makes possible a Jubilee.

Meditation as a prayer practice helps us to let go of old thinking that keeps us shackled to selfishness and self-preoccupation.

We dismantle rigid patterns that keep us in conflict. One must leave self behind and return to God.

It is a time to just let go, to leave fallow the mind and the heart so that one can begin to forgive and open oneself to God's abounding mercy.

We all need this liberation, this release, this recovery of clarity and freedom.

Meditation is a practice of cleaning the slate to begin again, every breath, new life, breathing as a practice of jubilation.

Breathing in the Spirit of God that teaches us who Christ is and transforms us into new Christs so that we too can bring good news to the poor!

FOURTH SUNDAY AFTER EPIPHANY (YEAR C)
Luke 4:20–30

Seeing in the Dark

BY PAUL WOOD

I had only just turned six when I was sent away to boarding school, and there, I learned how to be a naughty boy—but a harmless one! I learned how to sneak out of the dormitory at night and explore the empty school buildings in the dark, across the playing fields, down the orchard, or have a swim, but always avoided the cemetery! In those days, we didn't leave lights on at night, and as the school was out in the Rhodesian bush, if the light of the moon or stars was hidden behind clouds, it could be very, very dark. One thing I learned when very young was how to see in the dark, and I discovered that if you look directly at what you want to see, then you will not see it, but if you see with your peripheral vision, not looking directly at what you want to look at, but rather, seeing out of the edges of your eyes, so to speak, then you can see enough to navigate successfully.

(Of course, I need to reflect on how that behaviour relates to my psychology, why I did it as a little boy but also what effect it has had on my ongoing life. But that's all my business, and it is something that I reflect on.) Nonetheless, I do think this is a very good metaphor for the spiritual life. Where one navigates not as if one is in broad daylight. If one is too sure of oneself, if one only looks directly, too literally, too intently, too assuredly, then one might miss the point all together! One must pay attention to what is in the margins and on the edges, where there are doubts and uncertainty and strange happenings, those places on ancient maps that are inhabited by sea monsters, dragons and other strange creatures.

You see, isn't it interesting that instead of all the sincere religious men and scholars of the Law who studied the prophecies of the coming Messiah, it was some uneducated shepherds living close to nature (who don't have PhDs!) living on the peripherals of the towns who were the only ones who came to see the Christ Child!

How is that?

And who would have thought that the Magi, who came from a strange land and a foreign culture that was outside the covenant of God, pagans who studied the stars of all things, would be the only ones to come and worship the Christ Child! Why wasn't it the religious leaders and teachers of the covenant of Moses?

This seems to be a pattern that repeats time and again in the Scriptures. 'He came to what was his own, and his own people did not accept him.'[259] The very ones who should be able to see are the very ones who are blind. At one point, Jesus says in desperation to the Pharisees, 'the tax collectors and the prostitutes are going into the kingdom of God ahead of you … and even after you saw it, you did not change your minds and believe him.'[260] And again: 'You search the Scriptures because you think that in them you have eternal life; and it is they that testify on my behalf. Yet you refuse to come to me to have life.'[261] There is a very long history of very earnest and serious religious people missing the presence of Christ, whereas those who are seemingly on the outside, those living on the peripherals, actually 'get it!'

I suspect the reason is something like this. God, by definition, is outside of the box of our expectations, outside of the box of our control and over the horizon of our ego awareness, and so, if we try to fit God into the box of our consciousness, into what we already know, then the chance is that we will get it wrong!

And the whole task of meditation is about letting go of what we know, our fixations and familiar tram tracks, and attending to that which is other than what we normally are, that which is outside, outside of our conceptualisations.

Come, Lord Jesus!

Maranatha—Come Lord!

One image that I carry is of sitting and looking out to sea, sitting at the edge of consciousness, looking beyond, to the distant the horizon, over there, expectant of Christ's return.

Come Lord Jesus!

Maranatha

But really, meditation is not about the mind; we try and still that, but rather, it is about the heart.

It's about the orientation of the heart.

A heart that is open, receptive and attentive

For when God acts, God will always be a surprise.

For Christ will come when we least expect and from somewhere we do not know.

Maranatha.

We wait—we sit.

Still: still in body, still in mind, but with an open, receptive heart.

Maranatha.

---

259   John 1:11.
260   Matt. 21:31–32.
261   John 5:39–40.

FIFTH SUNDAY AFTER EPIPHANY (YEAR C)
Luke 5:1–11

Put Out into Deep Water

BY MICHELLE WOOD

> *The sea was a choppy dark blue, the sky pale, with a smooth gleaming buff-coloured cloud just above the horizon like a long tatter of silk … I began to study the sea … I searched the restless, white-flecked surface with an increasing anxiety, realizing that what I was now looking for and expecting momently to behold was my snake-necked sea monster.*[262]

The sea is often used as a symbol of the unconscious because we see its vast surface but not what is underneath. Silent meditation is a prayer practice about going underneath. You even feel that somewhat as you close your eyes. The bright lights of the surface fade, and we are in the dark.

Sometimes sitting with ourselves in silence can feel like waiting for our very own snake-necked sea monster to appear. Once, someone said to me that they could never meditate because they might discover something scary lurking in the silent depths of their mind, like a sea monster.

But for Swiss psychologist Carl Jung, 'The sea was his favourite symbol for the unconscious, representing the mother of all that lives.'[263] He wrote: 'like the sea itself, the unconscious yields an endless and self-replenishing abundance of creatures, a wealth beyond our fathoming'.[264]

In tonight's sacred story, Jesus is in a boat on the Sea of Galilee and instructs Simon Peter to 'Put out into the deep water and let down your nets for a catch.'[265]

For Simon Peter and the fishermen of the day, going out into the deep water was a terrifying invitation. The sea in ancient culture was that place where death and sea monsters like the leviathan lurked.

But deep water is a space of God's mysterious creativity. It is primal. In Genesis, we are told, 'In the beginning when God created the heavens and the

---

262 Iris Murdoch, *The Sea, the Sea* (London: Chatto & Windus, 1973), 266.
263 S. B. Parker, 'Carl Jung: The Sea and the Unconscious,' Jung Currents, 30 January 2022, http://jungcurrents.com/jung-sea-unconscious.
264 C. G. Jung, 'Psychology of the Transference', in *The Collected Works of C. G. Jung*, vol. 16, *The Practice of Psychotherapy: Essays on the Psychology of the Transference and Other Subjects*, 2nd ed. (London: Routledge and Kegan Paul, 1946), 177.
265 Luke 5:4.

earth, the earth was a formless void and darkness covered the face of deep, while a wind from God swept over the face of the waters.'[266]

The Spirit moves over the waters, and it is from the waters that God brings forth swarms of living creatures.

Going out into the deep water is about not only facing our fears but also opening to the creative, unfathomable, swirling of God within us.

For what looks empty and scary on the surface is plentiful underneath. The call is to go deep and let down one's net. To not be afraid.

Letting down one's net in meditation practice could be akin to following one's breath into the depths, or one's mantra or prayer word. A tool that combs through the silence like a net through the sea.

After the bell dings, our meditation net fills with so much in any one moment, from fishy thoughts that need to be cast away to fragments of pirates' gold.

We sit in the deep, listening and resting in the givenness of God. This is our practice.

From time to time, we may get momentary glimpses of our own sea monsters that make us want to fall on our knees and cry out like Simon Peter, 'Go away from me, Lord, for I am a sinful … !'[267]

Whatever happens as we push on into the deep water, we are invited by Christ to not be afraid. In our little meditation boat, our vehicle of discovery, we proceed in faith with a sense that Christ is always with us, cheering us on like an eager grandfather who can't wait for us to catch something real! He yearns for us to catch so much that our nets might break![268]

SIXTH SUNDAY AFTER EPIPHANY (YEAR C)
Luke 6:17–26

The Silence of the Beginning
BY PAUL WOOD

Our gospel reading is the Sermon on the Plain when Jesus gives a series of blessings and a series of woes, and so, I would like to begin by reminding ourselves about the power of words.

Words of blessing and words of woe.

Words can give life, and words can tear it down.

---

266   Gen. 1:1–2.
267   Luke 5:8.
268   Luke 5:6.

There is a story of the engineer and the Christian philosopher gazing at a magnificent building. The engineer is thinking, 'How many bricks are in this, how much cement and tons of concrete, and how many trees were cut down and sawn into logs and planks that were needed to build such a wonderful construction?' The Christian philosopher, he's not thinking about bricks, he is thinking about words: 'How many words did it take to build such a wonderful building?' Words that name things, words strung into sentences, making concepts, meanings, explanations, communication and plans, ordering this and ordering that—this beautiful building could not have been constructed without a lot of words—impossible!

Words—they have real power and they create realities.

Remember, in our Christian narrative God created the universe through words!

'Let there be light!'

'Let dry land appear'.

Ordering this and naming that, creating distinctions and then blessing it all as good.

So also, the prophets of the Old Testament moulded the children of Israel into shape through words, 'Thus says the Lord', they cried, and so they moulded the nation into God's children.

Words have power, which is why blessings work and good words produce life-giving results.

But similarly, because we live in a fallen universe, this is how curses work also. A curse brings destruction and destroys what is life-giving.

Words matter—like the ripples made by a pebble thrown into a pond, the ripples made by spoken words go out into space—but also up through time, and so, our words will affect future generations. It matters what we say and how we speak.

This is the gospel, the good news, the good spell, the ευαγγελιον

Now if we accept the reality of the power of words, we will also know that we are the embodiment of all the words spoken to us. That our souls are like an echo chamber that have captured every word spoken to us—even the first words from our childhood still echo around inside. And so, we carry within our souls many blessings and many woes that affect us for better and for worse.

Which is why we can look on with great concern as we see teenagers caught up in a sea of flattery and insults unleashed by social media.

We recognise that these blessings and curses flow all around us, but the thing about meditation is that it is a detox from words; meditation is to cleanse us from the clutter of words!

Remember, our Christian narrative does not begin with the word. It begins with the silence before the word.

'In the beginning when God created the heavens and the earth, the earth was a formless void and darkness covered the face of the deep, while a wind from God swept over the face of the waters.'[269]

All this was before the first words, 'Let there be light.'

When we meditate, we enter into a place in the Christian narrative that precedes the word, the place of the silence of the beginning.

A place of emptiness,

A place where the Spirit of God gently brushes over the waters.

And the wonderful thing about being in this place of emptiness is that the next thing that happens must be, by definition, an act of God, because nothing else exists yet—what comes into being is, therefore, pristine and fresh.

In meditation, we stive to enter into the stillness, into silence, into the emptiness, before the first word, so that we can become aware of that which is new, pristine and fresh and that which is life-giving and from God.

So, let us meditate, and let us enter the place before words.

Let us close our eyes, let us become silent.

Let us become still: in body and also in the mind.

Except for our breathing, the spirit of life flows in and out of its own accord.

And here we sit in emptiness.

You may use a simple prayer phrase to bring your active and moving mind to heel. If you use the word *maranatha*, say it steadily in four equal syllables: *ma-ra-na-tha*.

Stillness, simplicity, emptiness: for twenty minutes.

SEVENTH SUNDAY AFTER EPIPHANY (YEAR C)
Luke 6:27–36

Mercy and the Moulin Rouge
BY MICHELLE WOOD

I went to the Moulin Rouge the other week with my two daughters. We got all dressed up and headed down Collins Street to the Regent Theatre in Melbourne. On the way, a man stopped us, a hunched-over little man carrying a heavy cloth sack and with a long dark beard like Rasputin's. He asked politely if we had any money because he needed to find some accommodation to do his washing.

The three of us immediately started rummaging through our bags and purses, while the patiently waiting man told us about his struggles. Since ours

---

[269] Gen. 1:1–3.

is such a cashless society, my eldest daughter and I only had a purse full of useless plastic. But my youngest daughter, who has just finished university and has not yet started in her first job, pulled out a fifty-dollar note from her mobile phone case. The man recoiled and said, 'I can't take that. I am just grateful that you have listened to me.' But she gently insisted and said kindly, 'No, it's ok, please have it.'

He smiled a dignified smile, offered his thanks and proceeded on his way.

My eldest daughter turned and said to her younger sister, 'That is a lot of money to give away, Clara, it is better to buy food.' But she just replied, 'Oh look at us, we have everything, and we are going out together … I don't care what he chooses to spend the money on if it brings him some happiness. I don't need to judge.'

We knew she was right, and we loved her all the more for it.

She has the gift of mercy.

In this week's sacred story, we are instructed to:

Be merciful, just as your Father is merciful.[270]

In the practice of silent meditation, we are sitting in the mercy of God.

I wonder how you sense the mercy of God.

Scriptures depict it in four words: *hesed, rahamim, hanan* and *oiktirmos*.

Hesed reflects a profound sense of goodness and is love in action. It is to do with loyalty and relational bonds. Like God's love conversation with the people of Israel throughout the Old Testament.

God's mercy is hesed, love in action; it is faithful but can be broken.

When mercy ceases to be judicial, it flowers into this even more beautiful word, *rahamim*.

Pope John Paul II wrote when unpacking God's mercy, '*rahamim*, in its very root, denotes the love of a mother (rehem = mother's womb). It reflects a deep and original bond—indeed the unity—that links a mother to her child there springs a particular relationship to the child, a particular love.'[271]

It is completely gratuitous, not merited and from the heart.

God's mercy is rahamim, like a mother's womb.

Ever-widening God's mercy is also *hanan*, a constant predisposition to be generous, benevolent and merciful. St Augustine wrote that it is easier for God to withhold anger than mercy. Just like it is impossible for the sun to hold back its rays of light.

God's mercy is hanan, a constant, generous flow of goodness.

In this week's sacred story, we are instructed to:

---

270   Luke 6:36.
271   Francis. *Misericordiae Vultus Bull of Indiction of the Extraordinary Jubilee of Mercy*, 12 February 2022, https://www.vatican.va/content/francesco/en/apost_letters/documents/papa-francesco_bolla_20150411_misericordiae-vultus.html.

Be merciful, just as your Father is merciful.[272]
In Greek, the language of the New Testament:
Be *oiktirmos*, just as your father is *oiktirmos*.

While the Greek word is translated into English as mercy, it is important to remember, as Pope John Paul II points out, that the New Testament builds upon the wealth and depth that already marked the Old.

What is interesting is that in the Old Testament the quality of mercy is only ever ascribed to God; however, in the New Testament, Jesus, the human face of God, impels us all to grow in this capacity.

So, if the full semantic reach of the translations of mercy are gathered, it is quite a magnificent mercy that we are called to be:

> *Be deeply compassionate as your Father is compassionate.*
> *Be profoundly good,*
> *be love in action,*
> *be a womb of love,*
> *be a source of indiscriminate goodness,*
> *be an outpouring, a generous flow of grace.*
> *Be merciful as your Father is merciful.*
> *Feel it within you and be it in the world.*
> *In this time of silent meditation, may you be blessed by God's mercy.*

EIGHT SUNDAY AFTER EPIPHANY (YEAR C)
Luke 6:27–36

Love Your Enemies, How…?
BY MICHELLE WOOD

To access kindness and mercy in times when you feel angry, betrayed and hurt is extremely difficult. It's one thing to say,

> *Love your enemies; do good to those who hate you; bless those who curse you; pray for those who mistreat you.*[273]

But how do we actually do it? When people are hurtful and hateful towards us or those whom we love, two of the strongest human emotions—anger and fear—are set off like firecrackers.

---

272 Luke 6:36.
273 Luke 6:27–28.

In the 1960s, the Black American writer James Baldwin wrote a letter to his nephew, eloquently expressing why love is necessary:

> *There is no reason for you to try to become like white people and there is no basis whatever for their impertinent assumption that they must accept you. The terrible thing, old buddy, is that you must accept them. And I mean that very seriously. You must accept them and accept them with love. For these innocent people have no other hope. They are, in effect, still trapped in a history which they do not understand; and until they understand it, they cannot be released from it. They have had to believe for many years, and for innumerable reasons, that black men are inferior to white men. Many of them, indeed, know better, but, as you will discover, people find it very difficult to act on what they know.*[274]

To love one's enemy is a compelling and beautiful ideal, but what can an ordinary person do to prepare themselves and their psychology to live a life of love and mercy? It will require more than pronouncements from pulpits or listening to literature. It is very difficult to stay centred in love when someone is violating your family and culture or slyly ruining your reputation from the edges, like a thief whose fingerprints are barely seen. When anger, righteousness and retaliation burn hot, how do we stay loving and generous? And how might the regular practice of silent meditation benefit us at these times?

In my own life, I have been trying to cool and heal an experience where someone wronged me. Their actions robbed me of something very precious. And I am sure each of us can recall such an experience. At first, when I experienced the other person's actions, I didn't really understand what had happened. I was driven to think about it—a lot. I was consumed by it, going over and over it in my head. How could they have done this to me? Why? What kind of person does this? They don't even know me. How could they say such things about me? This person is a liar, hypocritical, out to feather their own nest. They can't be trusted. How do they sleep at night?

On and on this chatter went, flaming my passions, raising the temperature. So much so, that if this person's name was mentioned, it had a palpable effect on me: I could feel instant anxious heat in my body, and my own stubborn indignation rose. Needless to say, this is a tortuous place to live from. In reality, this person was not even a part of my day-to-day life. But still, their presence loomed like a dark thunderstorm about to break.

And even though I know all too well the teaching, 'Love your enemies, do good to those who mistreat you', I couldn't access it in any meaningful way. I was struggling.

---

274 James Baldwin, *The Fire Next Time* (London: Penguin Random House, 2017), 16–17.

So, I decided to do a little self-experiment regarding the practice of silent meditation (and other forms of prayer) to notice if these might assist me. I noted that it was easier for me to pray for this person and their wellbeing than it was to be free of the negative emotional effects that I felt their actions had on my life. Perhaps my prayers were a shallow dish of offering rather than a deep heartfelt well. Perhaps they reflected a conceptual response out of the 'right ethic' in my head, but I noticed that my heart had not really caught up. If you are to live love, kindness, generosity and mercy, your heart space or spaciousness is vital.

The practice of silent meditation is one of purifying the heart. It is a practice of meeting the irritants of our lives and making space for them. Above all, it is an altar of truthfulness. We can hide many unacceptable parts of ourselves from others, and everyone does, but when we sit in silence in the presence of God, we are truly naked. The deeper we go on this journey, the more awareness we have of our nakedness. Although this may be daunting, it is accompanied by our awareness of the mercy and kindness of God.

Silent meditation is a practice of cooling the passions of anger. It is like a shady quiet forest filled with dappled light. It allows for release and relief from the thinking mind and inflamed emotions. It helps us to return to our centre of being, a Christlike fulcrum where there is an ease of being. Through a return to this centre, this source, and cultivation of this peace, we gain an increased capacity for clear seeing and wise reflection.

The period after silent meditation is a good time to contemplate our blockages to love, kindness and mercy. We can analyse situations where we feel stuck and ask: what is really going on here? Why does this person wind me up? What is this all about? What situations does this incident reflect in my wider life and histories that enable it to have so much energy and power? We may feel that we don't really have enemies or that we don't want to murder anyone, but what about our tendencies to think unkind thoughts, say unkind things, fly off the handle or make excuses for our heatedness, voice-raising and intolerance. We all need wise guidance and cooling practices to help us move towards loving our enemies.

For our work on improvement, I gained some wise advice from a great Buddhist teacher, Luang Por Munindo:

1. Contemplate past situations with coolness and wise reflection.
2. Because the same situation will come up again, get some plans to try ahead of time: be predictive.
3. If, in the situation, the heat of anger rises, contain the heat. Don't let it spill out into words or actions. Just notice it, make room for it and care for it. Ask questions about it—what is this energy?

4. Endure it—push your tongue up to your mouth and grit your teeth. Don't act; don't fuel. It will pass.
5. This ability to deal with your internal obstructions of peace doesn't just happen overnight. Trust the teachings.[275]

I end this reflection by returning to this week's teachings by Jesus,

But I say to you who are listening: Love your enemies; do good to those who hate you; bless those who curse you; pray for those who mistreat you. If anyone strikes you on the cheek, offer the other also, and from anyone who takes away your coat do not withhold even your shirt. ³⁰ Give to everyone who asks of you, and if anyone takes away what is yours, do not ask for it back again. ³¹ Do to others as you would have them do to you… be children of the Most High, for he himself is kind to the ungrateful and the wicked. ³⁶ Be merciful, just as your Father is merciful.[276]

PS. Although I am still a work in progress, the gift of silent meditation practice has been invaluable for equipping me with a real path towards these most profound teachings of Jesus.

LAST SUNDAY AFTER EPIPHANY (YEAR C)
Luke 9:28–36

A Cloud of Grace
BY PAUL WOOD

I would like to start with some random thoughts about veils and coverings.

It is interesting to trace this narrative in the Bible. Clothes are not about keeping you warm as much as they are about covering your nakedness. This narrative ranges from the Garden of Eden, where Adam and Eve were naked and unashamed,[277] to their using fig leaves to cover their shame[278] and then to their using skins, for which an animal had to die to cover their shame.[279] This theme of the shame of nakedness develops further with Noah's drunken nakedness and how Shem and Japheth covered their father's shame.[280] It is

---

275 Luang Por Munindo, 'Meeting our Anger', audio recording, 1 January 2001, https://ratanagiri.org.uk/teachings/talks/meeting-our-anger.
276 Luke 6:27–31, 36.
277 Gen. 2:25.
278 Gen. 3:7–11.
279 Gen. 3:21.
280 Gen. 9:20–27.

interesting to note that one of the Hebrew words for 'forgiveness' also means 'to cover' *(kaphar)*, because when you forgive someone you choose not to look on their exposed shame, but instead, you cover them. It is an act of grace. You can trace this narrative of covering all the way through the Old Testament up to St Paul in the New Testament, who explains how the 'righteousness of God' is imputed onto us as a gift, and onto the Book of Revelation where a great multitude of the redeemed are clothed in robes of white.

Perhaps, this may be a good lens to understand one major difference between the Greek and the Hebrew cultures. Greeks glorified the human physique and celebrated nakedness, but the Hebrews covered it. Christianity is in some ways an amalgamation of both these cultures.

I suggest a parallel narrative to this story of covering is the story about how God is veiled. No one has ever seen God. When Moses went up the mountain to commune with God, he was enveloped by the cloud and the darkness. The cloud is God's veil, and it exists for our own protection. For without the cloud, God would be too much for us: our conscience could not stand it. It is like trying to look into the sun—to stand before the face of infinite goodness would mean that we would be destroyed by our own shame.

And so, the cloud that veils God is there for our protection. And the deeper we venture into God, the more our normal understanding mind is confounded in the cloud and we cannot see.

But the thing is this—you cannot see in the cloud—but you can still hear! You can still hear the narrative even though you cannot see the path. Remember, God's voice comes from out of the cloud.

I have heard it said that the Greek way of knowing is related to the eye, what you can see and observe, whereas the Hebrew way of knowing is related to the ear, and what you can hear, understand and be faithful to. Perhaps this also describes some of the differences between science and religion. Two pathways and two different kinds of knowledge. And Christianity amalgamates both.

This Sunday, the gospel story is the story of the Transfiguration of Jesus up the mountain.

Let us remember that when we meditate, we also have to climb a mountain, for not only must we untangle ourselves from the hustle and bustle of the world and find a lonely spot to pray in secret, but we must also rise higher, to a higher plane of consciousness, which is more spacious and from where we can see further.

As we rise to such a place, we too may realise that we are in communion with other great people, such as Moses or Elijah, who also went up a mountain to commune with God.

But then comes the cloud, and as the disciples enter the cloud and are enveloped in it, there is initial confusion over Moses and Elijah, until there is the voice out of the cloud that says, 'This is my beloved Son, listen to him.'

Suddenly, this voice changes the narrative. Jesus is not subject to Moses or Elijah, he is not even their equal, no he is above all—the Christ, the eternal Son of God—listen to him.

Clarity comes through the voice: the narrative makes sense of the experience.

So let us now meditate where perhaps we may enter a kind of cloud, where seeing with the understanding of our everyday mind is not the important thing, but rather, it is important to listen with the heart and be open, receptive and faithful to the narrative coming from the invisible, ever-present Creator.

Lent (Year C)

FIRST SUNDAY IN LENT (YEAR C)
Luke 3:21–22, 4:1–12

The Beloved in the Wilderness
BY MICHELLE WOOD

The opening to this most holy season of Lent is the story of Jesus and the temptations in the wilderness.

We know that when it comes to narratives about the temptation of Jesus, some fundamentalist Christians love to speak about spiritual warfare with Satan, how sinful we are and how the world and women are evil tempters. They love to invoke fear and battle metaphors, terrorising our minds as Putin is terrorising Ukraine, but I would like to do something different.

I would like to explore the temptation of Jesus narrative within the frame of Jesus being called the *beloved of God* and link this with my explorations of the works of priest and mystic poet Thomas Traherne.

To set the scene, it is important to underscore that this time of deep prayer and solitude in the wilderness is directly after God names Jesus as 'my son the beloved'.

And perhaps Jesus' whole time of wandering in the wilderness was about coming to terms with what it means *to be the beloved of God.*

Jesus, the wandering beloved, goes into the wilderness, deeper into God's love, and the clearer the refusal of anything less becomes.

Jesus, the beloved, goes deeper into God's love, and fear falls away.

Jesus, the beloved, goes further away from the world deeper into the wilderness, into the singularity of God's love, and the ways of this world seem empty—full of froth and bubble.

English priest and seventeenth-century mystic poet Thomas Traherne, himself a wanderer, wanders into a spiritual wilderness that he names interior Beauty (he capitalises the 'B' as we do God). He speaks of getting there via the way of gentle peace and love. And when there,

> *the Sea itself floweth in your veins*
> *… your spirit filleth the whole world, and the stars are your jewels;*

> *... you are as familiar with the ways of God in*
> *All Ages as with your walk and table.*[281]

I wonder whether it could be that what Jesus did in wandering in the wilderness under the starry sky was to incarnate the sweetness of what it is to be the beloved of God.

I poetically imagine the stars of Abraham falling on his chest and breaking open his heart, him walking the paths like Moses on the lookout for a burning bush, in the footsteps of Elijah, towards that still small voice of calm.

Jesus, the wandering beloved, is experiencing what it is to take full and complete refuge in God.

> *To not fear the terror of the night,*
> *or the arrow that flies by day,*
> *or the pestilence that stalks in darkness,*
> *or the destruction that wastes at noonday.*[282]

He is incarnating how a human being can come to know such love so that he can teach us.

From being rooted in the love of God, he is able to blow the temptation questions away with the ease with which we blow a dandelion head.

Jesus knows the ancient stories: how the people of Israel did not put their trust in God, did not rest in God's love, grasped after cheap temporal assurance from the world and were quick to construct idols.

This is still what we humans do—but are desperately dissatisfied with.

Jesus, our teacher, points us towards our true identity as beloveds of God, in a world of great beauty and blessed with goodness.

Thomas Traherne believed we have a world of love inside us that is conveyed through invisible things that touch our soul and that we need to tend.[283]

Just recently, in my garden I felt the invisible ways that such things touch our souls in a fleeting moment and wrote:

> *Tea in a quiet garden*
> *Ant feet are silent and doves coo*
> *Cradling a yellow milk jug*
> *Under bulbous magenta crepe myrtle*
> *Hands of rhubarb wave, Hello!*

---

281 Thomas Traherne, *Centuries of Meditations* (London, 1908), verse 29, https://www.ccel.org/ccel/traherne/centuries.i_1.html.
282 Ps. 91:5–7.
283 Thomas Traherne, *Centuries of Meditations*.

Often, there are sweet moments of ecstasy and love in our spiritual wilderness wanderings. The practice of silent meditation attunes us to them. It teaches the way of quiet observation, a feeling with what is unfolding around us, a way of experiencing God's love.

When we practice the prayer of silent meditation, we take refuge in God's love. We return to the centre of who we are: God's beloved in a world created out of love and for love.

SECOND SUNDAY IN LENT (YEAR C)
Luke 13:31–35

Jerusalem, Jerusalem
BY PAUL WOOD

Jesus laments, 'Jerusalem, Jerusalem, the city that kills the prophets and stones those who are sent to it! How often have I desired to gather your children together as a hen gathers her brood under her wings, and you were not willing!'[284]

His lament over Jerusalem is a sad reading, and it leaves me thinking about other places where there is conflict and the narratives in the endless meaning-making of human beings, who squabble over identities and names, histories and narratives, meanings and words. The long conflict over Jerusalem is not about something necessary, like food, no, it is about histories and identities, it's about stories and meanings.

Medieval maps placed Jerusalem in the centre of the world—such was her importance. A Jew had to face in the direction of Jerusalem when praying, and the Christian who had to face east to pray also had to turn towards Jerusalem and the rising Son.

There is no piece of real estate on the planet that is so filled with sacred importance to Christians, Jews and Muslims. It has been the site of so much argument but also bloodshed and violence.

And the strange thing is that its name is all about peace.

Salem = shalom, peace, completeness, wholeness

We encounter the name first in the Bible when Melchizedek, the King of Salem, shares bread and wine with Abraham.

Salem = Shalom, City of Peace

And the *Jeru* part seems to say, 'they will see awe'.

---

284 Luke 13:34.

What a powerful name! Seeing awe and being peace.//
It's a great vision—but she doesn't live up to it!

Oh Jerusalem, Jerusalem, oh vision of peace, you who kill the prophets and stone those who are sent to you.

So, my thoughts are:

Why do things become so easily the opposite of what they claim to be?

Why do we have such contradictions?

I see a Church that claims certain things but then does not do them—and is often blind to its own behaviour—and it makes us very angry.

I see it in secular politics also,

and I see the same in myself!

Contradictions.

Why? What is going on?

It's the nature of things. Words have shadows. The moment something is named, other things are not named, and so, the opposite is created and there is division.

If you call one thing 'good', then all the other things are 'not good'.

Not just names, but whole narratives and histories, they all have shadows,

and for every story there is always another story.

That's why the mind can never rest.

The nature of mind is that it is divided.

Good/bad, light/darkness, yes/no,

is it this or is it that?

Forever restless

until it comes to the gospel of grace,

because grace comes from a place deeper than the mind, the place of language and thoughts.

For it comes from the primal wilderness, which is before words, before thoughts.

It comes from the place of heart, the place of the centre.

And the gospel of grace comes from out of the wilderness.

Before Jesus began teaching and healing,

the first thing he did was to go out into the wilderness.

Away from the world of conflict and woe,

to a place of solitude

and a place of intimacy

with himself—and also his Heavenly Father

So, let us meditate now,

close the door to the battles of the mind and the opinions of the world

and 'Close the door' as Jesus teaches.

And pray to our Heavenly Father in secret.
In secret our Heavenly Father will reward us.
For just twenty minutes,
let us enter into that place that is before words,
into the wilderness of silence,
into the wilderness of stillness.
At the heart there are no words: just stillness,
a place of vast emptiness
where the only thing that moves is the wind,
and the breath.
It's ok! We will come back to the land of thoughts.
But not for twenty minutes—let us be in the wilderness.
Let's forget Jerusalem, forget Ukraine, forget the kids, forget our work!
Letting go of that restless, fluid mind,
forget the histories, and the stories, excuses and explanations.
And sink deeper
into the place of heart.
And come into the wilderness,
to the rocky ground avoided by so many.
And hear the emptiness of the air.
And see the radiance night sky.
And know that we, humans are made of the dust of the ground and formed into the image of God.

THIRD SUNDAY IN LENT (YEAR C)
Luke 13:6–9

The Secret Life Within
BY PAUL WOOD

I have been thinking about organic growth.

When you build a house, you construct it from the outside; it grows but that is because some outside agent is building it.

But organic growth grows of itself from the inside out and there is no external agent.

When you make a car, you build it from the outside in.

But in organic growth, all living things grow from the inside out.

And organic growth is a great mystery.

The Gospel of Mark says it like this: 'The kingdom of God is as if someone would scatter seed on the ground and would sleep and rise night and day, and the seed would sprout and grow, he does not know how. The earth produces of itself first the stalk, then the head, then the full grain in the head.'[285]

Organic growth is slow, silent and emerges from the inside, in secret.

Now it seems to me that the popular way of thinking about God is often as an outside agent who works on the world from the outside, and perhaps this is understandable when we speak of the Almighty God as creating through the word of command, creating through fiat; but thank goodness for the doctrine of the Trinity that also speaks of God as breath, the Spirit, breathed into every living creature and so creating living souls.

Living growth comes from the inside and it reaches outwards, upwards.

I like to think of the whole process of inside-outside as simply God speaking to God. The spirit is yearning through us to God beyond us and so we are caught up in the life of the Trinity. God speaking with God.

Now the Bible often speaks about organic growth, for example, when referring to the growth of knowledge, or a dynasty or a nation—it grows by itself like a vine or like a tree.

So, Israel is called forth from out of the earth and grows into a mighty nation, but like all forms of life, she struggles to survive through the seasons, some branches are cut off, new shoots appear and the growth continues so long as it is not uprooted.

When Jesus condemns the fig tree, it is because he sees a nation and a religion full of leaves showing off its works of the Law, but not fulfilling its divine purpose by having fruit. All works and no fruit, all work but no nourishment. The significance of fruit is that it is for the next generation; fruit is never for the benefit of the current growth but always for the benefit of something other than itself—whether it be sprouting another life after its own kind or simply being nourishment for others.

And Jesus sees a religion that is displaying proudly its leaves (works of the Law) but producing no fruit and see such growth as wasteful and condemns it accordingly.

In the gospel this weekend, Jesus recommends withholding judgement, giving time and a bit of care, digging around it and giving it a bit of manure, so that the tree can find its created purpose and produce fruit.

So, let us meditate and let us care for ourselves and our growth and come back to the idea of organic growth, which grows out of itself, from out of the silence and the secrecy of the inside.

---

285   Mark 4:26–28.

Let us gently close the door on the outside world and enter the secrecy of our own inner lives with God. Let us allow our consciousness to observe how our secret life has grown all by itself, without the push and shove of ego control.

Observe this life:

- How curious is it?
- Allow it to be.
- Be kind to it, dig around it and maybe give it manure—but let it be—for, in time, it will produce fruit after its own kind for the nourishment of others.

FOURTH SUNDAY IN LENT (YEAR C)
Luke 15:11–32

All That Is Mine Is Yours
BY MICHELLE WOOD

This week's reading is about the prodigal son and his brother. The story of a wasteful, lavish, dissolute, oversexed son and his responsible, dutiful, hardworking, loyal brother. Jesus tells this story in response to a crowd that has gathered around him.

A crowd that consists of upright, law-abiding Pharisees: learned, earnest, rigid and righteous 'men' and sinners—fallen women, tax collectors, prostitutes, adulterers, drunkards, addicts, people caught up in the ways of the world, in the afflictions of desires, in the demons of excess, and out-of-control outcasts, those tainted and shunned by the superior few.

You could almost imagine him looking out over this sea of faces and thinking what kind of story could bring such people so divided and limited in their sense of the abundant goodness and compassion of God to further awareness.

So, he takes a breath and tells a seemingly simple story with insights into the nature of God and how we as humans can bring into union our dualistic and contradictory tendencies. A tale that we as humans will be able to tell until the end of time.

'There was a man who had two sons.'[286]

---

286 Luke 15:11.

For us who are exploring the interior life, the way of paying attention, in the breaths between the plots of this story, we may notice that there is gradual growth in inner awareness that propels both sons towards God.

Both sons are at some distance from the father. Both are out of relationship and a long way off from the reality of their father's abundant compassion and desire to share all.

The prodigal son is a long way off because of his preoccupations with the external world. He travels to distant lands and is caught in the net of insatiable afflictions of desire.

The stay-at-home brother is a long way off because his internal world is full of anger, resentment, a sense of entrapment and jealousy.

We, like them, can be at a distance from God through external preoccupations or internal ones.

We can also enact a false sense of closeness to God by physically going to church or participating in some official ways but be at a distance because our hearts are clogged up with the poisons of anger, jealousy, bitterness and resentment.

Kind of like a marriage that someone stays in out of righteousness but, in doing so, poisons themselves and those around them with bitterness. It is a false strategy of closeness or doing the right thing.

In the story, the father has healing balm for both brothers. Drawing them both into intimacy by compassion. Enacted by an embrace, a kiss and some powerful words to soothe the sense of unfair displacement, he says, 'you are always with me, and all that is mine is yours'.[287]

In the prayer of silence, we are returning and staying with God so that we can feel this flow of compassion drawing us all into an intimacy, a primal gift.

You are always with me, and all that is mine is yours.

We trek inwards away from the distractions of the external world, *aware of our need* and our failings.

We trek further inwards, letting go of our thoughts and resentments towards a deeper reality.

As we enter the silence and begin our journey back to God, leaving behind the external world and its distractions and the internal world of thoughts, may we—

> *Come into to our inner room.*
> *Come into the reality of this moment.*
> *Let the silence carry us into the reconciling embrace of God.*

---

287   Luke 15:31.

If your mind drifts, anchor it to your breath and your prayer word: *maranatha* or the Jesus Prayer.

Come into the presence of the God who greets our anger, jealousies, fears and mistakes with a kiss.

Who is always there to welcome us.

Who declares with love,

> *All that is mine*
> *Is yours*

FIFTH SUNDAY IN LENT (YEAR C)
John 12:1–8

The Devotional Life
BY PAUL WOOD

When Michelle and I went to the Greek islands, we loved it so much. This is the way I remember it:

The dry summer landscape is sparse and rocky, and the mountain slopes are outcropped with villages of white houses stepping all the way down to the deep blue of the Mediterranean. This panorama stretches a far way off to the distant horizon and, up overhead, forming the huge sapphire sky-dome under which we dwell.

And under this dome, in among all the whitewashed houses, we walk the winding, narrow streets and occasionally come across an Orthodox Church. Its central dome is painted in a deep azure hue and everywhere is the echo of blue and white.

Entering the doors of the church is like visiting an art gallery devoted to spirituality. Inside the central dome, when we look up we see a huge image of Jesus Christ, the Word of God, the Logos, through whom the whole world is held together, gazing down upon us. Around the dome, there are numerous icons of the Apostles and saints.

And one realises that one has entered into a sacred place, a precious place, a place set apart to tell a grand narrative to live by, a narrative that stretches from eternity to eternity. It tells us who we are, where we have come from and to where we shall go after our short mortal span of time. It speaks of transcendence and of our belonging, and it speaks through the lavish and costly language of art and beauty.

It is not utilitarian, it is not practical, it does not produce anything, it is not a factory, it does not alleviate poverty, but what it does do is that it ennobles the human spirit, it invokes one to look higher, to look for something more. And although the making of beauty is costly, it nonetheless ennobles humanity, it lifts us up and transports our aspirations to a higher purpose and greater meanings.

I realised that here is a place of silent devotion that has come to us from the old world, the Byzantine world, when common people were not able to read and write, a time when the structure of faith was held together by small acts of religious devotion to this icon or that icon, rather than reading.

In among all this creative and costly beauty, a devout little lady dressed in widow's black comes limping in with her stick and approaches one of the many icons. She zooms out the sign of the Cross in two quick zigzags and leans forward to kiss the icon, as she has done thousands of times before.

What is her story, what is her connection? For here are stories of families, being born and dying, stories of lives lived, of ancestors, of saints and perhaps even of relics that connect living people organically back through time to when the Son of God walked upon the face of this earth.

And so, I ponder this world of religious beauty, and these acts of pious devotion that come from the old world. I ponder its place in our modern, enlightened, rationalistic, materialistic, stressed-out functional existence.

And I ponder: What is the function of beauty?

And: What is the point of devotion?

Does it teach us to touch the mystery of the transcendent?

Upon reflection, I think one of the wonderful things about the religious devotional life is that devotion is invoked freely, not by fear, nor need, nor conformity, nor by threat, but rather, devotion is invoked by beauty and by truth freely given.

I would hope that part of what we do when we meditate together in silence is that we share a quiet and simple devotion. A devotion to the beauty and truth of our Lord Jesus Christ, who calls forth from within us a higher consciousness and a nobler spirit. When we meditate, we put aside our restless earthly worries and open our hearts to the beauty of Christ, and we allow the mystery of our love to flow through ourselves, and so it returns to the source from whence it came.

And so let us now meditate.

And let us close our eyes and so close the door on the busy, noisy world outside,

let us become silent,

let us become still,

completely still, as still as a clay vessel,

and with open hearts,
and allow the fragrance of the perfume
to rise
like incense
before the one we love.

PASSION SUNDAY (YEAR C)
The Gardens of Eden, Gethsemane and Paradise
BY MICHELLE WOOD

We enter this Holy Week through the garden of autumn. The '*Season of mists and mellow fruitfulness*'[288] as described by the poet Keats. I spend a lot of time in my garden—sketching the latest growth bursts, writing a few lines of poetry, absorbing the sunshine, the colours, the breeze, smelling the butterfly bushes, under the canopy of blue, watching the shapes of the clouds. I can fully understand why Emily Dickinson wrote:

> *Some keep the Sabbath going to Church –*
> *I keep it staying at Home –*
> *With a bobolink for a Chorister –*
> *And an Orchard, for a Dome.*[289]

A garden, if we are lucky enough to have one, is an enclosed, protected space, away from the chores of the house or the work of the workplace. It is a place full of God—bursting forth from tiny ants to textured tree arms. In a garden, when drinking in its beauty and aliveness and contemplating the interrelationships between plants and animals, earth and sun, water and wind, bird and butterfly, bees and flowers, you can full appreciate the expression that after Creation, 'God saw that it was good.'[290]

At this time of year, we begin our trek through autumn where the maturing sun fills the 'fruit with ripeness and plumps the hazel shells'.[291]

We see the Easter story unfold all around us. The letting go and dying is beginning.

---

288 John Keats, 'To Autumn', Poetry Foundation, https://www.poetryfoundation.org/poems/44484/to-autumn.
289 Emily Dickinson, *The Poems of Emily Dickinson*, ed. R.W. Franklin (Cambridge: Belknap Press, 1998), 259.
290 Gen. 1:12
291 Keats, 'To Autumn'.

In the biblical drama of Creation, Fall and Redemption, the most central scenes are performed in gardens.

The Scriptures take us from primeval innocence and The Fall in the Garden of Eden, through to the travails in the Garden of Gethsemane, and finally, to our re-creation in the Garden of Paradise—the New Jerusalem.

The Garden of Eden in the Scriptures is God's first gift to humankind after the gift of life. And whenever we are in the beauty of God's Creation, we touch this narrative.

The Garden of Gethsemane is that place where Jesus comes to the edge of himself, in the dark of night. It is in this garden that he finds a quiet space to express his fears and pray to God. In the busy city of Jerusalem, he seeks a garden. And perhaps by being in the garden close to Creation, he is more able to entrust himself to the goodness of God.

The Garden of Paradise is the place of the pristine new when all has been healed.

The place 'where every tear will be wiped away and death will be no more'.[292] Where all living creatures and humankind will live in peace, cooperation and harmony.

So, as we prepare for this time of silent prayer, may we come into our own inner garden regardless of whether it feels more like Eden or Gethsemane, let us come into that place of beauty, safety and the presence of God.

---

292   Rev. 21:4

Easter (Year C)

EASTER SUNDAY (YEAR C)

The Resurrection Life: What Is It?
BY PAUL WOOD

The resurrection life—what is it?

We can think of this in three different ways:

First, there is the resurrection of Christ as told in the gospels, and I think the important thing to note is that Christ was not brought back from the dead, back to this world, in his familiar body, as this would be 'Resuscitation', but rather, Christ was transformed through death into a new bodily form that was not always recognisable and he could appear and disappear at will for forty days before he was gathered up into heaven. Now, how do we make sense of that? Rationally, factually, materialistically and scientifically?

Well, maybe we are still babies. Maybe in another ten or twenty thousand years, we will understand more of the secrets of existence and death. Why should we assume that our modern world has somehow peak understanding of the mysteries of death, and of space and time, and of consciousness, life, God and resurrection? I suspect there is much we do not yet understand but will discover in time—maybe we are still infants and only at the beginning of the great human journey.

So, first, though we cannot make sense of it yet, there is the bodily resurrection of Jesus as narrated in the gospels.

Second, there is the idea of the great resurrection harvest of all humanity at the end of time. Because Christ is the first fruits and we are the rest of the harvest. In the gathering up, each life lived is gathered up by the angels with sickles reaping the earth, and so, we are gathered into God and into a higher order of life, a new world.

Perhaps this is just the second great movement in the grand narrative of humanity—'we come from God and we return to God'. These are two great movements—entering in and gathering up. Just as one scoops water from out of the sea. We plunge into this world of experience and then are gathered up back into God.

Perhaps this is an accurate map for the whole of life; in the morning of life, we enter into Creation, discover, incarnate into this world, and in the afternoon, we begin to look up, learn to detach, learn to let go and gradually become translucent and gathered up and return to God.

So, the second way to view resurrection is that of the general resurrection of the whole of humanity.

But the third way of viewing resurrection is that it is not tied to something in past or the future, but rather, it is experiential now. Resurrection is not a narrative to believe in but rather an experience in the present moment.

As Jesus said, 'Very truly, I tell you, the hour is coming, and is now here, when the dead will hear the voice of the Son of God, and those who hear will live.'[293]

So, 'the hour is coming and is now here' when we can pass from death into life, now while in our current bodies, living in this world, before we physically die, and we can be awakened to a new consciousness, from darkness into light, from death into new life.

If Christ is the first fruits, it means that there is already a bit of humanity in the new world, there is already a part of us that belongs to eternity, that we are already connected to our resurrected future and already seated with Christ in heavenly places.

Perhaps this is the basis of our contemplation and our meditation in silence. That through silence, we are becoming more aware of that part of ourselves that is eternal, that part of ourselves that is already seated with Christ in the heavenly realm, that part of ourselves that has already overcome the sufferings and trials of this world, that part of ourselves that is already resting with Christ in the new world that is to come.

SECOND SUNDAY OF EASTER (YEAR C)
John 20:19–23

Resurrection from the Inside
BY PAUL WOOD

See meditation for Year A on page 41.

---

[293] John 5:25.

THIRD SUNDAY OF EASTER (YEAR C)
John 21:1–19

Boundless Love
BY MICHELLE WOOD

Johannine scholar Bruce Vater wrote, 'For the love of God is boundless, and who ever has truly received this revelation of love must love boundlessly in turn.'[294]

I often come home from work and say to Paul, 'I love the people I am counselling. I love all of them.'

Even the trickiest. I am thinking in particular of a twenty-four-year-old man who has participated in some horrendous violence—he has broken people's bones and has held a man at knifepoint and watched him wet himself in front of two small children—he has done some terrible things.

But he sits before me lost, lonely, incredibly sad, guilt-ridden, remorseful and vulnerable, but trying to make a new path. Initially, I ask myself when I meet him in these stories:

Can I love him?

Can I keep going with him despite my recoiling?

Can I access some deeper part of this boundless love revelation to hang in there for some sort of healing not only for him but also for myself and others, for we all live in a world where we are at the mercy of such forces?

How does the practice of silent meditation help anchor me in faithfulness to boundless love? So that I can truly care for, tend to and feed the other?

One thing silent meditation has taught me is to pay attention, and so, I look carefully. I look with my heart into the face of another human being who has been loved so little.

When I look at him, I see a face with big blue eyes round as a lake: still, searching, seeking connection. I see masses of dark curly hair like tea tree beach shrubs jutting out all over the place and a sun-kissed bronze face, with a few broken teeth behind a shy smile.

I see him as the image of God that he was before all his hurts and all his acts of violence. It is a good seeing. Sometimes, if I look a little harder, I can see the child that he once was before he first raised his hand to harm another or defend himself.

---

[294] Bruce Vater, 'Johannine Theology', in *The Jerome Biblical Commentary*, eds. Raymond E. Brown, Joseph. A Fitzmyer and Roland E. Murphy (Englewood Cliffs, NJ: Prentice-Hall, 1968), 833.

Silent meditation has taught me to slow down and look for hints of resurrection. Resurrection to me is to live from the love of Christ. To be continually dying to self and living, however smally, from this bigger boundless flow of love. Jesus described it like this while praying to God: 'I made your name known to them, and I will make it known, so that the love with which you have loved me may be in them, and I in them.'[295]

Another thing silent meditation has taught me is to listen with attention from the depths of my heart.

I heard this week an Orthodox priest teach that 'to be dead to the world and alive to Christ is to respond with love and not react'. The world is full of quick reactions that seek to alienate people from one another and from our common humanity.

Silent meditation has taught me to observe my reactions, put them aside if they are not helpful and respond where possible with love. It has taught me about the necessary space I need to be aware of myself and my own worldly reactions. Through this slowing down and quietening, I can try a little harder to stay with this young man, even when I recoil inside, or seek a way out or want to push him away.

John Main described the practice of silent meditation as one that 'opens us to the infinite expansion of love'.[296] That is what we are training in. A boot camp for boundless love.

FOURTH SUNDAY OF EASTER (YEAR C)
John 10:22–30

Finding Your Way

BY PAUL WOOD

According to St Peter, Jesus is 'the Shepherd and the guardian of our souls',[297] but as Jesus is no longer physically with us, how are we guided by the Good Shepherd?

Traditionally, Anglicanism recognises three authorities through which we follow Christ:

- the Scriptures
- the Church

---

295 John 17:26.
296 Main, *Inner Christ*, 117–18.
297 1 Pet. 2:25.

- the Inner Witness (reason, conscience and experience).

First, the Scriptures. If one is a Protestant, then the Scriptures are the number one place to go when seeking guidance. However, because nobody is an island unto themselves and one may be prone to delusions, one also needs to consider how the rest of the Church reads the Scriptures, and one also needs to be consistent with one's own reason, conscience and experience. Thus, for a Protestant, the Scriptures come first, which must also be backed up by the Church and with one's inner witness.

However, if one is seeking guidance as a Catholic or an Orthodox, then one's first point of call is the Church. The Church's liturgy, teachings, creeds and councils, together with the bishops and priests, but also taking into consideration what your brothers and sisters in Christ also believe. However, that should not stand alone, because the Church as a human institution is prone to corruption, and therefore, one's understanding must also be consistent with one's own reason, conscience and experience, but also be supported with knowledge of the Scriptures.

However, if one is more of a contemplative in nature, then one will tend to appeal to the inner witness first by reason, conscience and experience and because all are prone to delusion, one must also find corresponding support for one's reasonings with both the teachings of the Church and the authority of the Scriptures.

These three authorities, the Church, the Scriptures and the Inner Witness, exist in all Christians but because everybody is different, we all have these as different priorities and strengths. But the point is that all three are all there and are in dialogue with each other. This is one reason, I suspect, why Anglicans so often appear unclear about what they believe because they're in a process and there is an ongoing dynamic dialogue between these three authorities.

When we come to meditation and contemplation, I would suggest that contemplatives can only be contemplatives if they trust the inner witness first. It's like learning to catch a ball: written instructions are not enough, and the only way you're going to learn to catch a ball is by actually doing it. It is something one learns through experience. Instruction can only take you so far, but the real teaching comes through personal experience.

One can build a boat with help from the Church and the Scriptures, but then, one has to get into it and row it across the ocean. This is the work of contemplation.

It seems clear that Jesus teaches us to go beyond simply obeying the letter of the law and teaches us to be empowered by the Holy Spirit within, which will lead us into all truth.

FIFTH SUNDAY OF EASTER (YEAR C)
John 13:31–35

A New Commandment
BY PAUL WOOD

Love is such a wide-ranging word that embraces all kinds of feelings and actions, from children's pink hearts to teenage infatuations; from deep longings in life to courageous journeys; from sexual explorations to pure selfless charity; from the bonding love between brothers and sisters, to a mother's nurturing love of her children, or a father's selfless strengthening care; from love of country and heritage, which engenders respect and love of truth, love of beauty and love of goodness, to the highest form of love, the redemptive love of Christ; from *eros* to *agapē*; love in all its crazy and wild forms.

So, what is love?

I suggest two ideas. First, whatever physical life is to the body, love is to the soul. Take life out of the body and the body dies; take love out of the soul and the soul dies. Love is the energy that animates the soul, both mind and the heart. No human can live without love. In this way, life and love are very closely related.

The second idea is that love requires another. It cannot exist by itself. It only exists when there is a relationship to the other. Love requires two or more souls, heart to heart, mind to mind, because we exist in a matrix of relationships.

Now, the Old Testament requires us to love God. And this is usually thought of as a vertical relationship between the self and God, but Jesus takes us a step further. Jesus, the incarnated, visible form of God, says, 'I give you a new commandment.'[298] This new aspect of this commandment is to love each other in the same way as he has loved us, which Jesus has supremely demonstrated through redemptive love in his acts of servanthood and sacrifice.

So, here the field is widened considerably. The love of God is not just between the individual and God, in a private and vertical relationship, but also spread horizontally among our neighbours. The final judgement of humanity is based upon this principle. 'Then he will answer them, "Truly I tell you, just as you did not do it to one of the least of these, you did not do it to me."'[299] Thus, it is clear that how we have treated the least among us is how we have treated Christ. This incarnated form of love is further made real when Jesus

---

298 John 13:34.
299 Matt. 25:45.

says, 'For where two or three are gathered together in my name, I am there among them.'[300]

And so, we get a sense that love is the energy that brings life not just to the individual soul, but also to community. Therefore, when St John writes: 'God is love',[301] we understand that God is present in and among us and is the very thing that creates and sustains life both individually and corporately.

This means that we can complete the picture. It is not just that God loves us through his Son, from the top down as it were, but also that the Spirit of God, breathed into humanity at the beginning of Creation, empowers us to enact this love, prompts us from within to act and to love others and to love God.

Thus, God speaks to God. So, the complete picture is that we are caught up in the sharing of the life/love relationship of the eternal Trinity. God loves us through the Son, and we love God through the Spirit, enabling us to love God in return.

When we enter into the prayer of meditation, we become more conscious of our participation in the community of love on the level of the soul rather than the physical level. As we sit with ourselves, we become less divided between mine and yours, us and them, my stuff and their stuff, and in time, through the discipline of focused attention and carrying discomfort, we may begin to enter into the wholeness of the soul, which is sharing in the life/love of God.

SIXTH SUNDAY OF EASTER (YEAR C)
John 14:23–40

On the Edge
BY PAUL WOOD

It has become very clear to me over my years of being a parish priest, and my many attempts to introduce silent meditation to congregations, in various ways, that this is not something the mainstream is interested in or wants to understand. I have tried and failed many times.

I suspect that this has always been the case in the Church, that those who practice silence are contemplatives, monastics, hermits, solitaries and oddballs, people who live on the edge, in isolation and are not part of mainstream life. The movement of solitaries in the early Church was criticised by some as 'the

---

300   Matt. 18:20.
301   1 John 4:8.

flight of the alone into the alone', borrowing a phrase from Plotinus, the great Greek pagan philosopher.[302]

So, to ensure that we are not seen as people who have 'lost our way' and losing touch, it is important that we can show our habits are absolutely rooted in the life and teachings of Jesus and have a long history of practice in the Church.

Here are three things that root us solidly in the gospel.

First: The Wilderness

Jesus was part of a long biblical tradition of the wilderness. He was a wilderness man, not just his forty days and nights in the wilderness, but also rhythmically throughout his busy ministry, he always went off by himself to pray, seeking solitude, up a mountain, in a garden or some other quiet, secluded place.

In the same way, whenever we meditate, we are seeking solitude because when we are in the world of people, we are also in the world of projections that mould us and shape us, and sometimes, we can lose ourselves. But in the wilderness, we come closer to the truth of our natural selves, just as we really are, before God, as God really is. The wilderness in the Bible is the place of transformation and formation. It is 'The Academy of Soul Making' as described by Alan Jones.[303]

Second: Jesus Teaching Us to Pray

He says, 'But whenever you pray, go into your room and shut the door and pray to your Father who is in secret, and your Father who sees in secret will reward you.'[304]

This is radical, for most people in Jesus' day understood prayer to be something that is said publicly and 'out loud' for others to hear and certainly not 'in secret'.

In the same way, each time we meditate, we close the door on the world and, for a while, we are in our 'secret place' as Jesus teaches.

Third: The Internal Guide

When Jesus leaves this world, he also leaves us with the gift of the Holy Spirit, as our advocate and guide.

Now this is noteworthy, because the Holy Spirit is an internal authority, a guide you meet on the inside of yourself, unseen from the outside; it is an internal witness.

---

302 Daniel J. Tolan, 'The Flight of the All-One to the All-One: The phygē monu pros monon as the Basis of Plotinian Altruism, *Harvard Theological Review* 114, no. 4 (2021), 469–90. https://doi.org/10.1017/S0017816021000316.
303 Jones, *Soul Making*.
304 Matt. 6:6.

Isn't it interesting that when Jesus leaves this world, he does not give his Apostles any external guides to follow? He did not write anything down and say 'now you follow that'; he entrusted his teachings to the winds of the spirit as it morphs in the individual lives of each disciple. Nor did he point to Peter and say, 'now you obey Peter here, and he will lead you into all truth'. Jesus actually gave no external authority as our guide, but instead, he said that 'the advocate' will come to us and will be with us forever. The Spirit of Truth will come dwell within you; it will be your guide and lead you into all truth.

In silent meditation, we do not follow any external guide; rather, we listen to the internal guidance of the Holy Spirit.

Now this does not mean that we ignore the external authority of either the Scriptures or the Church's teachings, for if we do that, then we are likely to become isolated from our Christian sisters and brothers. Rather, what it means is that our times of silence are formative and authoritative together with the Bible and the Church's teachings.

One final point. There are many differing traditions of silence in Christianity.

This practice of using a single prayer word as a point of focus to bring stillness and silence is a tradition taught by John Main, the founder of the World Community for Christian Meditation. This tradition traces its origins all the way back to the first Christians, who went out as solitaries into the Egyptian desert to imitate and learn the prayer habits of Jesus. This movement became known as the Desert Mothers and the Desert Fathers.

So, let us now follow this practice and, through silence, enter into intimacy with God for the formation of our souls.

SEVENTH SUNDAY OF EASTER (YEAR C)
John 17:20–26

Making Known Love
BY MICHELLE WOOD

Some sentences are like flowers—you want to stoop down, look at their delicacy and inhale their scent deeply.

Like a line from tonight's sacred story, 'I made your name known to them, and I will make it known, so that the love with which you have loved me may be in them and I in them.'[305]

---

305   John 17:26.

Or the line from *La Traviata*, Verdi's opera, 'Love is the pulse of the whole world.'[306]

Or Van Gough's expression that '…the best way of knowing God is to love many things'[307]—from the symphony of yellows in a wheat field to the swirls of stars in a midnight blue sky. A face, a chair, boots, a sunflower, a teapot, an onion, a candle, a chestnut pipe—*to know life is to love many things*. To see bedazzling beauty in it all.

With Van Gough, each paint stroke is an expression of love.

He felt he'd painted sunflowers so much that they were in a strange kind of way his—he lived in them and they in him. Through a concentrated loving gaze, he came to know them in both an earthly and mystical way.

Van Gough makes the invisible known to us through art.

Jesus makes the invisible God known to us through love.

Before Jesus made known God's name as Love, the God of the Old Testament was unnameable, so big, so mysterious, so beyond human comprehension. When Moses encounters God from the burning bush, he asks God that when he goes to the Israelites and tells them that God has sent him, if they ask him 'What is his name?', what he should tell them. God replies that he should tell them, 'I AM … has sent me to you.'[308]

Moses's relationship to God is anything but intimate.

When Jesus encounters God at his baptism, he is called 'my beloved son'. It is a relationship marked with intimacy.

From this relationship, as God's beloved Son, Jesus teaches his disciples not to pray to an unknowable, abstract, ineffable mystery but to an intimate Father in heaven.

> *Our Father*
> *In heaven*
> *Hallowed be your name*[309]

Now, not everyone can relate to the metaphor of a father in an easy way. Some people have not had very good experiences of an earthly father. But the radical nature of Jesus making known to us God as intimate love, as love that is the pulse of the whole universe, is such an important shift for humankind.

I can only get somewhat near this concept when I think of my love for my two children, whose lives in the beginning were so fragile and dependent

---

306 Giuseppe Verdi, 'La Traviata Libretto English Translation', Opera-Arias.com, accessed 20 January 2024, https://www.opera-arias.com/verdi/la-traviata/libretto/english/.
307 Vincent Van Gogh, *The Letters of Vincent Van Gough*, ed. Roland de Leeuw, trans. Arnold Pomerans (London: Penguin Books, 1996), 72.
308 Exo. 3:13–15.
309 Luke 11:2–4.

upon me, even in the womb. For me, how I love them and come to know the extent of love through them is one of the most powerful ways of experiencing this Christian mystery.

In tonight's sacred story, Jesus is praying for his disciples, praying that this pulse of love that flows from God to him and from him to them may continue. Just like we might hope that some of the love that flows from us to our children may flow on through them to others.

Jesus is praying that they become love bearers, flames of love from within carrying both his love for them and God's. This love bearing will be the very thing that lives on that has eternal life. It is only through love that one can reveal anything about the nature of God.

It is in this spirit that Benedictine monk John Main crafted a beautiful prayer for practitioners of silent meditation: 'Heavenly Father, open our hearts to the silent presence of the Spirit of your Son. Lead us into that mysterious silence where your love is revealed to all who call, "Maranatha, Come, Lord Jesus".'[310]

Let us prepare for twenty minutes of journeying into that mysterious silence where love pulses and connects us to the whole divine harmony.

ASCENSION DAY (YEAR C)
Acts of the Apostles 1:1–14

The Great Silence of God
BY PAUL WOOD

See meditation for Year B on page 136.

---

[310] World Community for Christian Meditation, 'Opening Prayer', https://wccm.org/meditation-resources/online-meditation-readings-11-june/#:~:text=2)%20OPENING%20PRAYER%20AND%20MEDITATION,Maranatha%2C%20Come%20Lord%20Jesus.

Pentecost (Year C)

DAY OF PENTECOST (YEAR C)
Acts of the Apostles 2:1–4

Breath
BY PAUL WOOD

See meditation for Year A on page 50.

TRINITY SUNDAY (YEAR C)
John 16:12–15

The Glint of God within Us
BY MICHELLE WOOD

If you watch an artist paint and catch the last brushstroke they make, you will see that it is usually the one that pulls the whole painting together. For example, just the addition of a white dot in the corner of an eye creates a glint and, all of a sudden, the portrait comes to life.

If the early gospel bearers were painters, what do you think would be the last stroke they would make to bring together the whole biblical narrative that had been gestating for approximately 3,400 years?

What is this mark, dot, dash, the one word that brings the overarching biblical narrative to completion? Well, to understand this, it took a few hundred years of working through the meanings of Jesus' teachings on the relationships between himself, God and humanity, which are reflected in statements such as:

> *As you, Father, are in me and I am in you, may they also be in us.*[311]
> *I made your name known to them, and I will make it known, so that the love with which you have loved me may be in them and I in them.*[312]
> *When the Advocate comes, whom I will send to you from the Father, the Spirit of Truth who comes from the Father, will testify on my behalf.*[313]

---

311 John 17:21.
312 John 17:26.
313 John 15:26.

It took many conversations to put the glint in the eye of the gospel and this glint is—the word Trinity.

'Trinity' refers to the relationships of God, the Son and the Holy Spirit with us.

These holy relationships draw us authentically to the fullness of who we are and who we are becoming.

The Triune God of the gospel is transforming us from within and drawing us into divine intimacy.

The vision of this relationship is that we are made in the image of God and develop a consciousness of Christ through a process of continual re-creation by the Spirit.

Jesus describes more closely the transformative work of the Spirit. He makes clear that the Spirit of Truth 'will take what is mine and declare it to you'.[314]

He tells his disciples, 'the Spirit of Truth …will guide you into all the truth; for he [she] will not speak on his [her] own, but will speak whatever he [she] hears'.[315]

Like a secret love letter from Christ himself, she will arrive with a message, a nudge, a prick of conscience, a creative impulse … that beckons us towards some greater truth than we could have come up with ourselves.

The Spirit of Truth is a guide that leads us away from small-minded, divisive polemics, petty quarrels with our loved ones and greedy fights that gobble up goodness.

Like a well-paced yoga pose, this guide will stretch us a little further away from the 'me and my interests' perspective towards a universal love and truth.

> *The Spirit of Truth will guide you into all the truth; for she will not speak on her own, but will speak whatever she hears.*

She will whisper things that you may not want to hear, like—'give them another go', 'perhaps you didn't need to hear it like that', 'try to see it from their perspective'…

Silent meditation is a practice of shutting up and returning to this ritual of awakening to that presence of the Spirit of Truth within us. Not necessarily to hear declarations within the still, silent sitting but more so to remember that this is a space we need to bring into our everyday lives so that we can resist speaking from our own petty interests and hear a deeper language of

---

314 John 16:14.
315 John 16:13. The brackets indicate the use of feminine pronouns that reflect the feminine metaphors used to describe the Spirit throughout the Scriptures, such as in Proverbs, Psalms, Song of Songs.

love. The Spirit of Truth, as St Paul tells us, brings life and peace.[316] It is, as I see it, the glint of God within us.

SUNDAY BETWEEN 5 AND 11 JUNE (YEAR C)
Luke 7:11–17

Compassion in the Temple of the Holy Spirit
BY PAUL WOOD

*When the Lord saw her, he had compassion for
her and said to her, 'Do not weep'.*

I wish to take this opportunity to reflect on this Greek word for compassion.

Splagchnizomai is a strong visceral verb meaning being moved deeply in the bowels. Its root word, *splanchna*, simply means guts or entrails. It is the same word used that describes the wretched end of Judas, who fell in a field, and all his intestines or bowels (his *splanchna*) burst out.

It seems that this visceral compassion sometimes drove Jesus beyond normal expectations. For example, there were times when Jesus was exhausted and sought rest and quietude, but because the crowd were 'like sheep without a shepherd', his compassion—that is, his *splanchna*—compelled him to care for them.[317]

In the same way, it was his *splanchna* that moved him to stretch out his hand and touch the leper.[318]

It was his *splanchna* that moved him to feed the people in the wilderness.[319]

Perhaps these events can be put alongside other visceral events, such as when Jesus became angry or wept or was 'deeply troubled' in the garden. These events remind us that the eternal God is incarnate perfectly in Jesus with all the bodily sensations that we also have.

And so, for our meditation tonight, I wish to explore the theme of the body as the temple of the Holy Spirit.

The Bowels

Let us become conscious of our lower abdomen. This is the place of digestion, the stomach and gut, the bladder, the sexual organs and the womb.

---

316 Rom. 8:6.
317 Matt. 9:36.
318 Mark 1:41.
319 Mark 8:2.

The organs in this area are ones that experience a build-up and then demand release. Here is the origin of burps and farts.

This area, collectively known as the bowels, is in the Bible identified as the seat of deep primal visceral emotions. Fear, anger, disgust, jealousy, envy, hunger, cowardice, need, compulsion and lust: all the feelings that build up and demand release.

Sometimes, these demands are helpful, such as when we are moved deeply by a sense of compassion or awareness of injustice, a deep primal passion that forces us to act, sometimes even against the clear advice that comes from our heads!

But sometimes, these emotions, as with a burp or a fart, can be inappropriate.

The Head

Now, as we explore the temple of the Holy Spirit, let's move up higher, to the head. The head allows our primary communication with the external world. The head houses the face, eyes, ears, nose, mouth and tongue, through which it collects a great deal of data from the external world. The inside of the head is something like an echo chamber of all we have heard, spoken, seen, smelled and tasted. The inside of the head is full of memories, thoughts and stories. The reasoning function that brings these jumbled thoughts, memories and feelings into order is what we refer to as the intellect. The intellect enables us to create narratives and verbalise thoughts to communicate with others. Sometimes, we are so caught up in our heads that we think this is all there is. In fact, many people dwell entirely in their minds. This can cause them a lot of problems because the nature of the mind is that it can never rest. It works on binaries—light and dark, good and bad, right and wrong—and therefore, it can never rest. For every story, there is a counterstory, an endless monologue of explanations and justifications. People who live in this mental stress for too long can lose their way. In meditation, we learn to let go of the mind so that we can journey deeper, to the heart. This is usually done by focusing on a prayer word designed to keep the mind in one place; this enables us to let it go.

The Heart

Now, let's move to the heart. If I asked you to touch the place on your body that is the centre of your being, saying to yourself, 'This is me', I suspect you would touch the centre of your chest. You would not touch your head or your guts but your chest, which happens to be at an equal distance between the bowels and the intellect.

Here, in the centre of your being, are the lungs and the heart and, if you are a mother, also the breasts. This is the place of nurture, the place of life, the place of love.

Here are the lungs. Every living thing breathes. Breath is life from God. Everything in the animal kingdom, but also everything in the plant kingdom, breathes. We breathe in what they breathe out, and we breathe out what they breathe in. Breathing belongs to all living things: breathing in and then breathing out. This breath of life comes from God.

Nestled in and between the lungs is the living heart. Our spiritual tradition understands the physical heart and the spiritual heart to be one and the same. Science tells us that the heart begins to form around four weeks after conception, and the first heartbeat can be detected even before many women know they are pregnant. The heart has been beating a rhythm within us from our primal beginnings. This is the rhythm of life.

Like the centre of a wheel, the heart is the pivotal point from which the spokes fan out to hold the whole perimeter together. The heart is the place of union, intuition, conscience and free will.

Further, the heart is relational. When we connect with others, the deepest connection we can have is heart-to-heart. A heart connection means receptivity to the other for the exchange of life.

So, the heart is the place of 'covenant with God'.

And hence, we find that the heart is a valve through which love flows between and among us.

Love is like the blood of God, and the heart pumps this blood around the whole mystical body of Christ.

The prayer of silence, also known as pure prayer, is meant to bring us into the heart.

Let me introduce our meditation this evening by reading a well-known liturgical prayer. As I read it slowly and meditatively, I ask that you allow it to lead you into our twenty minutes of silence meditation together.

Let us now meditate and use the Collect for Purity to bring us into silent prayer.

> *Almighty God, unto whom all hearts are open, all desires known, and from whom no secrets are hidden: cleanse the thoughts of our hearts by the inspiration of thy Holy Spirit, that we may perfectly love thee, and worthily magnify thy holy name: through Christ our Lord. Amen.*

SUNDAY BETWEEN 12 AND 18 JUNE (YEAR C)
Luke 7:36–8:3

Praying as a Woman Who Shows Great Love
BY MICHELLE WOOD

> She stood behind him at his feet, weeping, and began to bathe
> his feet with her tears and to dry them with her hair, kissing
> his feet and anointing them with the ointment.[320]

Odd, if not outlandish, is how biblical scholar Michael Patella OSB describes the woman's behaviour in this week's sacred story. She is introduced as a sinner from the city, and somehow, she has managed to break into the dinner party and scramble over many smelly feet to find Jesus. Patella reflects upon her complete abandonment of manners and social conventions to give such lavish love. With a singular and narrow focus, she excludes all obstacles: personal history, status as a woman and sinner, disapproval and potential punishment. Naught matters except the fulfilling of this act of devotion. With arrow-like precision, she expediently gets to the bullseye.

In many ways, this is what we are trying to do in our practice of silent meditation: push through all obstacles, practical, intellectual and social. We seek to cast off whatever weighs us down and concentrate with all our might. We scramble past smelly feet and the judgement of others to arrive at the centre of being, the Spirit of Christ within. To meditate wholeheartedly, we must be driven like this woman. We must bring all our being: body, mind, heart, tears, disgraces and fears. Love, like a propulsive force, draws us on and on, breath by breath, to the moment of encounter. In a moment of stillness where all else falls away, with the intimacy of a gentle lover, we offer all that we have to the Holy One. The Holy One recognises the fullness of such an offering and meets this generosity of being with the fullness of forgiveness and healing.

The Holy One teaches:

> Her many sins have been forgiven; hence she has shown great
> love. But the one to whom little is forgiven loves little.

This poetic proportionality echoes through many of Jesus' teachings, from the story of the prodigal son to his encounter with the woman at the well. Loving devotion is crucial for us to receive restoration.

---

320 Luke 7:38

Is it possible to see our practice of silent meditation as an expression of loving devotion, a practice of reaching towards healing, forgiveness and re-creation into wholeness by the divine? Could it be that by keeping our loving attention singularly on Christ, through the simplicity of our prayer word recitation or breath practice and narrowing of our gaze, we will be propelled by this desire alone to begin to really pray?

When St Evagrios responded to the question, 'How do you know you are praying?', he said:

> *When your intellect in its great longing for God gradually withdraws from the flesh and turns away from all thoughts that have their source in your sense-perception, memory of the soul-body temperament, and when it becomes full of reverence and joy then you can conclude that you are close to the frontiers of prayer.*[321]

This is how the woman prays. In our time of silent meditation, may we pray with such outlandish love, in full reverence and joy.

SUNDAY BETWEEN 19 AND 25 JUNE (YEAR C)
Luke 8:26–39

The Demoniac of the Gerasenes
BY PAUL WOOD

Jesus ventures outside the homeland of the Jews, to the other side of the Sea of Galilee, which is a pagan territory. Having crossed the stormy sea, Jesus steps out of the boat into a strange land and is met by the terrifying 'Demoniac of the Gerasenes'.

This man lived among the tombs, crazed and naked. And falling down at Jesus' feet, he cries out, 'What have you to do with me, Jesus, Son of the Most High God? I beg you, do not torment me.'[322]

I like to set this alongside other famous 'first encounters', like that of Captain Cook and the Aboriginals—and the consequences that follow. There is always a clash of cultures and complex ethics surrounding a meeting with 'The Other'.

I imagine Jesus arriving and being met in a foreign land, the outskirts of pagan territory, in an area where, according to scholars, there was a Roman garrison stationed. If that was the case, can you imagine how hard it was for

---

321 Nikodimos and Makarios, *Philokalia*, 62.
322 Mark 5:7.

the people of that city to have the Roman invaders, who had come to possess their native lands, set up in their patch!

Clearly, some people collaborated with the Romans. A legion of Roman soldiers would need food and resources. Can you imagine all the social problems that would entail?

The Romans loved the pig: they used a boar's head as a logo, they loved to eat pork and they needed food. But the Law of Moses says that pork is forbidden food, and so, perhaps some folk gave up their cultural principles and set up piggeries.

No doubt, they also needed women. Can you imagine all the social problems, the guilt and the shame?

Perhaps they also needed wine to keep them happy.

And no doubt, some folk could profit, but others, the vulnerable, were exploited. The clash of cultures and values would soon include bribes, shady deals and broken promises as the garrison gradually took over the area. And so, as guilt and shame inhabited the people, they also became easy pray for demons to come out from the abyss.

So, what did they do with all their guilt and shame? What did they do with all their darkness? They did what human beings have always done ever since Adam and Eve. They projected the blame onto others; there is always someone, who is at the bottom, who, for whatever reason, takes it all on board. And perhaps this is how this man became possessed by a whole legion of demons, for some people can become sponges for the darkness that others project onto them.

Driven out of town, he lives among the tombs of the dead, naked and stoning himself in deranged self-blame.

And so, this man, with a legion of demons, is 'living out' the darkness that the people of the city and the countryside refuse to acknowledge inside of themselves.

When Jesus meets the man, he sends these demons back into the abyss—and so, the man is found to be 'clothed and in his right mind'.[323]

'Clothed' means that his dignity is restored, he is no longer naked, no longer exposed.

Next, 'and in his right mind' means that he has his own thoughts back, his mind back, he is no longer controlled by the dark shadows of others.

What a beautiful picture! Clothed and in his right mind.

But it seems the people of the city were not so pleased, for Jesus was bad for business and had upset the cosy deal they had established between the Romans, the pigs and the man who carried their shame. And now, without

---

[323] Mark 5:15.

their scapegoat, they would have to become responsible for their own shady dealings and accept their own guilt and darkness.

In meditation, we sit and allow the light of Christ to cast the darkness out of our souls so that we too may be found clothed and in our right minds.

SUNDAY BETWEEN 26 JUNE AND 2 JULY (YEAR C)
Luke 9:51–62

To Follow without Distraction
BY MICHELLE WOOD

As they were going along the road, someone said to him, 'I will follow you wherever you go.' And Jesus said to him, 'Foxes have holes, and birds of the air have nests; but the Son of Man has nowhere to lay his head.' To another he said, 'Follow me.' But he said, 'Lord, first let me go and bury my father.' But Jesus said to him, 'Let the dead bury their own dead; but as for you, go and proclaim the kingdom of God.' Another said, 'I will follow you, Lord; but let me first say farewell to those at my home.' Jesus said to him, 'No one who puts a hand to the plow and looks back is fit for the kingdom of God.'[324]

On an unusual track from Galilee to Samaria, weaving down the Jordon Valley, Jesus and his friends are walking to Jerusalem. It is not the usual safe route, but the shortest and most direct, taking three days.

On this walk, he encounters three people and invites them to come and follow him.

Each of them has to dig into a question that I would like to explore with you tonight.

What do you want most, right now?

If we begin to entertain that question, we will be exploring our desires. And if we begin to explore our desires, we will notice that usually we never have one desire but many.

And as we turn that question over in our minds:

What do you want most, right now?

Our desires will start to gather around that question like seagulls around a bag chips.

What do you want, most, right now?

---

[324] Luke 9:57–62.

Looking at what desires are gathering; we will also perhaps see that some are at odds with others—I really want that but if I take that, I wouldn't be able to have this.

And so, we must choose. Like choosing to come here tonight to meditate instead of doing the myriad other things that you may also desire to do.

What do you want, most, right now?

And if you think this is a very modern, hedonistic type of question, it may benefit you to listen to the sacred story tonight with new ears.

Because, in fact, Jesus asks this question perhaps not as crudely as I have posed it but nevertheless, he asks it to three people.

What do you want, most, right now?

It is a question that calls one to action. And a question that calls one to attention within oneself.

It is a question worth contemplating before launching into silent meditation.

What do you want most, right now?

In meditation, we respond to this question moment by moment, breath by breath.

In tonight's sacred story, Jesus encounters three people who say they want to follow him, but all have a very important excuse as to why they can't. The first person wants to follow but doesn't want to take up the invitation of an itinerant life. The second wants to follow but must look after family first, and the third wants to follow but first wants to go home to say goodbye.

In following Jesus, like following your breath, you can't wait. You can't say 'I'll breathe; I'll breathe in a moment. I've first got to do this.' Meditation is a training ground for following—for letting go of the world and following the light of Christ.

What do you want, most, right now?

In noticing how we meditate, how we are in the silence, how we listen to the gospel, how we are with one another, we will notice what we want right now.

Like the fishermen who immediately lay down their nets to follow Jesus, we are called. It is simple, in a sense, for when something so loving and big compels us and we recognise it, we drop everything.

What do you want, most, right now?

Come, follow me is the invitation. Can you leave your nets, family, thoughts, worries and other important obligations and just follow for twenty minutes in silent prayer?

What do you want, most, right now?

SUNDAY BETWEEN 3 AND 9 JULY (YEAR C)
Luke 10:1–12, 17–24

Pairs of Love and Peace

BY MICHELLE WOOD

Jesus sends the seventy-two in pairs to be a living expression of the love commandment. When you see two people tend to each other in small acts of care and love—a couple, a mother and child or two friends, you witness something of the love of God. It is only in our relationships with another that we practice and evolve a way of love. We must listen, sometimes yield, sometimes assert and often overcome our failings to practice the art of love. Love is the central calling of the Christian life: loving God and loving our neighbour. So, Jesus sends them in pairs to model.

And this is why it is important to also practice silent meditation with others. Even the desert mothers and fathers who lived quiet solitary lives of meditation still lived within a network of monastic cells.

To sit in silence with others is an outward visible dissolving of self to sit within the body of Christ. It is an act of love to one another to turn up each week and support each other to pray in this way.

When the bells chime at the beginning of meditation, we leave everything and close our eyes. Just as instructed in this week's gospel, we go bare and empty. The silence holds us together like a skin.

And when we meditate in this way, together, we taste the first fruits of peace. Peace is woven into the very fabric of the practice, breath by breath.

It is very important to cultivate a rich, deep sense of peace because this is the first thing that we are instructed to offer to every household we enter.

Finally, through the daily practice of silent meditation we learn a simple orientation of heart towards the divine. This is important because in this week's readings, the disciples get so caught up in what they have managed to achieve and their success in a type of self-inflation and sophistication that Jesus needs to help them return their gaze to God and asks them to not rejoice in these apparent successes, these things in and of themselves but 'rejoice that your names are written in heaven'.[325]

So let us enter together enter the peace of the silence, going bare and empty, with a simple heart that is focused on God.

---

325 Luke 10:20.

SUNDAY BETWEEN 10 AND 16 JULY (YEAR C)
Luke 10:25–37

The Wounded Self
BY PAUL WOOD

Modern interpreters of this parable all focus on the ethical question of 'who is my neighbour'. But the early Church fathers used the parable as an allegory of the spiritual life, and this is the approach I wish to take.

We all have aspects of our selves, elements within our souls, that have been attacked, robbed and dumped on the side of the road of life and left as dead.

People who have been abused as children know this only too well, that they have been robbed and dumped, but, in fact, it happens to all of us. No one is free of this, for we live in a world of sin, and there is always a part within each one of us that is damaged, left behind and forgotten.

But there are also other aspects of ourselves that are doing quite fine, thank you very much. These are represented by 'the priest and the Levite'. The Levites were the priestly tribe of Jews, and their lives were all about caring for the sacred places, keeping things pure in a ritual sense, and so, the very last thing they want is to defile themselves and be caught up in this ugly scene on the side of the road.

Many people live like this; in their everyday ego life, they are like the priest and Levite; in their minds, they are pure and going about their important daily activities, but they are also not acknowledging that deep down inside of themselves is a person lying half dead in the dust of life.

It is a picture of the 'divided self', which is, after all, the universal condition of human beings.

Carl Jung, one of the founders of the field of psychoanalysis, would say that in order to redeem the lost elements of your soul, you must enter what he called the shadow self. The shadow self is made up of all the energies, feelings and memories within ourselves that we suppress and avoid because of fear or repulsion, the things that are part of us but that we sweep under the carpet, out of sight of our conscious mind, so that we do not have to deal with them.

And the way to healing is never by avoiding the shadow self, but always by facing it and gradually integrating its elements into our everyday consciousness. In this way, the divided self gradually becomes whole. And this is a lifelong journey, but it is a journey that we all must begin for our healing.

So here is the dilemma. There is a locked pairing between the priestly ego self, on one hand, and the wounded self, on the other.

We need something from outside the system to save us.

Remember, the Scriptures say that 'The stone that the builders rejected has become the chief cornerstone.'[326] Christ is always the one you least expect.

So, along comes a Samaritan, someone from outside the system, someone the priest and Levite reject as apostates, but when he sees the wounded man, he is 'moved with pity'[327] and becomes the Christ to the wounded man. Kneeling down beside him, cleaning his wounds with the wine of redemption and anointing his injuries with the soothing oil of grace, he bandages the man and carries his new friend on his donkey to an inn that can care for him.

One of the things I love about the story is that the healing is not a magic fix but is a journey of care to bring the wounded man back to full health. For this is very real, it takes time, organic time, and gradual healing through love, care and attention.

For this is how we must integrate the bits of ourselves, from the shadows, in order to heal the divided self and become whole. Through love, care and attention.

In meditation, we open our wounded self before Christ and allow our wound to be, so that the wine and oil of Christ's love may gently soothe and heal us.

SUNDAY BETWEEN 17 AND 23 JULY (YEAR C)
Luke 10:38–42

There Is Need of Only One Thing
BY MICHELLE WOOD

In this week's sacred story, Jesus visits the home of two sisters, Martha and Mary. And you may be familiar with the dynamics this story portrays. Mary sits at the feet of Jesus listening and being with him, while Martha dashes about organising the meal and completing all the jobs. Eventually Martha gets upset and complains to Jesus, who says to her: 'Martha, Martha, you are worried and distracted by many things; there is need of only one thing. Mary has chosen the better part, which will not be taken away from her.'[328]

Bouncing off this redirection by Jesus, I would like to ask you some questions: Who calls you back to what is really important in life? Who holds up a mirror and helps you see how you inhabit life, so that you can call into question the distractions and worry habits that you get caught up in?

---

326 Ps. 118:22–23.
327 Luke 10:33.
328 Luke 10:41–42.

Who calls you by name, back into reality?

Who is that person who invites you to hit the pause button—stop at the feet of life and listen?

The gift of great spiritual teachers from Jesus to Thich Nat Hanh, Rowan Williams to Mary Oliver, Julian of Norwich to Thomas Merton, St Benedict to John Main is that they interrupt the busyness of our lives with a compelling, soft invitation to sit at the feet of life and love.

It is also the gift of a small child who invites you to stop cooking in the kitchen and look at a bird's nest that they have found in the garden.

There is need of only one thing… Listen! Shshshshshush…

Look at the miracle of this life, the love arriving … an unexpected moment to sit at the feet of Christ.

The practice of silent meditation is one of sitting at the feet of Jesus and giving our undivided attention to his presence. By practising this posture, we are able to look for this in a more outward way in our everyday lives for he is always there calling us deeper. He beckons, saying: *Pay attention, I have come so that you may have life and life to its full. Everything else is stocking fillers.*

In our busy cosmopolitan lives, we are all too much Martha and silent meditation is our Mary, it is our better part.

I try to develop these Mary practices in my everyday life and silent meditation is the well from which they spring. I wonder if you have any such practices.

Every day at work, after the morning counselling sessions, I set out for a walk, no matter the weather for the weather is God drenching me. I have to earnestly cross the threshold of my office door and leave the therapist behind. It is a discipline and a Mary practice.

If I didn't do this, the therapist and all her stress, questions, agitations, dilemmas, stories and emotions would dominate the walk. In fact, I would have been better off staying in the office because I wouldn't notice the walk.

Instead, aligned with my Mary practice, I walk down Dean Street and feel the icy winter wind slap my cheek like a Zen master and the sun gently warm my face.

I see a man dressed in bright disco colours eating a hamburger, and I smile.

I arrive at the art gallery café where a woman with Egyptian painted eyes makes me a coffee.

Her inner forearm has a tattoo that reads '*To make flowers you need the rain*', which is my gospel.

I sit at a table outside, against the sun-warmed glass of the building, looking at St Matthews Church. Like a compass point, it reminds me of the greater story in which my life and all life is held. I see the lime-green lichen spread across the slates of the pitched roof, decorating it for the glory of God, and the rose-coloured cross at the top of the steeple. This cross stretches above all those humanmade buildings towards the heavens. It opens me.

I listen to what life has given to me in this moment, from French pop accordion tunes to a couple arguing and a man leaving, saying 'f' you. I am present, mindful and think whether I need to do anything—alert, attentive.

I lower my gaze to the leaves, ruby and glistening on the ground.

You should always keep something beautiful in your mind, Paschal wrote.

I think about Jesus' expression 'there is need of only one thing'[329] and wonder: What is the one thing?

If you let yourself be open to wonder, I mean really open yourself to receive it, it's the closest thing to falling in love said poet Aimee Nezhutmatathil.

I wonder constantly about Christ, his teachings and how to stay close to his wisdom and peace. This wondering quest is a journey of infinite expansion into love.

And although it is a mystery to me, I observe that everything connects and flows better with him as my centre. He is my anchor of peace, my fixed point of ethics, my rootedness to love and I offer myself each day in this small way of silent meditation to sit at his feet.

So let us enter this period of silent meditation letting go of our Martha and leaning a little more deeply into our Mary.

Leaving our worries and distractions, let's sit at the feet of life, and love and just listen.

SUNDAY BETWEEN 24 AND 30 JULY (YEAR C)
Luke 11:1-13

The Lord's Prayer as a Ladder
BY PAUL WOOD

Whenever we pray, we enter into an intertidal zone between this world and the divine world. Prayer can be understood as the reciprocal feeding between earth and heaven. There is a mystical tradition of a ladder extending all the way from earth up to heaven (see 'Second Sunday after Epiphany [Year B]'), and with this in mind, I would like to suggest something strange. The disciples ask, 'Lord teach us to pray' and Jesus lets down this ladder. Let's imagine, in our minds eye, the Lord's Prayer as a great ladder, let down from heaven to the earth for us to climb up. Let us start, therefore, at the bottom, which means

---

329   Luke 10:42.

reading the Lord's Prayer backwards, and let us see what it teaches us.[330]

The doxology:

For the kingdom, the power and the glory are yours now and forever. AMEN.

The doxology is not found in either of the versions in the gospels although it is found in the early writings, such as the Didache. As the doxology is a liturgical device at the end of the Lord's Prayer, I do not use it in this reflection.

Step One

Here is the first rung of the ladder. Let us meditate on each petition

Save us from the time of trial and deliver us from evil.

This is the bottom rung at the base of the ladder. Firmly placed at the lowest place on earth to reach the most wretched of all. There is no lower place than this 'deliver us from evil'. Even death is higher up the ladder, for one can die a good death but there is nothing good in evil. This then offers us a first step no matter how low and wretched we might be as the ladder reaches down to our most base need. It is only then that have we the right orientation of heart to begin to look upwards and begin the ascent.

Step Two

Forgive us our sins as we forgive those who sin against us.

Having renounced evil but still being human, we will continue to sin. So, we must learn about forgiveness, to both give and receive it. When we receive forgiveness, we are acknowledging our wrongdoing and when we forgive another, we release them and ourselves from the weight of guilt. This is how we engender a light heart. This is how we rise higher and is like ballooning where we throw out some sandbags in order to rise. Meditation is a disciplined practice of letting go of heaviness, and this means forgiveness. Both the giving and receiving of forgiveness.

Step Three

Give us today our daily bread.

On our spiritual journey, we seek only the basic nourishment, our daily bread. Nourishment that is sufficient for the day allows for a sense of freedom from the clutter and anxiety that can bog our lives down in gluttony, greed and avarice. These first three of the seven deadly sins are the root of all the others and will weigh us down and render us unable to journey higher into

---

[330] There are two versions of this prayer in Luke 11:2–4 and the second and longer version in Matt. 6:9–13. For this purpose, I will use the English translation of the Lord's Prayer from The English Language Liturgical Commission. This is the usual form in Anglican prayer books. English Language Liturgical Commission, 'The Lord's Prayer', 1988, https://www.englishtexts.org/the-lords-prayer.

the subtler levels of being. Stay simple, slim and free with just a basic diet and keep the climb. The practice of meditation should be free from clutter for the essence of meditation is simplicity.

Step Four

Your kingdom come, your will be done, on earth as in heaven.

Here, we meet the intertidal zone where there is feeding across two worlds.

Our deepest desire is that God's will be done on earth. This means that everything is fulfilling its created purpose, being what it is and not in conflict with the rest of Creation or its Creator. It is a petition for the vision of peace for all.

The meditator is a member of the priesthood of all believers. It is a priesthood that spans the two worlds of dust and breath, matter and spirit. This is how the priesthood becomes a bridge for life to flow from heaven to earth and from earth to heaven. The priesthood is passionate for God and passionate for humanity, and it becomes a means through which the cries of humanity can be caught up into God and through which the life of God may be made incarnate into the dust of humanity. Can we hold this in-between space?

Step Five

Hallowed be your name.

The Christian mystic traditions of the Eastern Church differentiate between the energies and the essence of God. The essence of God is truly unknowable and beyond the capacity of earthly concepts. To believe in the essence of God is an act of faith, for what we can say about God is beyond our minds' ability to know. But we can perceive his energies, the power and glory that emanates from his essence; we can see and sense his presence through his energies. 'Hallowed be thy name' is like the glory, like the halo, like the light that shines from the hidden unknowable being of God. 'Hallowed be thy name' is a good place to hover and participate in. To see this light that shines from the invisible Creator in all of Creation is the goal of every contemplative.

Step Six

Our Father in heaven.

Although the essence of God is unknowable to the mind and so we cannot conceptualise God, nonetheless, God is knowable with the heart. One can trust the mystery, in the same way as an infant can trust its parents who it cannot yet recognise. I would suggest that the image of God as a heavenly Abba does not belong to the conceptualising mind, for it is rather a perception that belongs to the heart of a child; it speaks of intimacy, and of trust that life is benevolent, that grace exists and that love is the purpose. That the whole of existence is held by the intimacy of goodness and love.

SUNDAY BETWEEN 31 JULY AND 6 AUGUST (YEAR C)
Luke 12:13–21

Being Rich towards God
BY MICHELLE WOOD

I wonder what you think being rich towards God might be.

In this week's sacred story, a large crowd has gathered, by the thousands, we are told. People who had just witnessed Jesus taking a stand against the corrupt power of the Pharisees and lawyers. People are drawn to his message of freedom, truth, genuine help, empowerment and love. Like moths to a flame, they are amassing.

They are trampling to get closer to him, like crowds overcome with Beatle mania or Beaver fever. Perhaps like a desperate crowd at an Oprah Winfrey show, they are seeking help and answers to everyday problems.

Someone from this crowd calls out to Jesus, Teacher, tell my brother to divide the family inheritance with me.'[331]

The crowd await a reply from the one whose name is love.

Jesus opens his response by calling the questioner 'friend'—so radical an address, so equal, mutual and respectful unlike the Pharisees and their claims of superiority.

Jesus answers by telling a story about a man and his greed, his abundance of possessions and his barns.

Now this is not a dig at a prudent farmer who stores things in case of drought or famine to care for his stock and family when there is a shortage but rather, an illustration of miserly greed. It is a story of a man with a lot of treasure who does not share it. A man possessed by his possessions. A man seeking to control, stockpile and accumulate. A man whose mind is so fixated on his big barns and setting himself up for enjoyment that he does not even notice the needs of his family and neighbours or the poverty in his community.

The punch line in the story is death. Jesus says, 'God told him, "You fool! This very night your life is being demanded of you. And the things you have prepared, whose will they be?" So it is with those who store up treasures for themselves but are not rich toward God.'[332]

---
[331] Luke 12–13.
[332] Luke 12:20–21.

So, back to my original question—what does it mean to be rich towards God?

I wonder from reflecting on 'The Parable of the Rich Fool' whether to be rich towards God is to have a generous and open heart, one that sees good fortune as God's gift to be shared. Our personal generosity is really a passing on of God's generosity to us.

If we are clear about the order of things, we will understand that we cannot control or hold onto anything. Everything is from God and returns to God. And that can seem scary for we live in a world that highly prizes and indoctrinates us with ideas of individual autonomy, control, ownership, personal achievement and wealth and the glamour of success.

The consumerist world calls us every moment to be rich towards its corporations—buy this car, that appliance, this travel package, this stock, etc. Build bigger barns is its motto.

How can we turn a little more to be rich towards God?

Etty Hillesum is someone who can teach us about being rich towards God. In 1943, at age 29 years, she was deported with her family from a concentration camp in Westerbork to Auschwitz. In the concentration camp of Westerbork, she had experiences of spiritual awakenings and insight.

She wrote, 'Those two months behind barbed wire have been the two richest and most intense months of my life, in which my highest values were so deeply confirmed'.[333]

Hillesum addressed God repeatedly in her diaries (1941–42), regarding God not as a saviour, but as a vulnerable power we must nurture inside of us.

She wrote, 'Alas, there doesn't seem to be much You Yourself can do about our circumstances, about our lives. Neither do I hold You responsible. You cannot help us, but we must help You and defend Your dwelling place inside us to the last.'[334]

Her time at Westerbork, as reflected in her diaries, portrays the redemption of her spirit, although her body was captured and eventually murdered. She neither denies the horror of the Nazi terror, nor identifies with victimhood. She writes 'Against every new outrage and every fresh horror, we shall put up one more piece of love and goodness, drawing strength from within ourselves. We may suffer but we must not succumb'.[335]

Amid extreme conditions, Hillesum develops an awareness of the indestructible beauty of this world. She writes, 'The sky is full of birds, the purple lupins stand up so regally and peacefully, two little old women have

---

333 Hillesum, *Interrupted Life*, 205.
334 Hillesum, *Interrupted Life*, 178.
335 Hillesum, *Interrupted Life*, 294.

sat down for a chat, the sun is shining on my face—and right before our eyes, mass murder. ... The whole thing is simply beyond comprehension.'[336]

Etty Hillesum wasn't just wandering around in a Wordsworth Romanticism; she volunteered to care for the most vulnerable and needy in the camp, and her presence was described as radiant and luminous in this most dark place.

In her being rich towards God, she was able to live more fully the love commandment: to love God with all her heart and her neighbour as herself.

She seems to me someone who knew where her treasure was and how to place her attention on that no matter what.

Silent meditation, quiet contemplation, praying with our heart, reverently receiving communion, writing in diaries, reading the gospel, practising open generous love, staying close and open to the pulse and beat of life in nature and caring for the poorest and most needy are all ways of guiding the heart towards God.

Being rich towards God is a way of untangling ourselves from the consumerist objectification of this beautiful world so that we stop and consider it with Jesus' eyes.

Remembering that the best things in life are indeed free and beyond our control: the sky, the sunlight, beauty, the flowers, love…

I made noticing these things my prayer practice this week and experienced:

> *the sound of running water*
> *winter bird song*
> *orange blossoms*
> *tiny seeds*
> *wind bending a blade of grass*
> *shadows of pruned rose bushes on the curb side recycle bin*
> *sunlight on flowers of orange trumpets*
> *a breeze filled with jonquils exploding in my nose*
> *and a sky of violets under my feet.*

We are so rich with a purse that never empties.

Be rich towards God is our teaching today: Be trusting, generous of heart, bask in the created beauty, knowing we need no more than the love of God—who is our everlasting treasure.

---

336   Hillesum, *Interrupted Life*, 274.

SUNDAY BETWEEN 7 AND 13 AUGUST (YEAR C)
Luke 12:32–40

Making Purses for the Kingdom

BY PAUL WOOD

I do love Jesus' teachings about the coming kingdom of God, for they are unique. Our sacred reading today is full of tenderness—and it brings us a wonderful promise: 'Do not be afraid, little flock, for it is your Father's good pleasure to give you the kingdom.'[337]

'Do not be afraid, little flock' in a big world full of conflict and woe!

'For it is the Father's good pleasure'—it is the Father's joy! To give you the kingdom.

This reading is all grace: it's all love.

I guess some people might read this as 'when we die or at the end of the world, we will get the kingdom', whereas the notion is that the kingdom is more like a parallel universe, which is present with us now, within us and among us, now, but is unseen and unknown because it is overladen by the cares and troubles of this world. But the kingdom is present and very near, and it is the Father's good pleasure to give us the fullness of this kingdom—this is Jesus' teaching.

It is beautiful.

Then, Jesus goes on to encourage us to de-possess ourselves of the clutter and weight of this world: 'Sell your possessions'.[338] And, in many ways, meditation consists of doing just this—de-possessing ourselves of worldly stuff so that we are free, open and receptive to God.

But then, Jesus goes further to add something, and this is what interests me: he tells us to acquire something. He says, 'Make purses for yourselves that do not wear out.'[339] Money bags that never wear out!

So, do we have 'money bags in the kingdom'? Let's think about that—Why are they there?

It introduces to me this idea of an economy of spiritual currency, in giving and exchanging, in taking and receiving. Salvation is never an individual thing; no one exists by themselves; we exist with a community and in an environment where life is shared and flows from one to the other, and so, perhaps the kingdom of God is an economy, represented sometimes as the heavenly Jerusalem. A place to live in community. The king is at the centre,

---

337   Luke 12:32.
338   Luke 12:33.
339   Luke 12:33.

and the Law is love and within that community every individual soul gives and receives, lays down and takes up, confesses and forgives, like breathing in and out, in this ever-moving flow of the exchange of life from one to the other within the community. The free flow of life, of the spirit, participating in the life of the Trinity. From the Father, in the Spirit, through the body of Christ. Our money bags that never wear out enable us to participate in the eternal economy of the kingdom.

One of the things that Michelle and I have been working on in our meditation sessions of Quiet Communion is trying to develop, after our meditation, a method of community meaning-making whereby all voices can participate, instead of just one expert telling everyone else what they should know.

Because the problem with 'experts' is that when they speak others are often disempowered. This happens in church; the expert preaches from the pulpit, and everyone else too easily become passive, sitting on hard wooden benches. I have met people who have attended church all their lives and yet are unable to say what they believe when asked. This is no way to learn and to grow. One grows not just by listening to experts, but by participation and by daring to take the risk, by putting into words, or putting into practice, what one is trying to grasp, what moves within one, what insights the Holy Spirit is revealing. One grows through 'the risk of practice' within a community.

And so, the economy of the kingdom can only run if the structures support it—which are respect, taking risks, encouragement, listening, understanding, acknowledgement, compassion, openness, confession, forgiveness, acceptance, empathy and so on.

Perhaps virtues like these are the very stuff out of which our purses 'that never wear out' are made. Perhaps out of virtues like these the life of the kingdom is shared among us.

Of course, the Church fails miserably, just as we often do in our meditation, but nonetheless, we, living in this world of shadows, do capture a glimpse and we get a sense every now and then that the kingdom of God is very close, just beyond this thin veneer of the world.

So let us remember: 'Little flock, it is the Father's good pleasure to give you the kingdom.'

SUNDAY BETWEEN 14 AND 20 AUGUST (YEAR C)
Luke 12:49–59

Silent Meditation and Eternal Time
BY MICHELLE WOOD

I wonder about your experiences of time as you practice silent meditation.

Perhaps it drags on and on and you experience some agitation or desperation for the bells to dong and move onto the next.

Perhaps sometimes after a busy, hurried day, your sense of time slows and becomes more like a leisurely drive down a country lane where you can wind down the window, feel the breeze and take in all that is around you.

Perhaps you are pulled into the future—the meal to be prepared next, the jobs on the to-do list, the daydreams, what's coming up socially…

In tonight's sacred story, Jesus asks us to consider how we interpret time.

How are we to understand the relationship between the present moment and the eternal? The reality of God incarnate and the kingdom of God that is yet to come.

There is often a disjuncture between our awareness of the ever-presentness of God and daily life. How do we make sense of this and how might the practice of silent meditation help us?

We all live and construct our lives through a cultural prism of historical time, and it is not surprising that this is full of conflict and division. It is like living in the dark with a low-battery torch defining a partial seeing. We look over here and see this bit of life and over there and see that bit of life and narrate a story that joins the two, but really, we move from partial dot to partial dot attempting to draw some sort of picture of reality.

As human beings, we are limited in itsy-bitsy ways of living and classifying our lives in accordance with worldly time and a distracted busyness.

Filling up all the space with tasks and conflicts, desires and ideas.

But sometimes, we have these moments where something more eternal breaks through. Zarah Parker writes that the poet William Wordsworth named such moments as '"a spot of time," and describes them as a moment in your life when it's as if you feel the order of the universe as God created it.'[340]

Once, after meditating on the banks of the Murray River in the evening, I opened my eyes, my being so still, my awareness so expanded that I experienced what I can only describe as one thousand eyes twinkling at me. Of course,

---

340 Zarah Parker, 'Wordsworth's Spots of Time', Memoir of a Writer, 11 August 2017, https://thememoirofawriter.com/2017/08/11/wordsworths-spots-of-time/.

what I saw was the sun light bouncing off each little water crest of the river. But it was like looking with the lights all turned on and not some dim little torch. I was receiving everything at once in what felt like a God ever-present moment, a timeless, eternal moment.

In the book *In Search of Lost Time*, such a moment comes for Proust when he dips a Madeleine cake into a cup of tea. All of a sudden, his consciousness expands and he is flooded with childhood memories and has a sense of his being across time. He stops living in the itsy-bitsy sense of reality and touches something more transcendent and whole.

Perhaps these two moments reflect something of an entry into the kingdom of God. A perceiving from a deep centre, a clearer reality, where the lights are all switched on, where the beauty of Creation and the wholeness of our being is expanded and expressed in relationship to all time, eternal time.

John Main wrote, 'the purpose of meditation to lead us to full awareness of who we are, where we are'.[341]

In other words, we have to stop hovering in the realms of itsy-bitsy time and this continuous postponement of the kingdom of God until later and enter it.

For Jesus teaches, 'The kingdom of God is not coming with things that can be observed; nor will they say, "Look, here it is!" or "There it is!" For, in fact, the kingdom of God is among you.'[342]

John Main instructs that to realise this teaching, 'You must let your consciousness expand and your awareness develop. …We must realise the persons we already are, … [and that] we are already in the sphere of God's grace because the Spirit has been sent into our hearts.'[343]

Whether we find a door to enter the kingdom of God via the practice of silent meditation, or by being blown open by nature, or receiving the sacrament of Holy Communion, or dipping a cake in a cup of tea, what matters is the realisation that

The kingdom of God is within us, the kingdom of God is among us.

Silent meditation is a prayer bridge to help us step out of itsy-bitsy time and its preoccupations, to the extent that we can, to consciously enter the presence of the ever-present, eternal God.

---

341   Main, *Inner Christ*.
342   Luke 17:20–21 (New Revised Standard Version); or 'within you'.
343   Main, *Inner Christ*, 87.

SUNDAY BETWEEN 21 AND 27 AUGUST (YEAR C)
Luke 13:10–17

A Sabbath Rest

BY PAUL WOOD

Our sacred story today is an example of when the legalistic mind gets in the way of a beautiful life-giving principle. And that beautiful life-giving principle is one of the Ten Commandments. 'Remember the Sabbath day and keep it holy', and then how the lawyers loved to nitpick around what exactly this means.

Let's reflect on the Sabbath.

We get our sense of time from the rhythms of nature based upon the sun and the moon. From the sun we get days, and from the moon we get months. A month has twenty-eight days in it, which can be divided into four bite-sized chunks that we call weeks.

And as we enter into the world of human affairs, the seven-day week is marked by Sabbath keeping. We must: 'Remember the Sabbath day and keep it holy. Six days you shall labour and do all your work. but the seventh day is a Sabbath to the Lord your God; you shall not do any work—you, your son or your daughter, your male or female slave, your livestock, or the alien resident in your towns. For in six days the Lord made heaven and earth, the sea, and all that is in them, but rested the seventh day; therefore, the Lord blessed the Sabbath day and consecrated it.'[344]

What a beautiful principle this is. Six days of creative work and then a day of rest, a Holy Day, a day of re-creation.

Because we are created in the image of God, we have the God-like powers of creating, and for six days we work at creating, creating this and creating that, ensuring we have food, warmth and shelter. But we also create with words and stories, questioning this and then that, what's next, who is who, judging measuring, moulding and shaping things, what about this, what about that. And so, we busy ourselves, and life is hard, and it requires a lot of work to sustain our lives, and we can be totally consumed by this work,

But then, occasionally we must stop or be stopped, refrain from all busyness and work, and we must remember that we are not creators; rather, we are the created!

Let us stop and remember that God created and placed us in this beautiful world that we did not make, with its rivers, mountains, seas, the dew of the morning, the warmth of the sun, the glitter on the waters and the cooling

---

344   Exo. 20:8–11.

evening breeze in summer. We did not give ourselves the breath of life—all is given, and all is gift. Created and sustained by a good power that is beyond our knowing, the Almighty, the Creator, our Heavenly Father.

Let us remember the great mystery of the givenness of life amid our busyness in the world.

When I was a young man, I lived in the bush in Southern Tasmania. I had built a house of wattle and daub and my neighbours through the trees were Seventh-Day Adventists, a religious group of Sabbath keepers. Their church differs from mainstream churches that celebrate on Sunday, the day of the resurrection, the first day of the week. For them, Saturday is the last day of the week, and each Saturday, they would gather, bringing together the produce from their gardens and their various kitchens, and it was a day of lying about on the grass in the sun, gazing up at a blue sky, not far from a little bay. The day was spent sipping herbal teas and talking about the Bible and spirituality while being immersed in the great beauty of God's work, the distant crashing of waves, the trees, fruits and flowers, colours and smells. It was all a gift before returning to the week's hard work of earning a living, which included eight hours a day on the jackhammer at a local limestone quarry. It was a beautiful, restful break from hard physical work.

Now, meditation is a little bit like a Sabbath, except it is practised on the level of our individual consciousness, rather than on the level of a social community group.

Meditation is a time to have a break from our 'normal everyday conscious working mind'—when we detach ourselves from the worries and clutter of everyday and bring our busy minds to a place of rest, and as we untangle, we become still, open and receptive to the 'eternal other' out of which this great beautiful mystery of life arrives before us—and here we are.

Receptive—*maranatha*—Come Lord

Open—Lord Jesus have mercy

Alert and attentive in this restful space, so that we can return to the world refreshed to heal, teach and participate in the great creative work of redeeming the world. For the fruits of meditation are not so much enjoyed during the meditation itself, as much as later, in how it affects the rest of our lives and how it touches others with a sense of spaciousness, of something more and of something other and eternal.

'Remember the Sabbath day and keep it holy.'

SUNDAY BETWEEN 28 AUGUST AND 3 SEPTEMBER (YEAR C)
Luke 14:7–14

Vying for a Place at the Head of the Table
BY MICHELLE WOOD

In the practice of silent meditation, some speak of the silent observer or witness who notices when we wander off-course and gently brings our attention back to prayer.

The practice of silent meditation helps us to notice what we give our attention to, what thoughts and emotions are vying for space at the head of the table. As soon as we begin to turn our attention solely towards God, in those thoughts strut, wrangling for the best seats in the house. Can you notice what sorts of thoughts turn up and what sort of psychological dynamics they demand? What thoughts are easy to sit down in the back recesses of our mind, and what type of thoughts huff, puff and pull until they are at the head of the table? How can the poor, lame, marginalised aspects of self ever be seen and heard in this cacophony of clamouring? How can we experience the wholeness of our created identity in God?

In the fourth century, the desert fathers and mothers went out to remote and uninhabited Egyptian and Syrian deserts to examine, in solitude, what was going on in their minds. They were the pioneers of the prayer of silence. They sought to confront their falsehoods, fears of being nothing and self-oriented ego desires. Russian theologian Evdokimov wrote that 'one goes into the desert to vomit up the interior phantom'.[345]

Encouragingly, he wrote that the men and women of this desert tradition paved the way for us to go into our own interior desert, a place of deep transformation.

The practice of silent meditation is our interior desert, our place of transformation where, if we are on the right track, we will experience 'a heart inflamed with charity for the entire Creation' according to seventh-century desert father Isaac of Nineveh.[346]

In tonight's sacred story, Jesus notices how people's interior phantoms behave at a dinner party. Jesus is a master noticer.

He inflames their hearts and calls them back to the loving, humble and inclusive table of God via storytelling. In his story about vying for a seat at

---

345 Rowan Williams, *A Silent Action: Engagements with Thomas Merton* (London: SPCK, 2013), 24.
346 Williams, *Silent Action*, 31.

the head of the table, he portrays a bigger ordering system, helping them and us relate from our identity-in-God, rather than human artifices of prestige and power.

He paints a beautiful vision of how our identity-in-God is marked by humility, authentic generosity and a universal inclusivism.

Silent meditation is a practice of noticing so that we can notice, as Jesus notices. By noticing with tenderness and love the neglected bits of ourselves—where we are blind, lame and poor. From this noticing, we can proceed from a springboard of authenticity of being rather than vie for a place at the head of the table with our superficial personas that seek an ego stroke from the world.

In the prayer of silence, we are seeking a humble heart, one that can look beyond the conventions of the world to see more clearly and decline the practices of exclusivism and egoism. We are growing a heart that makes space for the whole of humanity, trusting in the abundance of God.

In this time of silence, let us enter our interior desert with vulnerability and poverty of heart. Trusting in Christ who is our host and the head of our table, who gently invites us to notice that we are seated, for twenty silent minutes, at a most wonderful banquet in communion with all, held in love by the creative wisdom of God.

SUNDAY BETWEEN 4 AND 10 SEPTEMBER (YEAR C)
Luke 14:25–35

Meditation and Dying
BY PAUL WOOD

I have a very short reflection this week.

But first of all, let me set the context: Jesus is on a journey to the final moment of his life, his sacrificial death. Crowds are following him, and he turns to say, 'Whoever comes to me and does not hate father and mother, wife and children, brothers and sisters, yes, and even life itself, cannot be my disciple. Whoever does not carry the cross and follow me cannot be my disciple.'[347] Scholars say that Jesus' use of the word 'hate' is hyperbole in order to contrast the absolute importance of putting Christ above all others, especially now on the approach to death.

So, I would like to meditate on death, not as something negative but rather as something natural, wholesome and good and even beautiful.

---

347 Luke 14:26–27.

The Journey into Death

When we meditate, we are learning how to die, so that when we actually do die, we will do it well.

What happens if we die well when we die is that we gently let go the things of this world and we surrender ourselves into God. 'Father, into your hands I commend my spirit.'[348]

It is the same when we meditate; we gently let go the things of this world (our thoughts and attachments) and we surrender into God.

This is dying.

Let us now have twenty minutes in the practice of dying—so that when we actually do die, we will do it well.

You might wish to use the prayer phrase, 'Father, into your hands I commit my spirit', which you can use as an anchor to keep your attention focused on God.

After this, we will read the sacred story for this week.

Let us pray:

'Father, into your hands I commit my spirit.'

SUNDAY BETWEEN 11 AND 17 SEPTEMBER (YEAR C)

Season of Creation Special

Luke 12:22–31

The Marriage of Creation and Christ as Centre and Climax of our Salvation

BY MICHELLE WOOD

A wise Trappist Monk wrote in his journal in 1965, 'Looking at the hills and recovering the freedom of true prayer … I realised that what is important is not my house, not the hermit image, but my own self, and my sonship as a child of God.'[349]

That monk was Thomas Merton.

And as we gather at the end of this day in springtide, we contemplate the revelation of God in the beauty unfolding around us. A psalmist sees how nature praises God:

> You magnificent magnolia cups with your bone white bells of soft pink hues,
> praising God.

---

348   Luke 23:46.
349   Williams, *Silent Action*, 78.

You golden branches of wattles, bursting with balls of sun,
praising God.
You willy-wagtails and blue wrens bouncing on branches with your
tiny feet clasping in choral evensong, as beautiful as a choir,
praising God.
You bees with tiny mouths that suck the sweetness
from the flowers to make gold,
praising God.

We gather to meditate to return to God in whom all has life.

Our being, just by breathing, praises God and offers the thanksgiving prayer: I am because of the love of God.

In his book, *Jesus Christ: The Unanswered Questions*, Rowan Williams writes that we need in this modern world a new way of being, a new spirituality—founded on a relationship between the doctrine of Christ and the doctrine of Creation.

The way he sees it, if I could roughly summarise, is that for human beings to come to the fullness of their humanity, to be the creatures that God made us to be, we need the created world to be all that is created to be.

The wellbeing of the physical world and our wellbeing is intimately linked in what Rowan Williams calls the *toing and froing of gift*.

We depend on the physical world for our wellbeing, and the wellbeing of the physical world depends on us.

There is a toing and froing of gift between us and God's Creation.

God made us to be human and has given us a unique role within Creation to become fully human.

Our humanness can only be understood and realised within the reality of the whole Creation—and each one of us, although a unique and precious creation, is only a very small part of this body of Christ.

Our full humanness in God's Creation should not diminish or deplete or demean the Creation.

If we are to align with William's premise, then what is the Christian to make of this current environmental crisis?

Rowan Williams reflects theologically that this crisis of relationship with the material world is a failure of having a doctrine of Christ that is intimately in dialogue with a doctrine of Creation.

Historical institutional Christianity, for a variety of reasons, has divorced itself from Creation and thus, holds unhealthy and unbalanced views on sex, women and nature.

But what if in this modern era, we centre on a dialogue of the doctrine of Christ and the doctrine of Creation, as Rowan Williams suggests?

What if we were really to believe that actually we can't really be in relationship with Christ without this—what would we do differently, in our lives of prayer, worship and ways of living in this beautiful world?

What would Christianity look like if we were to seriously marry the two?

We may not know the answer to this, but we do know it would be radically different.

Hence, Williams posits that a new way of being, a new spirituality is needed for Christianity.

It's perhaps not so new, really, for if we consider the gospel reading tonight, we get a whiff that it has always been there: Jesus' message of learning how to live simply as a creature in God's Creation without worry.

If we look to the Creation and look to Christ, could we find an authentic life as Christians?

A life that plays its part in ecological harmony with the whole.

Being a creature in Creation is our calling, our primal identity; it is, as Thomas Merton puts it, the only serious reality worth worrying about.

For Creation isn't some beautiful China teacup that we take out of the display cabinet to exclaim 'Oh, how quaint! Isn't she pretty?' every now and then, say, on St Francis Day or during a designated liturgical season; rather, it is a litmus test regarding where we are up to in salvation. For the more fully human we become, the more in relational balance with every bit of God's Creation we will be. Recognising as God does the importance of the useless wild ass, the unwise ostrich and the unclean raven. We will value all the diverse creations' ways of praising God as much as our own. Allowing them due space and voice.

In the life of Jesus, we see the union of Creator and creature. The marriage of Creation and Christ is the centre and climax of our salvation. A rediscovery of this centre would inspire a Christianity not bound up in buildings and fights over sexuality and money but one that seeks the transformation of its seekers as lovers of God's Creation.

Each time we sit in silent meditation, we are being re-created as God's creatures, perfected by our pioneer Christ. May we be sustained to live in joyful sacramental harmony with the whole of God's Creation, attentive to its wellbeing, not taking too much or giving too little. Let us look after Creation as much as our own wellbeing. This is our vocation as evolving Christians. This is our salvation.

SUNDAY BETWEEN 18 AND 24 SEPTEMBER (YEAR C)
Luke 16:1–13

Meditation – A Single Point of Focus
BY PAUL WOOD

Jesus says 'No slave can serve two masters, for a slave will either hate the one and love the other, or be devoted to the one and despise the other. You cannot serve God and wealth.'[350]

One awareness that we develop as meditators is that we know that thinking and paying attention are not the same thing!

In meditation, we are learning to pay attention, and this is not about thinking. We do a lot of thinking in normal everyday consciousness but often at the expense of paying attention.

Meditation is about learning to be attentive. It is easy to be attentive to something novel and dramatic, but it is difficult to sustain our attention on the familiar, the small and the everyday,; yet, this is what meditation requires.

Paying attention is the basis of not just meditation but also of prayer in the wider sense. If we are to form a relationship with anything, we must first give it our attention, and prayer can be described as 'our loving attention toward God'. It is also what worship is. Ascribing worth to God, the highest good, the sacred. Thus, loving attention towards God is the essence of worship.

The thing about biblical monotheism is that there is just this one transcendent Creator—one single point of focus. Whereas in polytheism (many gods), one asks this god for that and then asks that god for this. Here, there are many different focal points and none of them is the whole, only bits and pieces of the whole. But in monotheism, there is only one focal point, which contains the whole.

'No slave can serve two masters', says Jesus, just as a wheel cannot have two centres.

Perhaps, this is what Jesus meant when he said 'Blessed are the pure in heart, for they will see God'.[351] A heart of fidelity is a heart of single focus. It is an uncluttered heart, a heart without distractions.

Of course, in our everyday consciousness, our attention is usually all over the place, but during our meditation at least, we might achieve this single focus even if it is momentarily. And a little bit of sacred meditation each day,

---

350 Luke 16:13.
351 Matt. 5:8.

or a little bit of prayer and worship each day, keeps our lives oriented towards the sacred, and this brings order in our lives.

The biblical Creation story is about a single authority bringing order. Polytheistic creation stories are about drama, jealousy and warfare among the gods and so on. But in monotheism, God creates by the word of command. 'Let there be light', and there was no conflict nor cosmic battle, no violence, just a gentle result—and there was light. Thus, the Creation story is a gentle story of making distinctions and bringing things together, creating order out of the primal chaos.

Here are the traditional orders of Creation.

Highest of all is the uncreated God, the Creator of all.

Beneath God are the invisible powers that belong to the created order. Therefore, they are lower than God who alone is uncreated. The created powers are the angels, who are the invisible forces that govern circumstances and the destiny of nations.

And below these angelic powers is the world of human beings and their affairs. Then, beneath the world of humans is the animal kingdom, below which is the plant kingdom, and below it is the mineral kingdom.

In traditional cosmology, in the Great Chain of Being everything has its place within the orders of Creation. Each of the orders is ontologically unique. Each has its place, and so, when things find their rightful place within the orders, when all things fulfil their created purposes within God, then, there is order and peace like on the first day of Creation.

In meditation, our single focus is towards God, the one uncreated eternal Creator.

And here we sit with all our disordered, confused thoughts and feelings that belong to our world.

We sit still, with a single focus, under the one Creator, God.

O God, you inspire the hearts of the faithful with a single longing,
grant your people to love what you command and to desire what you promise,
so that in all the changes and chances of this uncertain world,
our hearts may surely there be fixed where true joys are to be found;
through Jesus Christ who is alive with you,
in the unity of the Holy Spirit,
one God, now and for ever. **Amen.**[352]

---

[352] The Collect for Easter 5 in the tradition of *The Book of Common Prayer*, reworked by Rev. Bosco Peters, 'Ordinary 21 (Fifth Sunday of Easter)', liturgy, https://liturgy.co.nz/reflections/easter5.

SUNDAY BETWEEN 25 SEPTEMBER AND 1 OCTOBER (YEAR C)

Luke 16:19–31

The Little Girl at My Gate

BY MICHELLE WOOD

Have you ever had a wake-up call? Something that made you realise that you need to change the way you do something, to avoid a problem in the future?

My earliest memory of a significant wake-up call was when I was in Grade 4, around eight years old. I attended a very poor state school and in this school were all sorts of colourful characters.

There was Andreas who wore a stolen black leather jacket too big for his bony body and had a diamond stud earring, the first boy I'd ever seen with such a thing.

There was an obese Dutch boy who could not speak English and whose lunchbox stench of sausage and dried meats was the source of bullying ridicule by tough, cool, vegemite-on-white-bread kind of kids.

And there was Teresa Dunlop, who was called 'the dunny'. She came to school smelling of urine and had nicotine-stained yellow teeth, unbrushed matted hair and red, scabby sores that covered her face, arms and legs. She had long, unclipped nails filled with dirt, which she used as a weapon of self-defence.

At lunchtime, she sat alone at the end of a long wooden bench, hunched into a ball like a cat, and every day, the other children would take turns to run by her, calling her the dunny and warning other children not to sit on that bench as they would get 'dunny germs'. Sometimes, she would hiss back at them or reach out to try to touch them, and they would run away screaming. I would regularly notice this type of taunting and walk past to find a quiet spot with my two little friends.

Anyway, one day she came to school looking even more dishevelled than normal. Her sores were inflamed and bleeding as if she had been violently scratching them.

She sat in a tighter ball. And the children upped their teasing as if to match her decline. I couldn't bear it and had my first wake-up call. I left my little group of friends, went over to the bench, stood next to her and asked her whether she was okay, and she reached out to scratch me with her long nails.

I didn't run away but sat on the bench, not too close but close enough. I didn't really know what to say, so I didn't say anything, I just sat there in silence. The bell went and I went off to my classroom, but she remained.

She didn't come to school the next day, nor the next. In fact, I have never seen her again. And to be honest, I never really thought about her again until much later when I began to work with children who had been violently abused and neglected by their parents. How I worried for her and what became of her, who now, if she were still alive, would be in her fifties!

Every three years when we read this gospel passage, I remember that little girl with her sores and I lament: Could I have done more for the little girl sitting at my gate?

And what about now? Now that I am not so poor and under-resourced, how do I live in the awareness of what a Christian is called to be: a communicator of the gospel to our neighbour in word and action.

At present, I am reading a book by Rowan Williams, titled *Silence and Honey Cakes: The Wisdom of the Desert*. In it, he conveys many pithy sayings and stories from the desert fathers and mothers. These examples centralise how 'one's own awareness of failure and weakness is indispensable to communicating the gospel to my neighbour'.[353]

The practice of silent meditation, as the desert fathers and mothers saw it, was a practice of addressing one's inattention, one's failure to see what is truly there in front of one because of a vision clouded by self-obsession or self-satisfaction.[354]

As they say, 'You flee to the desert not to escape neighbours but to grasp more fully what the neighbour is—the way to life for you, to the degree that put yourself at their disposal in connecting them to God.'[355]

Jesus teaches that we will not find our access to real life, eternal life, true happiness in materialism, but rather in our awareness of the great flow of love from God by opening to it and letting it flow through us to our neighbour.

In tonight's sacred story, the rich man was inattentive to the needs of Lazarus, and it cost him eternal peace and rest. The story serves as a wake-up call.

One aim of the practice of silent meditation is to grow a mind that does not cut anyone off from God, including ourselves. We can only do this by first stopping and paying attention to our thoughts. For only then can we be responsible for the thoughts rooted in self-obsession and self-satisfaction and not project these onto others.

In this interior desert, we practice a type of prayerful psychoanalysis of the soul to guard our attention, as a farmer their ripe grapes, a practice that helps us poke about and shoo crows, so that by removing the log from our

---

[353] Rowan Williams, *Silence and Honey Cakes: The Wisdom of the Desert* (Oxford: Medio Media, 2003), 25.
[354] Williams, *Silence and Honey Cakes*, 26.
[355] Williams, *Silence and Honey Cakes*, 39.

own eyes, we can open towards the infinite love of God so that we may see more clearly and love more dearly the neighbour at our gates.

SUNDAY BETWEEN 2 AND 8 OCTOBER (YEAR C)
Luke 17:5–10

Faith the Size of a Mustard Seed
BY PAUL WOOD

Faith the size of a mustard seed. That's all we need to uproot a deep-rooted problem like the invasive mulberry tree or to move a mountain of difficulty that lies along our path. With faith the size of a mustard seed—one achieves mighty things. Let's talk about faith.

Faith: what is it? It is usually thought of as a gift because it is not an act of the will; it comes by grace. Faith is basically a trust or confidence in something, and ultimately it is trust in God. Having confidence in God. Being confident that in spite of how the world seems to be to us, that God, who Jesus speaks of as our Heavenly Father, is nonetheless bringing all things their completion in love—and this gives us our life's meaning and purpose.

Faith means that in spite of how impossible things may seem to be to us now, we believe there is always something more going on, that there is always a greater story, beyond what we can now see and know. So, if we have faith in God and we are faced with an impossible situation, be it a mountain of troubles or a deep-rooted problem within ourselves, what then? Well, we can expect miracles to happen because God is greater than our limited awareness and the limits of our ego-bound perceptions. For miracles happen all the time, and the future is full of miracles and always surprises us with things we have never expected!

No one knows what will happen in the future, but something will happen! No one knows how the Russia–Ukraine war will play out over the next five to ten years. Who knows? Who knows what will happen in the Middle East or in Far East Asia? Who knows how will we manage the global warming crisis and whether we will care for the poor? Who knows whether we will manage to develop artificial intelligence safely and protect the world from runaway technology and the corruption of tyrants, criminals and dictators? Who knows when the next global pandemic will strike or what will happen in the next five to ten years? We are all in the dark—and it is dark because it is so very hard to see what is true, what is real and what is good. But with faith, we know that the future is still full of possibilities and full of miracles.

Faith is learning to walk in the dark. Faith is trusting in the goodness of God in spite of how difficult things seem to be from our perspective at this time. Knowing that—regardless of whether we are under the right hand of God to receive blessings or under the left hand of God to receive judgement—either way, we are in the loving care of God, who will bring us to completion in love.

I know that in this world of darkness many people suffer from anxiety or panic attacks, and others suffer from depression, self-doubt and self-hatred, but perhaps the worst of all is losing faith and falling into despair with no meaning.

I say that this is the worst of all because we can suffer many hardships so long as we retain faith and a sense of meaning and purpose—we can carry our cross, but if faith collapses, we also lose our meaning and reason to be.

Faith keeps us going in the face of the impossible, and we need just a little bit to get us through.

Personally, I find that the journey of ageing is a fascinating journey of faith, and the challenge is to keep a sense of meaning and beauty in the face of our gradual demise and death.

As we age, we become more and more translucent as the light of eternity begins to shine through our disintegrating bodies, and with faith, we are able to see the beauty of the darkness, filled with a sense of wonder. Stars are only seen when it is dark, and they shine forth like prophets proclaiming the way, into the unknown and into the heart of God. The only things we take with us are our faith, hope and love. And that's it. Just our slippery selves—nothing more when coming home to the house of the Lord. And although it is the most important journey of our lives, yet when we have done it, after we have moved that huge mountain, and uprooted that invasive tree, 'we have only done what we ought to have done' and nothing more.

So, as we sit in silence and practice our discipline of meditation.

Let us also be aware that beyond our ego awareness, is that 'darkness of unknowing' that is filled with the mystery and presence of God.

SUNDAY BETWEEN 9 AND 15 OCTOBER (YEAR C)
Luke 17:11–19

Returning to Give Thanks – My Prayer Practice This Week

BY MICHELLE WOOD

This week's sacred story is about Jesus walking to Jerusalem; he heals ten lepers but only one, in fact, the one who was not attached to the Jewish temple and priests, turns back to give thanks to God and with his healed body lies down at the feet of Jesus in deep gratitude.

So, this week I would like to reflect with you on the practice of turning back to give thanks to God.

I experienced a synchronicity this week. I finished reading the book *Silence and Honey Cakes: The Wisdom of the Desert* by Rowan Williams. A book that grew out of the John Main Seminar in Sydney in 2001 that Rowan led. This book has had a profound effect on me. I will turn back to trace how it ties into my synchronistic experience a little later.

On completing this book, like a monkey I swung to the next nearest reading branch: a book by Sister Benedicta, titled *The Sayings of the Desert Fathers: The Alphabetical Collection*.

I have this elaborate process of reading and notating things that are important to me. It is a spiritual practice and, as I see it, an extension of meditation, paying attention and giving thanks. It is a way of slowly digesting, being with the text, honouring the author and integrating learnings rather than consuming and moving on as this fast-paced world so encourages. So, throughout this book are my pink post-it notes sticking their heads up out of the pages, like a tongue out of a mouth, beckoning me to do something with these pearls of wisdom.

I developed this reading–notating system so I can read in the garden, by a river or in a café. The next stage is typing the notes. And although it chains me to my desk, it allows me to chew the cud once more and go over each saying letter by letter. I create an index based on my own quirky taxonomies, so that I can find these pearls of profundities again. I give them a name and slot it under an alphabetic ordering principle. For example,

G
Growth
'When the novice approaches the elder and says, in the usual formula, "Give me a word," he or she is not asking for either a command or a solution, but for a communication that can be received as a stimulus to grow into fuller life.'[356]

I
Identity
'God alone will tell me who I "really" am, and he will do so only in the lifelong process of bringing my thoughts and longings into his presence without fear and deception.'[357]

---

356 Benedicta Ward, trans., *The Sayings of the Desert Fathers* (Kentucky: Cistercian Publicans, 1975), 50.
357 Ward, *Desert Fathers*, 50.

Anyway, back to synchronicity. In the foreword to her book, Sr Benedicta writes that the *Apophthegmatic* is a collection of sayings compiled in Greek and arranged under both alphabetical and systematic headings—snap, I thought!

So, although I am not a desert mother, an Amma, of the fourth century, I am a sort of twentieth-century one, who goes to Abba Rowan asking poetically interiorly the formula 'give me a word' … a communication that can be received as a stimulus to grow into fuller life.

He fills my sack with honey cakes like this one:

He says, 'Those of us who have the freedom to do so need to go on asking where the unity of the church lies and in what that unity consists.'[358]

He tells me gently that unity comes from looking together into a mystery … it is not a unity based on an institutional matter.[359]

He writes, 'If there aren't enough people looking into the mystery, unity comes to be seen in functional terms—meetings for events, discharging obligations…etc.'

Most profoundly, he says that unity exists fundamentally in gazing towards Christ and through Christ into the mystery of God.[360]

So let us like the healed leper in tonight's story return to gaze into the mystery…

PS.

Under S

Silence

Abba Rowan reminds us that Meister Eckhart said, 'There is nothing so much like God as silence.'[361]

SUNDAY BETWEEN 16 AND 22 OCTOBER (YEAR C)
Luke 18:1–8

The Widow and the Corrupt Judge

BY PAUL WOOD

It seems to me that most people understand prayer as trying to change the external world by appealing to God for special favours. My own personal experience is that my prayer requests are seldom answered in that way.

---

[358] Williams, *Silence and Honey Cakes*, 110.
[359] Williams, *Silence and Honey Cakes*, 110.
[360] Williams, *Silence and Honey Cakes*, 110.
[361] Williams, *Silence and Honey Cakes*, 111.

Rather, I suspect that the power of prayer is about changing oneself first, about transforming one's own internal world, transforming one's consciousness and perceptions. This then enables one to not only to see things differently, including seeing the miraculous, but also to work towards changing the external world in a realistic way through one's own actions and influence. Prayer is a self-forming practice. Perhaps, prayer is doing the necessary internal work towards getting one's bearings in order to act in the world with greater wisdom. In this way, the internal and external work together, prayer and action are connected, our consciousness influences our behaviour and changes the world.

Now, as contemplatives we make a habit of looking inwards and observing our internal world, and as we do so you may note that it is always restless and that it is restless because there is a kind of a drama going on, quite like the drama of the widow and the corrupt judge. Where the widow represents the vulnerable within us seeking justice and the judge represents the world as it is.

We must note that the judge does not represent God, as some may first assume, because the judge is corrupt. The God presence is rather represented by the widow, as the vulnerable Christlike presence in an indifferent world. Jesus commends the persistence of the widow and says that she will get what she wants, not because the judge is good, but because of her persistence. So, Jesus encourages us not to give up, but to keep on at it and persevere in our prayers in spite of the state of things as they seem.

There is an Old Testament story about the patriarch Jacob who wrestles with an angel all night by the Brook of Jabbok, and the angel wounds him, but also blesses him, saying, 'You shall no longer be called Jacob, but Israel, for you have striven with God and with humans, and have prevailed.'[362] The name Israel means One who struggles with God, and the story of his descendants, the ten tribes of Israel, is the story of the Old Testament; it is the story of their struggle with God.

And so, we stand with the widow, just as Jesus stands with the vulnerable, and we continually seek justice before an egocentric Law man. Faith is a struggle, and we believe that the vulnerable will win in the end. Just as in the Book of Revelation the Lamb overthrows the dragon, and the meek inherit the earth and the last will be first. Because every sparrow fallen is known and loved and every hair is numbered, and in the end, our deepest desires will find their fulfilment and their completion in the great plan of God—so keep up the struggle—it is worth it.

What has this to do with silent meditation? Well, first of all, as we become silent on the outside, we become aware of the noise within ourselves and the internal ongoing struggle, but then, through meditation techniques, we seek

---

362   Gen. 32:28.

to quieten the internal drama, to find stillness and peace. Perhaps we should call silent meditation a 'strategic silence', a silence to cleanse our minds from endless chatter, so that we can hear afresh with pristine ears the call of God and reorient our hearts to true north, and then return to the world of drama once again—but this time with greater wisdom. Because the world of the drama is meaningful to Christians, it is the lives of people, we must continue the struggle for love and justice, but we also need respite, we need rest, we need a regular Sabbath, to recreate our lives. And so, silent meditation is like a Sabbath among the drama of life—for twenty minutes only—and then back into the fray, to stand with the widow, seeking justice before a dodgy judge.

SUNDAY BETWEEN 16 AND 22 OCTOBER (YEAR C)
Luke 18:9–14

Humility
BY MICHELLE WOOD

The thing that I am most curious about in tonight's sacred story is the distinction between where one stands and in what direction one looks when approaching the holy.

In the parable that Jesus tells, two people come to the temple to pray. One person feels they are living a very good life; they stand by themselves and narrate a story of their own goodness, braggingly talking to God as if lost in a type of self-congratulatory mirror. What they narrate interiorly could be seen, at best, as relief that they are not like others who are immoral or, at worst, a story of smug disdain for people who are struggling. This man even goes as far as moving his denouncing generalisations into a very personal diminishment of another person in the temple praying.

The other person praying in the temple is a tax collector, who feels corrupt, broken and ashamed. He stands far off and cannot even look up towards heaven. Beating his chest, he cries out for mercy, his whole being opening and stretching towards God.

I guess each of us must grapple with the question how close or far off do we stand in relation to the mystery of the holy, and how much of our prayer is directed towards self or God. Anyone sitting for twenty minutes in silent meditation can't help but sense that they are standing a long way off and will all too easily follow the musings of their own mind, entertaining all too readily their own self-talk.

Part of my own grappling is seen in my relationship over time to the *Jesus Prayer*.

When I first heard the Jesus Prayer—*Lord Jesus Christ, Son of God, have mercy on me, a sinner*—I thought, 'Oh, that's a bit harsh! What a downer, that's no way to relate to the God of love.' Now, I think it is the most truthful and perhaps the only authentic prayer I can offer.

Because behind my veneer of so-called goodness are so many failings, so many things that I am deeply ashamed of, so much pride and inner claims of superiority. I have done some very wrong things, and I've broken vows and hurt people I love and care about deeply.

But it is a wonderful thing to be truthful, *oh happy wound*, because that is how we grow.

The desert fathers speak of the importance of truth above sincerity because we can't grow if we just cover our faults and try to convince others to collude with our often distorted and avoidant self-responsibility. How many times do we enter into conflict with another and talk to someone else trying to convince them of our innocence and the other's guilt! The simplest relationships and global relationships are destroyed on this axiom of I am right, and you are wrong; I am good, and you are evil; and I am pure, and you are corrupt.

I love that in the rule of St Benedict there is a wise sentiment to remember that when trying to resolve conflict it is not a matter of who is right and who is wrong but who is offended and who needs to say sorry.

To get to the heart space where we can actually live this sentiment, we need the quality that St Benedict says is the greatest foundation for the spiritual life: humility. Humility, he writes, is 'the foundation for our relationship with God, our connectedness to others, our acceptance of ourselves, our way of using the goods of the earth and even our way of walking through the world, without arrogance, without domination, without scorn, without put-downs, without disdain, without self-centeredness'.[363]

Humility is perfection and, in the biblical sense, it is of having become mature, ripened and whole.

If the Pharisee in the parable had humility, he may have noticed the other's pain and dejection and offered a touch of mercy or inclusion, rather than being intoxicated with his pride.

And just in case some of the older readers in this book, through being brought up on a diet of being harsh on themselves, jump to criticise their own faults and lack of humility, I want to finish with a beautiful thought from the

---

[363] Joan Chittister, *The Rule of Benedict: A Spirituality for the 21st Century* (New York: Crossroad, 2010), 98.

Knitting Monk Br Aidan, a young monk from Holy Cross Monastery in New York. He was taught by his Novice Master that

> *Humility flowers into simplicity.*
> *The journey towards humility is to search out what is true*
> *to myself and live out of that so that I am fully alive.*
> *Humility is about being in touch with the fullest expression*
> *of who I am… my uniquely created self.*
> *It is a journey of growing some things and diminishing others.*
> *Owning my shortcomings so that I can live authentically*
> *and in proper relationship to God and other people.*
> *Humility asks, what do I have too much of or not enough of?*
> *Do I need more self-critique or more gentleness?*[364]

Silent meditation is an act of humility. Even the physicality of it steers us towards this spiritual foundation: we sit still in the presence of God, lower our eyes, cease our self-talk and diminish, as far as we are able, self-centredness.

John Main repeatedly taught that the essence of silent meditation is simplicity. You don't need any grand skills or to be perfect.

In each session, we attempt to quieten our pride and humbly come before God, giving our whole attention, our heart. Sitting with each other in compassion, we embrace and pass on the mercy of God to all whom we live in relation to, our neighbours.

SUNDAY BETWEEN 23 AND 29 OCTOBER (YEAR C)
Luke 18:15–30

Jesus Blesses Little Children
BY MICHELLE WOOD

Jesus says, 'whoever does not receive the kingdom of God like a little child will never enter it'.[365]

What does it mean to receive like a little child, and how might the practice of silent meditation assist us to do this? When researching these questions, I read a commentary by biblical scholar Michael Patella, OSB. He wrote, 'Jesus

---

364   Aidan Owen, 'Episode 9: On Humility', 15 January 2018, video, https://youtu.be/_77XATz3Kjs. Author Br Aidan Owen's website is https://alittlefire.org/the-knitting-monk/.
365   Luke 18:17.

draws attention to the unfettered openness of a child that can lead one into the kingdom of God.'[366]

So tonight, I would like to speak about silent meditation as a practice of unfettered openness. It seems as if most of life is about gatekeeping and working out what we allow in and out, standing in the doorways of doubt, afraid to take a risk. Contrastingly, recently I saw a film of two little children who were twins and commencing preschool. They had never been separated for any length of time. On their first day of school, they were separated for three hours; I think I saw the closest example of unfettered openness when they were reunited at morning playtime. The young girl caught the first glimpse of her brother and made the quickest dash down the corridor, pigtails swinging and a smile that erupted to set off fireworks of joy on her face. When her little brother saw her, he opened his arms to catch her like a ball. They both held one another, laughing and jumping up and down with excitement.

Directness, no thinking, pure response, being fully alive, zest in the present moment, unfettered openness, love, playfulness and joy. These are how a child receives, and 'whoever does not receive the kingdom of God like a little child will never enter it'.

Some scholars overstate, in my opinion, that this passage is about the innocence of children, but I think, in agreement with Patella, that the scene in the Gospel of Luke is far more about Jesus' elevation of overflowing, unfettered openness.

John Main wrote, 'Beginning the journey of meditation is to begin to understand that it is for joy that we have to learn to prepare ourselves and that our capacity to receive it with open, generous hearts depends on the generosity of our discipline.'[367]

So, get rid of highbrow, stuffy seriousness, judging and theorising, cut off all thoughts and get down low into the sandpit of simplicity; open your childlike heart in the silence, repeat your prayer word and open unfettered to receive the kingdom of peace, love and joy. Do not allow any authoritarian voices of moral stinginess to get in the way.

---

366   Michael Patella, 'Luke', in *The Jerome Biblical Commentary for the Twenty-First Century*, eds. John J. Collins, Gina Hens-Piazza, Barbara E. Reid and Donald Senior (London: T&T Clark, 2020), 1289–1362, 1342.
367   Main, *Inner Christ*, 247.

SUNDAY BETWEEN 30 OCTOBER AND 5 NOVEMBER (YEAR C)
Luke 19:1–10

Zacchaeus and Dehiscence

BY PAUL WOOD

Zacchaeus was a tax collector, and as the chief tax collector in the town, he was probably despised and seen as a traitor living for his own profit at their expense. And he also was a little man, so little that he could not see through the crowd that had gathered to welcome Jesus into town. So, in his enthusiasm he ran and climbed a tree so that he could see Jesus. It is his eagerness that brings him face to face with Jesus who befriends him and blesses him by coming into his house to the grumbling and complaints of a confused crowd. It sounds quite comic so far!

Then, Zacchaeus stood there and said, 'Look, half of my possessions, Lord, I will give to the poor; and if I have defrauded anyone of anything, I will pay back four times as much.'[368] Then Jesus said, 'Today salvation has come to this house.'[369] If Zachaeus actually follows through and does indeed do all this, then what a lovely story this is about a mean little taxman flowering into the fullness of being a true human being and finding salvation and becoming Christlike. What a great story! It is a story about being set free from the bonds of wealth and greed and coming into the fullness of being 'a good human being'. The flowering of 'a true human person' as Zacchaeus comes into the reality of who he is, created in the image of God. This is what repentance is all about!

Often people think that repentance is about bowing down to an external authority and saying sorry. Sometimes, it's true, reality teaches you that you were wrong, 'Oops, sorry, I thought there were ten but there are actually three!' People often think that that's all repentance is. 'Sorry, I've made a mistake, and so, I've changed my mind—sorry.' But repentance is also about growth into who we really are. 'Today salvation has come to this house', says Jesus, and there is joy and gladness because Zacchaeus 'got it'. Zacchaeus has 'woken up' and sees things in a new way! He is born again. It is a wonderful moment, brought to its completion through his enthusiasm and curiosity that made him climb a tree, which brings him into the presence of Jesus where the conditions are right and the little man wakes up, and so, we see him coming to a point of dehiscence.

---

368 Luke 19:8.
369 Luke 19:9.

In botany, dehiscence is when a seed pod finally bursts open spreading its seeds and fulfilling the purpose it has been growing towards all its life. Always growing from the inside outwards, and dehiscence is the moment when it finally erupts from within because the conditions are right to scatter itself.

I think the spiritual life is best understood when seen as natural organic growth. Life grows of itself from the inside outwards. It never grows from the outside inwards; that's how you build a house! or a car!—from the outside in, but living things always grow from the inside out. As the parable says, 'the earth produces of itself'.[370] From a place hidden, it grows slowly, little by little; while the farmer sleeps, it grows of itself—and each stage of its growth is connected to what it has come from, and it always grows beyond itself towards the light. It grows by being connected. And so, the leaves are connected to the twig, and the twig to the branch, and the branch to the trunk, and the trunk to the roots and the earth.

Organic growth is mysterious, it comes from the inside, and it grows towards the light. The Bible tells of how, over centuries, nations grow like trees and dynasties grow like vines. It also represents knowledge growing like a tree, 'the tree of the knowledge of what is good and what is evil', just so also is 'the tree of life'.[371]

The mystery of life is that it is organic, it comes from the inside and grows of itself towards the light. We must nurture it and tend it as it grows of itself.

This story of Zachaeus and his dehiscence is just one small story in the grand narrative of the Tree of Life, which grows and grows, from consciousness to consciousness, until it wakes up to the fullness of the kingdom of God.

Meditation and contemplation are important for they recognise that we grow from within. Welcome to Eden

SUNDAY BETWEEN 6 AND 12 NOVEMBER (YEAR C)
Luke 20:27–40

Stripping Away Intellectual Peacocking and Returning to a Living Centre of Love
BY MICHELLE WOOD

This week, I read a poem in which death and life continued to live alongside each other, and I was reminded of the last line in tonight's sacred story in

---

370   Mark 4:26–29.
371   Gen. 2:9.

which Jesus says, that God 'is God not of the dead, but of the living; for to him all of them are alive.'[372]

The poem was by Nigerian poet Saddiq Dzukogi about his daughter Baha who died just a few weeks after her first birthday. In the poem, he imagines her as a twelve-year old girl. He writes,

> *Today Baha is not dead;*
> *she is twelve years old,*
> *sits beside a flower vase,*
> *presses her thumb to the clay.*
> *Her heart buds into a magnificent sun,*
> *waterfalls its warmth all over her satin face.*
> *Taller than her classmates,*
> *in the corner she leans her*
> *head to white paper,*
> *carves moons out of her notebook,*
> *while other children*
> *sit and listen to the teacher.*[373]

I imagine this grieving father reading tonight's sacred story pushing past the intellectual peacocking, where the Sadducees try to outsmart Jesus on Torah technicalities, asking Jesus that if there are seven brothers and one is married and he dies, and according to the Torah, the next brother must marry his wife and he dies ... who will she be married to in the resurrection?

I imagine this grieving father would want to quickly get to the living heart of what Jesus says about death and resurrection.

He'd be impatient and perhaps intolerant of hyperbole displays of logic and the histories of who is right and wrong, or who is the cleverest or who knows the books of the Bible the best.

I see him pushing through the jungles of egoism and argument, away from contest and institutional claims, blowing off the dust of deductions, looking beyond the Sadducees and their superior, closed claims about the Torah.

I imagine him thrashing through this impersonal, objective, dead letter debate to get closer to the heartbeat of God—led by the soft little hand of a child, first a year old and then twelve years old. For this child lives in him who loves her just like we all live in God who never stops loving anything created.

He would ask Jesus to speak to him of the God of Love and about a reality beyond this book-bound, scroll-sealed version of the world. The grieving

---

[372] Luke 20:38.
[373] 'Learning about Constellations' is from Saddiq Dzukogi, *Your Crib, My Qibla* (Nebraska: University of Nebraska Press, 2021), 27.

father would urgently inquire, 'Tell me about the place of poetic holy mystery where angels and ancestors are children alive in God.'

And Jesus in tenderness would tell him that our God 'is a God not of the dead, but of the living; for to him all of them are alive'.

In our practice of silent meditation, we strip away all our intellectual peacocking and return to a living centre of love.

SUNDAY BETWEEN 20 AND 26 NOVEMBER (YEAR C)
Luke 23:33–43

The Feast of Christ the King
BY PAUL WOOD

See meditation for Year B on page 184.

Bibliography

Anglican Church of Australia. *A Prayer Book for Australia*. Mulgrave, Victoria: Broughton Publishing, 1995.

Atwell, Robert. *Celebrating the Saints*. London: Canterbury Press, 2016.

Augustine. *The Confessions of Saint Augustine*. Translated by E. B. Pusey. London: Global Grey, 2018.

Baldwin, James. *The Fire Next Time*. London: Penguin Random House, 2017.

Bourgeault, Cynthia. *Centering Prayer and Inner Awakening*. Lanham, MD: Cowley Publications, 2004.

Bourgeault, Cynthia. *Eye of the Heart: A Spiritual Journey into the Imaginal Realm*. Boulder, CO: Shambhala, 2020.

Boxall, Ian. 'Matthew'. In *The Jerome Biblical Commentary for the Twenty-First Century*, edited by John J. Collins, Gina Hens-Piazza, Barbara E. Reid and Donald Senior, 1168–1237. London: T&T Clark, 2020.

The Book of Common Prayer. Cambridge: Cambridge University Press. First published in 1662.

Carmichael, Alexander. *Carmina Gadelica: Hymns and Incantations*. Edinburgh: Floris Press, 1992.

Chittister, Joan. *The Rule of Benedict: A Spirituality for the 21st Century*. New York: Crossroad, 2010.

Clendenin, Dan. 'O Comforting Fire of Spirit'. Journey with Jesus. https://www.journeywithjesus.net/poemsandprayers/590-hildegard-of-bingen-o-comforting-fire-of-spirit.

Climacus, John. 'The Ladder of Divine Ascent: Step 27: On Holy Solitude of Body and Soul'. SermonIndex.net, n.d. https://www.sermonindex.net/modules/articles/index.php?view=article&aid=41415.

Cohen, Leonard. 'It Seemed the Better Way'. Recorded between April 2015 and July 2016. Track 7 on *You Want It Darker*. Columbia Records, compact disc.

Collins, John J., Gina Hens-Piazza, Barbera Reid and Donald Senior, eds. *The Jerome Biblical Commentary for the Twenty-First Century*. London: T&T Clark, 2020.

Coogan, Michael D., Marc Zvi Brettler, Carol A. Newsom and Pheme Perkins, eds. *The New Oxford Annotated Bible New Revised Standard Version with the Apocrypha*. Fully revised 4th ed. New York: Oxford University Press, 2010.

de Mello, Anthony. *Sadhana: A Way to God*. 19th ed. Anand, India: Gujarat Sahitya Prakash, 1988.

Dickinson, Emily. *The Poems of Emily Dickinson*, edited by R. W. Franklin. Cambridge: Belknap Press, 1998.

Division of Christian Education, trans. *New Revised Standard Version*. Washington, DC: National Council of Churches, 1989.

Dostoyevsky, Fyodor. 'Poor People'. In *Fyodor Dostoyevsky Stories*. Translated by Andrei Goncharov, 29–148. Moscow: Progress Publishers Moscow, 1977.

Dylan, Bob. 'Boots of Spanish Leather'. The Official Bob Dylan Site. Accessed 7 November 2023. https://www.bobdylan.com/songs/boots-spanish-leather/.

Dzukogi, Saddiq. *Your Crib, My Qibla*. Nebraska: University of Nebraska Press, 2021.

English Language Liturgical Commission. 'The Lord's Prayer'. https://www.englishtexts.org/the-lords-prayer.

Eudes, John. *The Sacred Heart of Jesus*. Fitzwilliam, NH: Loreto Publications, 2003.

Farjeon, Eleanor. 'Morning Has Broken'. In *Songs of Praise*, edited by Percy Dearmer, Ralph Vaughn Williams and Martin Shaw, 30. London: Oxford University Press, 1931.

Forrest, Jim. 'The Challenge of a 20th Century Saint, Maria Skobtsova'. Pravmir.com. Last modified 31 March 2015. https://www.pravmir.com/the-challenge-of-a-20th-century-saint-maria-skobtsova/.

France, R. T. *The New International Greek Testament Commentary: The Gospel of Mark*. Grand Rapids, MI: William B. Eerdmans, 2002.

Francis. *Apostolic Letter Desiderio Desideravi of the Holy Father Francis: To the Bishops, Priests and Deacons, to Consecrated Men and Women, and to the Lay Faithful: On the Liturgical Formation of the People of God*. Rome: Dicastero per la Comunicazione, Libreria Editrice Vaticana, 2022.

Francis. *Misericordiae Vultus Bull of Indiction of the Extraordinary Jubilee of Mercy*. 12 February 2022. https://www.vatican.va/content/francesco/en/apost_letters/documents/papa-francesco_bolla_20150411_misericordiae-vultus.html.

Gunaratana, Henepola. *Mindfulness in Plain English*. Boston, MA: Wisdom, 2011.

Hillesum, Etty. *An Interrupted Life: The Diaries, 1941-1943 and Letters from Westerbork*. New York: Holt, 1996.

International Bible Society. *The Holy Bible: New International Version of the New Testament, Psalms and Proverbs*. Grand Rapids, MI: Zondervan, 1984.

Jackson, Jill, and Sy Miller. 1955. *Let There Be Peace On Earth*. Jan-Lee Music. https://hymnary.org/text/let_there_be_peace_on_earth.

'John Main: Biography', The School of Meditation, archived from the original 8 May 2012, accessed 5 December 2021, theschoolofmeditation.org.

Jones, Alan W. *Soul Making: The Desert Way of Spirituality*. San Francisco, CA: Harper & Row, 1985.

Judd, Frank F., Jr. 2010. '"Be Ye Therefore Perfect": The Elusive Quest for Perfection'. In *The Sermon on the Mount in Latter-day Scripture*, edited by Gaye Strathearn, Thomas A. Wayment and Daniel L. Belnap, 123–39. Salt Lake City: Deseret Book, 2010.

Jung, C. G. 'Psychology of the Transference'. In *The Collected Works of C. G. Jung*. Vol. 16, *The Practice of Psychotherapy: Essays on the Psychology of the Transference and Other Subjects*. 2nd ed. London: Routledge and Kegan Paul, 1946, 177.

Keats, John. 'To Autumn'. Poetry Foundation. https://www.poetryfoundation.org/poems/44484/to-autumn.

Law, William. *The Spirit of Prayer*. n.d., ca. 1750. Available at: https://ccel.org/ccel/law/prayer/prayer.

Leech, Kenneth. *True God: An Exploration in Spiritual Theology*. London: Sheldon Press, 1985.

Main, John. *The Inner Christ*. London: Darton, Longman and Todd, 1987.

Manton, Karen Anita, and Lynne Muir. *The Gift of Julian of Norwich*. Mulgrave, Victoria: John Garratt Publishing, 2005.

Merton, Thomas. *Seeds of Contemplation*. Wheathampstead, Hertfordshire: Anthony Clarke Books, 1961.

Merton, Thomas. *The Way of Chuang Tzu*. New York: New Directions, 1996.

Munindo, Luang Por. 2001. 'Meeting our Anger'. Audio recording. 1 January 2001. https://ratanagiri.org.uk/teachings/talks/meeting-our-anger.

Murdoch, Iris. *The Sea, the Sea*. London: Chatto & Windus, 1973.

Nikodimos and Makarios. *The Philokalia: The Complete Text*. Vol. 1. Translated by G. E. H. Palmer, Philip Sherrard and Kallistos Ware. New York: Farrar, Straus and Giroux, 1979.

Owen, Aidan. 'Episode 9: On Humility'. 15 January 2018. Video. https://youtu.be/_77XATz3Kjs.

Park, Yeonmi, and Maryanne Vollers. *In Order to Live: A North Korean Girl's Journey to Freedom*. New York: Penguin Press, 2015.

Parker, S. B. 'Carl Jung: The Sea and the Unconscious.' Jung Currents, 30 January 2022. http://jungcurrents.com/jung-sea-unconscious.

Parker, Zarah. 'Wordsworth's Spots of Time'. Memoir of a Writer. 11 August 2017. https://thememoirofawriter.com/2017/08/11/wordsworths-spots-of-time/.

Patella, Michael. 'Luke'. In *The Jerome Biblical Commentary for the Twenty-First Century*, edited by John J. Collins, Gina Hens-Piazza, Barbara E. Reid and Donald Senior, 1289–1362. London: T&T Clark, 2020.

Peters, Bosco. 'Ordinary 21 (Fifth Sunday of Easter)'. Liturgy. https://liturgy.co.nz/reflections/easter5.

Premier Unbelievable? 'Tom Holland Tells NT Wright: Why I Changed My Mind about Christianity'. 17 July 2018. Video. https://www.youtube.com/watch?v=AIJ9gK47Ogw&t=5s.

Rahner, Karl. *The Practice of Faith*. London: SCM Press, 1985.

Rahner, Karl. *Theological Investigations*. Vol. 17. Translated by Margaret Kohl. Limerick, Ireland: Mary Immaculate College, University of Limerick Centre for Culture, Technology and Values, 2004.

Ramsey, Michael. *The Christian Priest Today*. Eugene: Wipf and Stock, 1982.

Sardello, Robert. *Silence: The Mystery of Wholeness*. Berkeley, CA: North Atlantic Books, 2011.

Schumacher, Ernst Friedrich. *Small Is Beautiful: A Study of Economics As If People Mattered*. London: Blond & Briggs, 1973.

Sheldrake, Rupert. 'Friedi Kühne'. https://www.sheldrake.org/videos/friedi-kuhne.

Siedentop, Larry. *Inventing the Individual: The Origins of Western Liberalism*. Cambridge, MA: Harvard University Press, 2014.

Skobtsova, Maria. *Mother Maria Skobtsova: Essential Writings*. Translated by Larissa Volokhonsky and Richard Pevear. Maryknoll, NY: Orbis Books, 2003.

Teihard de Chardin, Pierre. *Hymn of the Universe*. London: Collins Fontana Books, 1974.

Tolan, Daniel J. 'The Flight of the All-One to the All-One: The phygē monu pros monon as the Basis of Plotinian Altruism'. *Harvard Theological Review* 114, no. 4 (2021): 469–90, https://doi.org/10.1017/S0017816021000316.

Traherne, Thomas. *Centuries of Meditations* (London, 1908). Available at https://www.ccel.org/ccel/traherne/centuries.i_1.html.

Van Gogh, Vincent. *The Letters of Vincent Van Gough*. Edited by Roland de Leeuw. Translated by Arnold Pomerans. London: Penguin Books, 1996.

Vater, Bruce. 'Johannine Theology'. In *The Jerome Biblical Commentary*, edited by Raymond E. Brown, Joseph. A Fitzmyer and Roland E. Murphy, 828–839. Englewood Cliffs, New Jersey: Prentice-Hall, 1968.

Verdi, Giuseppe. 'La Traviata Libretto English Translation'. Opera-Arias.com, accessed 20 January 2024. https://www.opera-arias.com/verdi/la-traviata/libretto/english/.

Ward, Benedicta, trans. *The Sayings of the Desert Fathers: The Alphabetical Collection*. Collegeville, MN: Liturgical Press, 1975.

Weil, Simone. *Waiting for God*. Translated by Emma Craufurd. New York: Perennial Classics, 2001.

White, Richard. *The High Country: Australia*. Mansfield, Victoria: Zone I Productions, 2014.

Whyte, David. *House of Belonging*. Langley, WA: Many Rivers Press, 2002.

Wikipedia. 'Etty Hillesum'. Last modified 10 January 2024, 15:24 (UTC). https://en.wikipedia.org/wiki/Etty_Hillesum.

Wikipedia. 'Philip Huggins'. Last modified 21 August 2022, 06:06 (UTC). https://en.wikipedia.org/wiki/Philip_Huggins.

Williams, Rowan. *A Silent Action: Engagements with Thomas Merton*. London: SPCK, 2013.

Williams, Rowan. *Looking East in Winter: Contemporary Thought and the Eastern Christian Tradition*. London: Bloomsbury Continuum, 2021.

Williams, Rowan. *Silence and Honey Cakes: The Wisdom of the Desert*. Oxford: Medio Media, 2003.

Winton, Tim. *Breath*. London: Penguin Group, 2008.

Woodhouse, Patrick. 'Etty Hillesum: A Life Transformed'. YouTube, 5 July 2016. Video. https://www.youtube.com/watch?v=Ad7MjP7grCo.

World Community for Christian Meditation. 'Opening Prayer'. https://wccm.org/meditation-resources/online-meditation-readings-11-june/#:~:text=2)%20OPENING%20PRAYER%20AND%20MEDITATION,Maranatha%2C%20Come%20Lord%20Jesus.

www.ingramcontent.com/pod-product-compliance
Lightning Source LLC
Chambersburg PA
CBHW022036290426
44109CB00014B/874